Jewish Everyday Life in Medieval Northern Europe, 1080–1350

TEAMS

DOCUMENTS OF PRACTICE

General Editor
Joel Rosenthal, *State University of New York at Stony Brook*

Advisory Board
William Chester Jordan, *Princeton University*
Sara Lipton, *Stony Brook University*
Jonathan Rotondo-McCord, *Xavier University of Louisiana*

This publication has received funding from the European Research Council (ERC) under the European Union's Horizon 2020 research and innovation programme under Grant Agreement No. 681507.

The book is published open access at scholarworks.wmich.edu/mip_teamsdp/ licensed under the Creative Commons Attribution-NonCommercial-NoDerivatives 4.0 International License. For details go to https://creativecommons.org/licenses/by-nc-nd/4.0/.

Medieval Institute Publications is a program of
The Medieval Institute, College of Arts and Sciences

Jewish Everyday Life in Medieval Northern Europe, 1080–1350

A Source Book

edited by

Tzafrir Barzilay, Eyal Levinson,
and Elisheva Baumgarten

TEAMS

MEDIEVAL INSTITUTE PUBLICATIONS
Western Michigan University
Kalamazoo

Copyright © 2022 by the Board of Trustees of Western Michigan University

Library of Congress Cataloging-in-Publication Data

Title: Jewish everyday life in medieval northern Europe, 1080-1350 : a sourcebook / edited by Tzafrir Barzilay, Eyal Levinson, and Elisheva Baumgarten.

Description: Kalamazoo : Medieval Institute Publications, Western Michigan University, [2022] | Series: Teams : documents of practice | Includes bibliographical references and index. | Summary: "Designed to introduce students to the everyday lives of the Jews who lived in the German Empire, northern France, and England from the 11th to the mid-14th centuries, the volume consists of translations of primary sources written by or about medieval Jews. Each source is accompanied by an introduction that provides historical context. Through the sources, students can become familiar with the spaces that Jews frequented, their daily practices and rituals, and their thinking. The subject matter ranges from culinary preferences and even details of sexual lives, to garments, objects, and communal buildings. The documents testify to how Jews enacted their Sabbath and holidays, celebrated their weddings, births and other lifecycle events, and mourned their dead. Some of the sources focus on the relationships they had with their Christian neighbors, the local authorities, and the Church, while others shed light on their economic activities and professions"-- Provided by publisher.

Identifiers: LCCN 2022047959 (print) | LCCN 2022047960 (ebook) | ISBN 9781580444781 (paperbound) | ISBN 9781580444798 (hardbound) | ISBN 9781580444804 (e)

Subjects: LCSH: Ashkenazim--Europe--Social life and customs--To 1500--Sources. | Jews--Europe--Social life and customs--To 1500--Sources. | Europe--Social life and customs--To 1500--Sources.

Classification: LCC DS135.E81 J45 2022 (print) | LCC DS135.E81 (ebook) | DDC 940/.049240902--dc23/eng/20221011

LC record available at https://lccn.loc.gov/2022047959

LC

ISBN hardbound: 9781580444798
ISBN paperbound: 9781580444781
eISBN: 9781580444804

All rights reserved. Without limiting the rights under copyright reserved above, no part of this book may be reproduced, stored in, or introduced into a retrieval system, or transmitted, in any form, or by any means (electronic, mechanical, photocopying, recording or otherwise) without the written permission of both the copyright owner and the author of the book.

Every effort has been made to obtain permission to use all copyrighted illustrations reproduced in this book. Nonetheless, whosoever believes to have rights to this material is advised to contact the publisher.

Printed and bound by CPI Group (UK) Ltd, Croydon CR0 4YY

Contents

List of Illustrations ix

Introduction: Jewish Life in Medieval Europe..............................xi

1 – From Birth to Death and Throughout the Year:
   Life Cycle and Rituals... 1
   1A – Medieval Tombstones from Mainz 1
   1B – Food, Mourning, and the Jewish Life Cycle 4
   1C – The Establishment of the Speyer Community
         and Its Main Synagogue... 5
   1D – Map of Medieval Speyer and Its Jewish Sites 7
   1E – The Medieval Synagogue of Speyer 9
   1F – Marital Relations and the Laws of Penance
         (*Hilkhot Teshuvah*), Eleazar of Worms 10
   1G – The Language of Prayer..12
   1H – *Haroset*: A Sweet-Sour Memory of the Past.............12
   1I – The Fate of a Match—Love Magic by Isaac of Chinon 14
   1J – The Monumental *Mikveh* of Friedberg....................16
   1K – The Burial of a Man with Communal Funds 18
   1L – Mock Marriages: The Story of Nathan and Ganna 19
   1M – The Beginnings of Yiddish in Worms.......................21
   1N – R. Yom Tov's Suicide 22
   1O – Remembering Pietism in Ashkenaz from Spain 24
   1P – Piety Even in Death: Rabbeinu Bahya
         Commenting on Ashkenazi Custom 26
   1Q – Instructions to my Sons and Daughters:
         The Ethical Will of Eleazar 27
   1R – Tournaments and Medieval Jewish Weddings 33

vi   CONTENTS

2 – Living Arrangements: Family, Household, and the Home..............35

    2A – Absent Husbands and Lonely Wives.............................35

    2B – Guests, Golden Earrings, and Domestic Fatherhood 37

    2C – The Education of Girls 39

    2D – Co-habiting with Another Man's Widow 41

    2E – Celebrating the Sabbath at Home with Food and Song: A Song for the Sabbath Table from Northern France 43

    2F – Eating and Hospitality 45

    2G – The Sweetness of Learning Torah 46

    2H – Clearing Refuse in Medieval Cologne 48

    2I – Beyond Normative Sexuality: The Story of Arloga and Her Husband Rabbi Jonah 50

    2J – Late at Night in a Medieval Jewish Home: A Marriage that Went Astray...........................51

    2K – The Case of Levirate Marriage (*Yibbum*) Refusal...............53

    2L – Providing Her Sustenance: Local Customs and the Daily Meal 55

    2M – The Custom of Having Sexual Relations on Sabbath Eve 57

    2N – Travel on the Sabbath 59

    2O – Guardianship Agreement in Hebrew and Latin................60

    2P – Traveling and Friendship in the Middle Ages: *The Book of Abramelin* 61

3 – Making a Living: Money, Markets, and Professions.....................63

    3A – Women as Business Partners 63

    3B – Making Kosher Cheese in Northern France 64

    3C – The Economic Importance of River Travel......................66

    3D – Loans between Jewish Businesswomen 67

    3E – Traveling with Money on the Sabbath 70

3F – Stealing from Your Spouse..71
3G – Conflict over the Use of a Rented Room for Business.........72
3H – Using Your Wife's Money to Pay Your Bills......................74
3I – Networks of Communal Support and Trust:
      Who Stole the Missing Objects? 76
3J – A Record of Credit Transaction between Queen Elisabeth
      of Germany and the Jews of Würzburg.....................78
3K – Jewish Seals on a Receipt of Debt from Zurich 79
3L – A Receipt of Debt from Zurich 81
3M –Displays of Wealth: One Bishop's Account
      of a Jewish Wedding in Hereford 83
3N – Jews Assigned as Market Observers in Würzburg..............85

4 – Law and Order, Disruption and Crisis................................87
  4A – The Legal Rights Granted to the Jews of Speyer 87
  4B – Imperial Privilege Granted to the Jews of Speyer 89
  4C – The Forced Conversion of the Jews of Trier 93
  4D – Murder Accusations and Religious Devotion 100
  4E – The Attack on the Jews of York
        Reported in Christian Sources................................103
  4F – The Erfurt *Judeneid*..107
  4G – Jews in Customary Law 109
  4H – Jews in the Illustrations of Legal Codes..........................110
  4I – A Contract Between the City and
        the Jewish Community of Augsburg........................112
  4J – The Great Expulsion of the Jews of France
        Through the Eyes of a Christian Chronicler...............115
  4K – The Black Death and the Persecution of Jews 117
  4L – The Persecution of Jews in Nordhausen
        during the Black Death..118

5 – Jews and Christians: Neighbors, Partners, Adversaries 121

    5A – The Role of Converts in Jewish–Christian Relations 121

    5B – The Exchequer of the Jews in Twelfth-Century England....123

    5C – Conversion to Judaism: Acceptance and Status 126

    5D – Jews in the Law of the Church...................................128

    5E – Papal Incentives for Jewish Conversion to Christianity.....133

    5F – Jewish Women in a Christian Monastery......................135

    5G – The House of Converts (*Domus Conversorum*) in Medieval London 137

    5H – Medical Cooperation..138

    5I – Punishment for Relapsed Converts in Jewish and Christian Practice...........................140

    5J – Jewish–Christian Dispute over Dearest Rachel: A Tale of Child Conversion to Christianity 142

    5K – Jewish Anti-Christian Polemics: A Walk through the Market 144

    5L – "The French King David": Illumination of a Jewish Biblical King 146

    5M – Jews as Seen in Christian Eyes 148

    5N – Sharing Tales: Jews and the Stories of Alexander the Great 150

    5O – The Fountain of Life in a *Haggadah*..........................151

    5P – Dukus Horant: A Heroic Epic in Old Yiddish 153

    5Q – "An Old Yiddish Knightly Tale" Etched into a Slate 155

Glossary 157

Bibliography...161

List of Contributors..168

List of Illustrations

Figure 1: Worms cemetery xi

Figure 2: Ashkenazi script: alphabet copied
in a *Mahzor Vitry* manuscript xiii

Map 1: Jewish settlement in northern France and England
in the late thirteenth century xxiv

Map 2: Jewish settlement in the German Empire and the
Low Countries in the late thirteenth century xxiv

Figure 3: Tombstone of Hannah Tova of Mainz 3

Map 3: Medieval Speyer and its Jewish sites 8

Figure 4: The medieval Synagogue of Speyer 8

Figures 5 and 6: The Friedberg *Mikveh* 17

Figure 7: Yiddish in the Worms *Mahzor* 21

Figure 8: Jousting depicted in a Hebrew liturgical manuscript 32

Figure 9: Hebrew inscription at the Lyvermann house basement 49

Figure 10: A detail from the Luxembourg coat of arms
in the *Brunngasse* house 82

Figure 11: The Basilica of Constantine in Trier 98

Figure 12: The Erfurt *Judeneid*. Erfurt, Municipal Archives.......... 107

Figure 13: The *Saxon Mirror (Sachsenspiegel)*,
    Wolfenbüttel manuscript. 111

Figure 14: The Augsburg contract and seals. 113

Figure 15: Jews wearing the badge. 131

Figure 16: David playing the harp............................... 147

Figure 17: The Israelites in the desert............................ 149

Figure 18: The Fountain of Life. 152

Figure 19: Yiddish tale on a slate from Cologne. 155

Introduction:
Jewish Life in Medieval Europe

Tzafrir Barzilay, Eyal Levinson, and Elisheva Baumgarten

Figure 1: Worms cemetery, © Neta Bodner

STROLLING DOWN THE NARROW paths of the *Heiliger Sand* (lit. holy sand, meaning holy ground),[1] the Jewish cemetery in Worms, Germany, numerous tombstones dot the grassy terrain, the earliest of which dates to the mid-eleventh century. They are a reminder of the vibrant Jewish community that was once an integral part of this bustling Upper Rhine urban center during the high and late Middle Ages. A few sport the names of well-known medieval Jewish scholars, others those of respected men and women who held important communal roles, but the vast major-

---

[1] Photos of the cemetery can be seen in the official site of the city of Worms https://www.worms-erleben.de/erleben/entdecken-und-staunen/sehenswuerdigkeiten/heiliger-sand.php.

ity of the tombstones commemorate "ordinary people"; children, women, and men whose stories are forever lost to us. Although there are those who reached a ripe old age, living well into their seventies and even eighties, many died in their youth. Their tombstones, usually erected by their loved ones, reveal scant information—family ties, age, occasionally the reason for their death (usually in cases where the deceased had been murdered or martyred), sometimes a profession is mentioned, a communal position or other personal details emerge from the short inscriptions. Their names may sound familiar to us, as many are popular Jewish names still in use today, such as Abigail, Hannah, Moshe, Rebecca, Meir, Jacob, Isaac, and Nathan. These tantalizing bits of information leave us hungry for more. Who were these people? What can we learn about their lives, their homes, families, and communities?

The historical study of daily life—the quotidian practices, norms, and beliefs of people of past generations—has become an increasing focus of research over the past three decades. It is tempting to imagine oneself within past circumstances and to contemplate the similarities and differences between past and present. The obvious danger, of course, is anachronism. We often assume that people were essentially the same in every period and culture, and that they thought and behaved as we do, but in truth we can only speculate as to how the personal experiences of other individuals matches our own. This volume seeks to provide a glimpse into the life of the Jews of northern Europe in the medieval period by presenting primary sources: documents, literature, and visual material created by the people who lived there.

As one leading historian of everyday life has argued, it is crucial to realize "that the distance between 'us' and the 'others' is not something self-evident and given, but problematical; it may be possible to bridge the gulf, but it cannot be eliminated."[2] How, then, can we bridge this gap between "us," in the present, and "them," in the past? How can we familiarize ourselves with their lives? While the personal stories of most of the people buried in the *Heiliger Sand* remain unknown to us, this volume presents sources that will help us piece together various aspects of their lives, illuminating features of their material culture, the spaces they frequented, and their quotidian routines.

---

[2] Alf Lüdtke, *The History of Everyday Life: Reconstructing Historical Experiences and Ways of Life* (Princeton: Princeton University Press, 1995), 8.

INTRODUCTION: JEWISH LIFE IN MEDIEVAL EUROPE   xiii

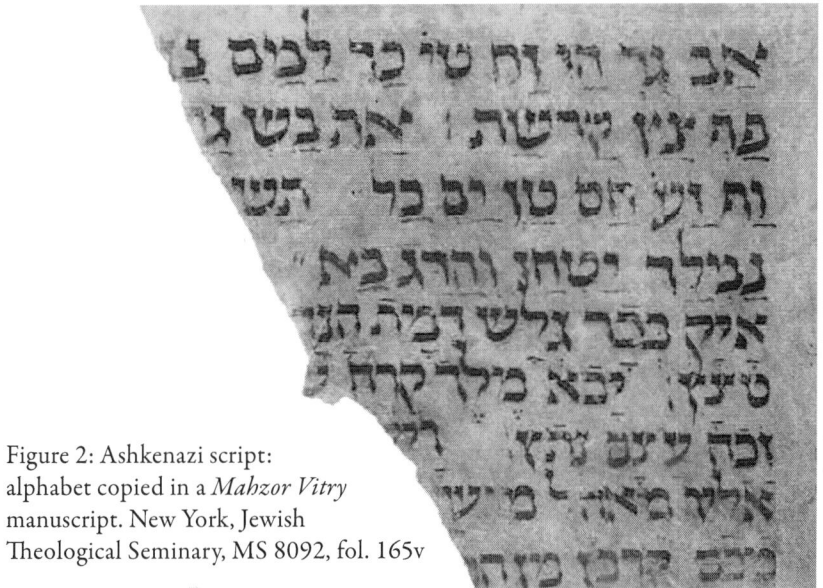

Figure 2: Ashkenazi script: alphabet copied in a *Mahzor Vitry* manuscript. New York, Jewish Theological Seminary, MS 8092, fol. 165v

The current volume focuses specifically on the Jews of Ashkenaz over the period 1080–1350. Ashkenaz is the name given to the geographical area that incorporated the German Empire, northern France, England and parts of Italy. These Jews shared customs. Later, these customs spread east, eventually reaching Poland as well. These lands of the European northwest had a similar climate and geography, which shaped and determined their patterns of agriculture and economy. It is thus not surprising that they also shared many social institutions during this period. Similarly, the Jewish communities of this geographical unit also shared numerous cultural traits which served to differentiate them in many respects from the Jews in Spain and those living along the European shores of the Mediterranean to the south of this geographic area.[3] These include unique customs and worldviews, a particular Hebrew script (called Ashkenazi script), and close and ongoing ties between the rabbinic authorities of the region. Most importantly, these medieval Jews often saw Ashkenaz as a distinct unit within the wider Jewish world. That being said, it was not a homogeneous society and there were important local differences between

---

[3] The Jews of north European descent are still known as Askenazim, those of Spain as Sepharadim (Spain is called Sepharad in Hebrew), and those of north Africa as Mizrahim (from the Hebrew word for East, Mizrah).

the communities, some of which will emerge clearly in the sources we present.

The majority of Ashkenazi Jews lived in relatively small urban communities, which often included dozens of families, with the larger ones comprising hundreds of individuals. While overall the Jews numbered 1 to 5 percent of the northern European population (as far as the limited demographic information available allows us to estimate), in many of the towns of the period they were a significant minority. In each town they tended to live close to each other, often in the center of the city near the palace of the local ruler who often protected them. In some towns there were streets, usually those on which the local synagogue, the *mikveh*, and other communal buildings stood, which were named *Judengasse* (Jews' street, German) or *Rue des juifs* (the Jews' alley, French). During this period Jews were not usually forced to live in walled-off areas (that were later to be called ghettoes), so Jews and Christians could mingle freely and traverse the urban space as they wished, and Jews were not usually limited in where they could purchase real estate. In this environment, in which Jews and Christians were neighbors, acquaintances, and business partners, some even formed close friendships. They surely knew each other well and sometimes shared political interests and cultural ideas. At the same time, relations were not always amicable, and violence at the hands of their Christian neighbors was a recurring threat for medieval Jews. These complex relationships between Jews and Christians shaped medieval urban daily life.

Little is known about the communities of the region prior to the eleventh century, beyond the existence of a few small Jewish settlements. Unfortunately, very little source material has survived from this earlier period, and this paucity has determined our start date of the year 1080. The latest sources in this collection are dated to the mid-fourteenth century, specifically 1347–1350, when the Black Death, a plague, swept the continent, killing about a third of the population, and resulting in significant political, social, and cultural upheaval. During these years the Jewish communities suffered not only the horrors of the plague itself, as non-Jews did, but were also subjected to murderous persecutions as a result of accusations that they caused the plague by poisoning wells. Over three hundred Jewish communities were decimated around the first outbreak of the plague, many completely destroyed. As a result, in the aftermath of the Black Death the size, organizational structure, and political status of the surviving communities were significantly changed. Even before the plague, however, Jewish existence in Ashkenaz faced major challenges. Jews were expelled from one location after the other. The Jews of England were expelled, not to return for centuries, in 1290. The Jews of France were expelled in 1182, and were then readmitted only to be expelled again, with the process being repeated in 1306 before the final expulsion in 1394. In Germany starting from the late thirteenth century, the Jewish communities were subjected to several waves of severe persecution before the Black Death, especially in 1298 and 1336, significantly more brutal and widespread than the occasional local violence of earlier centuries (with the exception of the massacres of 1096). The plague, therefore, marked the peak of a crisis that had been ongoing for several decades, at the end of which many of the Jewish communities of Ashkenaz were either completely destroyed or profoundly changed. The period of 1080–1350 therefore stands as a distinct political, social, and cultural period in the history of the Jews of northern Europe.

There are other sourcebooks that present documents written by Jews and about Jews—among them, *The Jew in the Medieval World, A Source Book: 315–1791*,[4] compiled by Jacob R. Marcus, is notable. However, none of these collections covers as defined a period of time and geographical area as does this volume, and none focuses on Jewish everyday life. Marcus's book, for example, spans a period of almost fifteen hundred years, from the Christianization of the Roman Empire to the French Revolution, and a vast geographical area that includes Europe, the Mediterranean, and the Middle East, and focuses on theology, politics, law, and ideology rather than on lived experience. The documents collected in this volume, on the other hand, relate in some way or another to "ordinary people": women and children, craftsmen, and paupers. It is true that many of the documents in this sourcebook either refer to Jews associated with the learned or economical elite or were themselves written by male scholars, because this is the nature of the vast majority of surviving sources. Our goal as social historians, however, is to use these documents to illuminate Jewish society at large. This is possible due to the multiple

---

[4] First edition: Jacob R. Marcus, *The Jew in the Medieval World, A Source Book: 315–1791* (Cincinnati: Sinai Press, 1938). Also see: Solomon Grayzel, ed., *The Church and the Jews in the XIIIth Century* (New York: Hermon, 1966); Amnon Linder, ed., *The Jews in the Legal Sources of the Early Middle Ages* (Detroit: Wayne State University Press, 1997); Olivia Remie Constable and Damian Zurro, eds., *Medieval Iberia: Readings from Christian, Muslim, and Jewish Sources* (Philadelphia: University of Pennsylvania Press, 2012).

ongoing social interactions between all segments of society reflected in the documents. Rich and poor, learned and less learned, women, men, and children, youth and adults—all saw and were in daily contact with one another. They met each other within their shared communal spaces: the synagogues, *mikvaot* (ritual baths), and the dance halls, during funerals, on the street and in the markets, or within each other's homes. Thus, a careful reading of these documents, even if written by and for the elite, can shed light on the everyday life of other sectors of the community.

What exactly do we mean by the term *everyday life*? Scholars have suggested several definitions, as during the twentieth century everyday life became a methodological concept used in such academic disciplines as anthropology, sociology, cultural studies, and, from the late 1970s on, also in historical research, where it was particularly popular in Germany. In the context of this sourcebook, the term *everyday life* refers to the ways in which people habitually act, think, and feel. It is about subjectivity and experience, about bringing to the fore those voices and experiences that were overlooked and undervalued by previous generations of historians. As historian Alf Lüdtke wrote, at the center of the history of everyday life "are the lives and sufferings of those who are frequently labeled, suggestively but imprecisely, as the 'small people.' It involves their work and non-work.[5] The picture includes housing and homelessness, clothing and nakedness; eating and hunger, love and hate." Lüdtke points out the connection of this definition with the (relatively) new academic focus on the history of non-elite people: "Beyond this, certain thematic emphases have emerged, such as the history of work, of gender relations, of the family, and especially of popular cultures. The attention is no longer focused on the deeds (and misdeeds) and pageantry of the great, the masters of church and state."[6] In short, the study of everyday life focuses on recurring practices and common spaces, especially in relation to the existence of the "ordinary people."

This volume offers students a sense of the spaces frequented by the Jews of Ashkenaz, their daily practices and rituals, and how they thought about all three. There are sources that discuss culinary preferences or details of intimate sexual relations, while others deal with clothes, objects,

---

[5] That is, regular activities not relating or involving paid work.

[6] Alf Lüdtke, "'Alltagsgeschichte': Verführung oder Chance? Zur Erforschung der Praxis historischer Subjekte," unpublished paper, cited by Geoff Eley in Lüdtke, *The History of Everyday Life*, ix.

or communal buildings. Some documents testify to how Jews observed Sabbaths and holidays, and held weddings and funerals, celebrated births, and other life cycle events. Others focus on the relationships with Christian neighbors, local authorities, and the Church. Still others offer details regarding daily economic activities, professions, and trade. All these different perspectives together provide answers to questions regarding medieval daily life directly from the words of the Jews themselves, albeit through the filters of translation and editing.

Our sourcebook is divided into five sections. The first, *From Birth to Death and Throughout the Year: Life Cycle and Rituals*, contains sources dealing with turning points in the life of a particular individual or family, such as births, coming of age, weddings, and deaths; as well as those relating to the cycle of the year in the community: holidays, fast days, and special communal events, such as the dedication of a synagogue. The focus in this section is on events that were regular occurrences in every community but that nonetheless carried deep emotional, social, and religious significance for those who participated in them. They thus represent central features of Jewish daily life.

The second part, *Living Arrangements: Family, Household, and the Home*, highlights the everyday activities that took place within Jewish households. The sources focus on where medieval Jews slept, what they ate, and the kinds of relationships they sustained with their family members. They deal more with common experiences and behaviors than with events.

In *Making a Living: Money, Markets, and Professions*, we present sources pertaining to the economics of medieval Jewish life. The Jews of Europe are often described as usurers, who made a living offering interest loans to their Christian neighbors (indeed, this notion often justified the violence and persecution carried out against them throughout this and later periods). While there were those who dealt in credit supply (as did many Christians), Jews also worked as traders, craftsmen, and service providers. The sources on the subject reveal the negative image that Christians often held regarding Jews in this context, but also the complex reality of their economic life and daily social interactions.

Law and Order, Disruption and Crisis focuses on select legal sources involving Jews, such as incidents in which Jews faced legal sanctions or suffered as a result of the violation of legal protections accorded them by rulers and local authorities. The documents include statutes and regulations from secular and Church law as well as court records, and shed light on the legal status of medieval Jews within Christian society: ranging from protected on the one hand, to marginalization on the other, with many alternatives in between. Also included are internal legal discussions of the Jewish communities. These reveal the highly legalistic nature of medieval Jewish society, in which Jewish law (*halakhah*) formed the basis for a variety of social norms and practices. These Hebrew sources, in conjunction with Latin and vernacular sources, allow a better understanding of medieval society.

The final section, *Jews and Christians: Neighbors, Partners, and Adversaries*, focuses on sources attesting to the connections between Jews and their Christian neighbors. Although this subject comes up often in other sections as well, it was such a central feature of medieval Jewish life that we felt it necessitated a separate section. Jews and Christians shared numerous business ties and exchanged cultural ideas and beliefs as well as having personal relationships. They also had a mutual distrust and animosity, and Jews were sometimes the victims of discrimination and horrifying violence at the hands of their Christian neighbors. Although there was a wide range of attitudes characterizing the relationship between the two communities within medieval society, the one constant was the fact that Jews were a minority within the cities and towns of northern Europe, and this dictated that, for better or worse, their relations with their Christian neighbors shaped much of their daily experience.

* * *

First developed as a distinct academic field in the mid-nineteenth century, the study of Jewish life in medieval Europe tended to focus on the broad strokes and major turning points of Jewish history: from the heights of intellectual innovation, sophisticated communal organization, and religious devotion to nadirs of marginalization, discrimination, and persecution. For many scholars, the high points were marked by the internal development of Jewish culture, while the lows evolved from challenges forced upon the Jews by the surrounding Christian society. The Jews were therefore often portrayed as a society within a society, and their tendency towards isolationism was overemphasized and even applauded. Enmity between Jews and Christians was considered the norm and cooperation and sharing of culture were seen as coincidental at best and shameful at worst. These scholars thus developed the basic outlines of the field under the assumption that Jews and Christians lived completely separate lives and maintained their distance when possible.

Their attitude was not completely far-fetched. In fact, according to available sources medieval Jews were indeed a marginalized, and sometimes persecuted, minority in northern Europe, and evidence of Christian enmity towards them is abundant (as the selection of sources in the following pages makes clear). However, in the 1920s Salo Wittmayer Baron, one of the great scholars of Jewish history, underlined a basic methodological problem with this attitude: its tendency to focus on major political events and prominent men. He noted, for example, that while the horrific persecutions of 1096 and 1348 had been the focus of much scholarship, periods of peace and prosperity merited little discussion. While medieval scholars and communal leaders such as Rashi and Meir of Rothenburg were (justifiably) portrayed as highly innovative and influential, the ordinary lives of the majority of Jews, who were not part of the rabbinic elite, were almost entirely overlooked. Baron made it his mission to write a conclusive history of the Jews that would go beyond lachrymose descriptions of Christian violence and internal intellectual developments of Judaism. The result was *A Social and Religious History of the Jews*, an eighteen-volume opus that took over thirty years to complete.[7]

Baron's work is a *tour de force* but, as several scholars have pointed out, because it sought to cover the entire history of the Jewish people—a history that spans over three millennia and the globe—it necessarily had to adopt a bird's-eye view on the development of Jewish culture. Major political events, influential intellectual movements, and elite men were thus still often the focus of attention. Since the turn of the twenty-first century, several historians have attempted to address other facets of Jewish existence, as Baron had originally intended, and although significant progress has been made in broadening the scope to include Jewish women and the Jewish family, none has successfully devised a practical way to deal with the issues that Baron's work raised.[8]

The work of Elisheva Baumgarten and the *Beyond the Elite* group (2016–2022) has offered a change in perspective, seeking to focus on the importance of routine everyday life, and on Jews who were not part of the

---

[7] Salo W. Baron, *A Social and Religious History of the Jews*, 18 vols. (New York: Columbia University Press, 1952–1983). The work of Israel Abrahams, the first to systematically discuss issues of everyday history of medieval Jews, should also be mentioned in this context: Abrahams, *Jewish Life in the Middle Ages* (London: Macmillan, 1896).

[8] For relevant bibliography, see bibliography section at the end of this volume.

elite. To do so, they moved away from the idea of portraying a complete history of the Jews (or even only of the Jews of a particular area or period). Instead, they published studies on the Jewish household and family, on the economic activity of Jews, on their rituals, their spaces, their objects, and their routines.[9] This approach is not intended to replace work focusing on political and intellectual phenomena, but to supplement it and thus provide a more comprehensive picture of Jewish life in medieval Ashkenaz.

This work is known in academic circles, but does not always find its way into popular culture or the classroom. One issue is that the experience of medieval daily life is not easily comprehensible for students. Many of the physical and cultural factors that shaped everyday experiences are absent from our contemporary world, and it is not easy to imagine them. In addition, some students are often more interested in "big events" than in everyday experience: political conspiracies, bloody battles, and formidable heroes tend to generate more excitement. This makes it challenging to paint a multifaceted picture of the past, and students are sometimes left with a black-and-white perception of medieval society. This volume offers an in-depth understanding of medieval Jewish life that demonstrates the complex realities in which these Jews lived. The primary sources allow readers access to the words and ideas of medieval people, providing students with a better and more immediate sense of quotidian life and the complex factors that shaped it. For professors, this volume is a tool that makes medieval sources on everyday life easily accessible for English-speaking students by providing translations from medieval Hebrew, Latin, and other vernacular languages. It provides a comprehensible first step into the field of medieval European Jewish history, with an emphasis on daily life.

Primary sources are the basis of any historical research. There are, after all, no live witnesses who can tell us about their experiences in the distant past and no photographs or movies that captured what life looked like. All that we have are documents and literary sources written at the time, along with paintings, objects, and buildings from the period. Interpreting these sources takes skill. Beyond issues of paleography (the study of historical handwriting) and translation, one has to consider the immediate contexts in which they were created as well as the cultural backgrounds of

---

[9] For publications and further information, see: https://beyond-the-elite.huji.ac.il.

their creators. Before presenting any general historical narratives, scholars have to analyze each primary source that serves as evidence for their arguments to ensure that they decipher and present it correctly. Thus, a sophisticated reading of primary sources is a crucial skill that every student of history must master. This current volume aims to facilitate that process.

To understand the relevant context for each primary source, historians must first consider a set of basic questions:

- Who wrote or created this source?
- For whom was it written?
- Where and when was it created, and how did these circumstances influence its content?
- What is its genre? How is it organized?
- Why was the source created? What was its purpose?
- In what language was the source written? Was it edited?
- What kind of information does it reveal, and which parts were apparently revealed unintentionally?

Having answered these basic questions, scholars can then determine the particular queries they would like to study based on the content of the source and their particular areas of interest. Let us take for example a list of contributions to a medieval synagogue made over the course of a century. One scholar could use it to study which items were considered valuable, or the wealth of certain donors. Another may focus on the names of donors to note how naming practices changed over time and ask what these changes teach us about the surrounding culture. A third scholar could note the date of each donation to understand which occasions were popular times for supporting communal enterprises. We can, of course, think of many more such ideas. Thus, the same source can be read in several ways and be utilized for different research projects. The introduction for each source presented in this volume provides some answers to the basic questions listed above. As for other historical queries, although this book suggests ways in which these sources can be read, readers are of course invited to pursue additional directions.

The sources contained in the volume consist of a variety of genres, languages, periods, and locations. They include archival sources such as court cases, official records, and notarial agreements; literary sources such as stories, poems, and chronicles; and legal sources such as law codes and legal correspondence. A unique genre for understanding Jewish daily life is *responsa* literature. These consist of questions people would send to a prominent rabbinic authority about specific situations relating to *halakhah* that were not covered in traditional sources, and the answers to their queries. While these questions and answers were often formulated as hypothetical cases, they still reveal much about the daily realities of medieval Jews.

Hebrew was the language in which medieval Jews usually wrote, and thus Hebrew sources constitute the majority of the material included in this volume. We have also included texts written by Christians for or about Jews that were written in Latin, the written language of high medieval Christian Europe, as well as some sources translated from vernacular languages—the particular languages of each region, which were spoken by both Jews and Christians. Temporally and spatially the sources span the entire period in question, 1080–1350, and the entire relevant geographical area: Germany, northern France, and England. In addition to the written sources, this volume includes images from medieval manuscripts, pictures of surviving medieval buildings and objects, and maps that illuminate the physical spaces in which Jews lived and operated in medieval northern Europe.

To facilitate the use of each source, each is accompanied by a brief explanation of its historical context. Words in Hebrew (or other medieval languages) are marked in italics and translated in the text. At the end of each source the reader can find up to four items for further reading, as well as a longer general list of such items at the end of the book. We have also included a standard index of terms, names, and places as well as a glossary of relevant terms. Each term that appears in the glossary is marked in bold throughout the book. Our intention was to design a source book that is useful for students with no prior knowledge of the field, while allowing more experienced students to broaden their horizons.

As always when deciding what to include, there is much that must unfortunately be left out. Works of Jewish philosophy and Hebrew grammar, common throughout the Middle Ages, have not been included. General tractates of law, biblical and talmudic commentaries, and liturgical works are also underrepresented, although they amount to the vast majority of surviving Hebrew manuscripts from this period. Given that these genres usually focus on general theoretical issues they therefore contain less information on daily life and we deemed them less relevant for our purposes. However, such sources have been translated in other books and articles, so a student who wishes to explore them should be able to do so with relative ease.[10] In addition, this is by no means a comprehensive compilation of relevant material, and there are of course many sources that reflect Jewish everyday life in medieval northern Europe that have not been included here. We invite researchers and students to delve into this field, and add new sources, insights, and discoveries to the growing scholarship.

This book is the fruit of the collaborative efforts of the research group *Beyond the Elite: Jewish Daily Life in Medieval Europe*, based at the Hebrew University in Jerusalem and supported by the European Research Council (Grant Agreement No. 681507). Led by Professor Elisheva Baumgarten, *Beyond the Elite* is a collaborative and interdisciplinary team that makes use of methodologies borrowed from fields such as sociology, anthropology, archaeology, gender studies, and art history, in addition to more traditional historical methods. The group's intention is to study a variety of quotidian practices and aspects of social and religious life pertaining to the Jewish communities of medieval northern Europe. Its goal is to broaden the scope of historical research regarding these communities and better understand the ways they created, manifested, and negotiated their religious identities within their medieval Christian environments. This volume is a further step towards this goal.

Each member of the *Beyond the Elite* team chose sources from his or her field of research, translated and edited them, and added introductory comments. This process, in which the unique skills of each member came into play, allowed this volume to cover a wide range of genres, languages, periods, and locations, which would have been beyond the scope of any single scholar working alone. The team members: Nureet Dermer, Aviya Doron, Miri Fenton, Etelle Kalaora, Adi Namia-Cohen, Andreas Lehnertz, Neta Bodner, Albert Kohn, Hannah Teddy Schachter, Amit Shafran, Tzafrir Barzilay, Eyal Levinson, and Elisheva Baumgarten, also wish to thank team member Audrey Fingherman, who has been responsible for much of the administrative work required for the compilation of this volume.

---

[10] See note 4 above, as well as the bibliography section at the end of this volume.

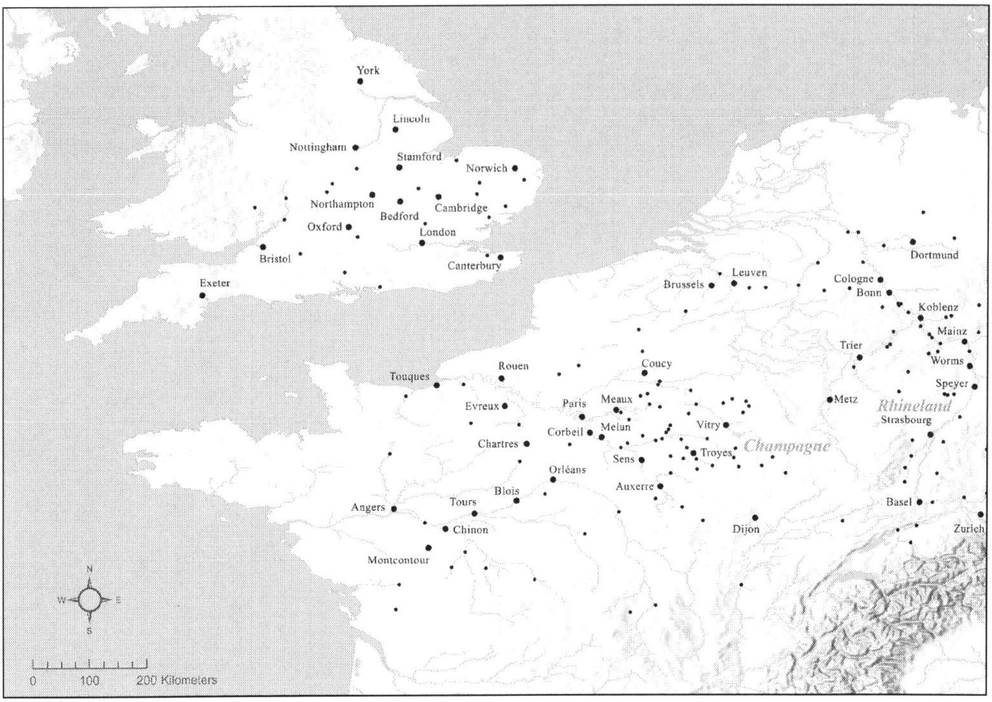

Map 1: Jewish settlement in northern France and England in the late thirteenth century. Map by Ruhama Bonfil.

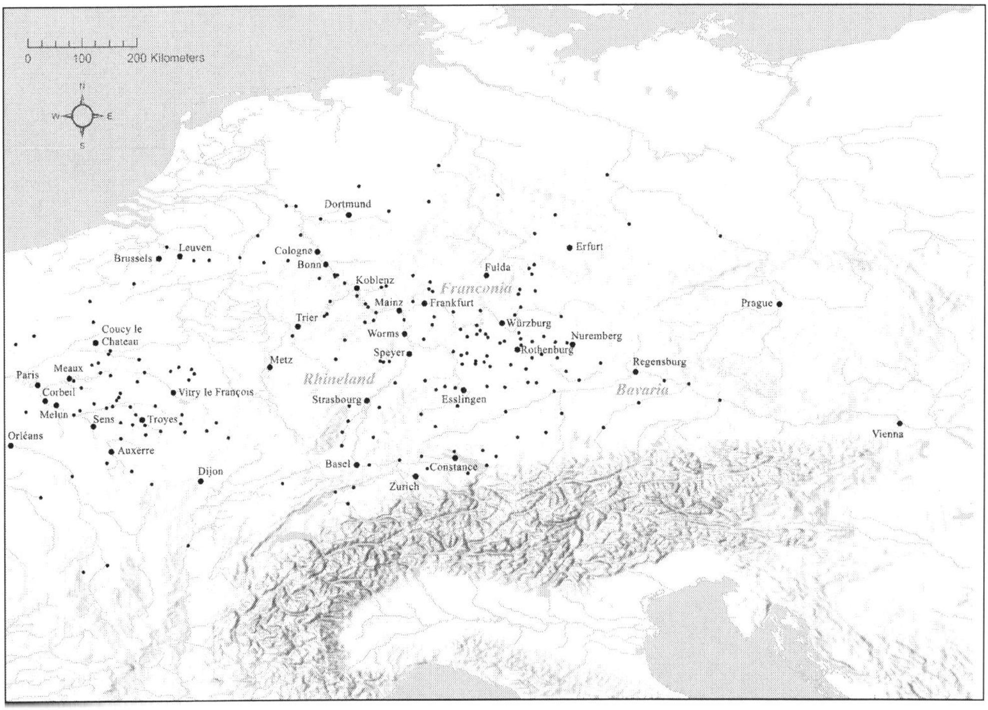

Map 2: Jewish settlement in the German Empire and the Low Countries in the late thirteenth century. Map by Ruhama Bonfil.

1 – From Birth to Death and Throughout the Year: Life Cycle and Rituals

1A – Medieval Tombstones from Mainz

Tombstones, and particularly their epitaphs, provide a glimpse into the values and conventions of a community. Epitaphs can tell us much about the way some individuals were commemorated, conceptions about the afterlife, and the values of the community. They also draw attention to many people otherwise not mentioned in more formal sources. On Jewish tombstones of the period an individual was referred to by their personal name and that of their father. Maternal connections are not noted.

Below are eleven tombstones from Mainz from the high Middle Ages. What can we learn from the epitaphs about the deceased and their world? What kind of deeds are they described as performing? What kinds of events are mentioned? The list below features some people who were learned and well known and others about whom we have no additional knowledge. All dates are written using the Hebrew lunar calendar. Note the names of the men and women, descriptions of their status, and any other traits depicted.

> This is the tombstone of our rabbi, Rabbi Judah son of Yakar[1] who died and went to heaven in the year 824 [1063].[2] May his soul be in Eden.[3]

> This is the tombstone of Marat [Mistress] Rebecca daughter of Isaac who died in 842 [1082] may she rest in Eden on the 6th of *Adar*.[4]

---

[1] Judah b. Yakar was a well-known rabbi from Mainz, a pupil of Gershom b. Judah, Light of the Exile.

[2] The Jewish year is calculated from what is considered the creation of the world. Here the year is 4824, usually just signified by the last digits. The numbers in brackets represent the date CE.

[3] A reference to the Garden of Eden, another term for heaven.

[4] A month in the Jewish calendar, roughly parallel to March.

Marat [Mistress] Hannah Tova daughter of R.[5] Joel the *Levite*,[6] the widow of Our Rabbi Eliezer died on 3rd of *Nissan*,[7] 849 [1089] may her soul rest under the Tree of Life.[8]

This stone is for the head of Marat Tzeruya daughter of R. Joel, the important woman who died in 928 [1167/8], may she rest in Eden.

This stone was erected for the head of R. Meshulam son of Kalonymous who died on the 12th of *Kislev*[9] 932 [1171] may he rest under the Tree of Life.

This stone was erected for the head of the groom, R. Judah son of Meir who died on the 7th of *Sivan*[10] 929 [1169], may he rest in the Garden of Eden.

The grave of Hakim haCohen,[11] the boy son of Meir who died in *Marheshvan*[12] in 967 [1206], may he rest in Eden.

This is the tombstone for R. Shemaryah son of Hakim who was killed under the roof in his house in *Adar* 1012 [1252] without hate, may his soul be kept in the bundle of the living (*beTsror haHaim*).[13]

This is the grave of the Rabbi, R. Meir son of Abraham haCohen the elderly who was killed **sanctifying the name of God** in 1041 [1281] on the 27th of *Sivan*, on the day the **synagogue** was burnt and **Torah scrolls** were torn, may he rest with honor.

This is a stone that commemorates Marat Hannah who died at the age of nineteen but was wise like an old woman, the daughter of R. Judah, the head of the pack and in her short years she rejoiced in God and bore her soul and scattered bread and honored those far and wide and

---

[5] When the word "Rabbi" is not written out, this signifies an appellation comparable to "Mr." The word "rabbi" signifies a learned authority.

[6] A Jewish male descendant of the tribe of Levi.

[7] A month in the Jewish calendar, roughly parallel to April.

[8] An expression for heaven.

[9] A month in the Jewish calendar, roughly parallel to December.

[10] A month in the Jewish calendar, roughly parallel to May.

[11] Cohen—a decedent of one of the families that served as priests in the ancient temple of Jerusalem (destroyed 70 CE).

[12] A month in the Jewish calendar, roughly parallel to October.

[13] An expression customarily added to a deceased Jewish person and often written on Jewish tombstones.

she died on the day of the destruction of the temple (9ᵗʰ of *Av*)¹⁴ in the year 1052 [1292] and as she is gathered to God we must repent, may she dwell with women in the tent.

This is the tombstone of Marat Pesslin, the pious and old woman, the daughter of R. Moses who died on the 18ᵗʰ of *Nissan* on Friday in the year 1080 [1320], may her soul be bundled in the bundle of life. Amen, Amen, Sela.

SOURCE: Epidat, epigraphische Datenbank
http://www.steinheim-institut.de/cgi-bin/epidat.

Here is a picture of the Marat (Mistress) Hannah Tova daughter of R. Joel tombstone, standing in the old Jewish cemetery of Mainz. Note the Hebrew script, still legible today.

E. B.

Figure 3: Tombstone of Hannah Tova of Mainz

Further Reading

Horowitz, Elliott. "Speaking to the Dead: Cemetery Prayer in Medieval and Early Modern Jewry." *Journal of Jewish Thought and Philosophy* 8 (1999): 303–17.

Raspe, Lucia. "Sacred Space, Local History and Diasporic Identity: The Graves of the Righteous in Medieval and Early Modern Ashkenaz." In *Jewish Studies at the Crossroads of Anthropology and History*, ed. Ra'anan Boustan, Oren Kosansky, and Maria Rustow, 147–63. Philadelphia: University of Pennsylvania Press, 2011.

Reiner, Avraham (Rami). "The Dead as Living History: On the Publication of Die Grabsteine vom jüdischen Friedhof in Würzburg 1147–1346." In *Death in Jewish Life: Burial and Mourning Customs Among Jews of Europe and Nearby Communities*, ed. Stefan C. Reif, Andreas Lehnardt, and Avriel Bar-Levav, 199–211. Berlin: de Gruyter, 2014.

---

¹⁴ A month in the Jewish calendar, roughly parallel to July.

1B – Food, Mourning, and the Jewish Life Cycle

Attributing symbolic meanings to foods used in life cycle rituals was (and still is) a common practice in many cultures. For the Jews of medieval Ashkenaz, sharing meals with the local community was a common practice whether before and/or after life cycle ceremonies. The *Seudat Havra'ah* (lit. meal of health or recovery) was the meal eaten right after the funeral of a loved one. Eaten after the mourners returned from the gravesite, the meal was provided by the neighbors and consumed in the mourner's house. It consisted of simple food and included bread and boiled eggs. This meal is documented in the biblical exegesis of Rashi (Solomon son of Isaac of Troyes; ca. 1040–1105). In Rashi's commentary on Esau's sale of his birthright to Jacob for a stew made of lentils (Gen. 25:30), he quotes a midrash that refers to the **talmudic** preference to eat lentils at the *Seudat Havra'ah*: eating lentils was a known custom throughout the Roman Empire, for Jews as well as for non-Jews, in antiquity, for their symbolic meaning as representing the life cycle. Rashi's commentary reveals that in medieval Ashkenaz Jews ate eggs rather than lentils at the beginning of this meal. The eating of an egg as the food of consolation was not only symbolic but also nutritional, as eggs were considered especially nourishing, and had the added advantage of being easily attainable.

> And on that day, Abraham died ... and Jacob cooked the lentils to feed the mourner [his father, Isaac]. And why lentils? Which resemble a wheel, for mourning is like a wheel turning in the world. And what else? Lentils have no mouth and so the mourner has no mouth, for he is prohibited from speaking. Therefore, it is customary to feed the mourner with eggs at the beginning of his meal, since they are round and have no mouth. So too, a mourner has no mouth.
>
> SOURCE: Rashi, Gen. 25:30. "MeHaAdom Adom."

A. N. C.

Further Reading

Reif, Stefan C., Andreas Lehnardt, and Avriel Bar-Levav, eds. *Death in Jewish Life: Burial and Mourning Customs among Jews of Europe and Nearby Communities*. Berlin and Boston: de Gruyter, 2014.

Rubin, Nissan. *Time and Life Cycle in Talmud and Midrash: Socio-anthropological Perspectives*. Boston: Academic Studies Press, 2008.

1C – The Establishment of the Speyer Community and Its Main Synagogue

Solomon son of Samson (*Shlomo bar Shimshon*) of Mainz, who, in a work dated to the 1140s, described the massacre of the Jews that had taken place place during the First Crusade in 1096, added the passage below into his **chronicle**. The passage, written sometime earlier by an anonymous author from Speyer, reports on the establishment of the Speyer community and its **synagogue**. The community was established in 1084 by Jewish refugees from Mainz, under the protection of Speyer's **bishop**. The bishops of Speyer continued to provide protection for the Jews, including during the persecution of 1096. However, tensions with some of the local Christians forced the Jews to move from the outskirts of the city to its center, closer to the bishop's palace. In 1104 the building of a new synagogue, parts of which can still be seen today, was completed in the new location. Thus, this short passage contains many details pertaining to the communal history of the Jews of Speyer, as well as to their relations with the local Christians.

> In the beginning, we came to prop up our tents, whose stakes will never be plucked up,[15] to this [city of] Speyer. And this was because of the fire which struck the city of Mainz. Because the city of Mainz is our hometown, the place of our ancestors, the most ancient, laudable, and commendable community of all the communities of the kingdom; And the entire neighborhood of the Jews and their street was burnt, and we were in great fear of the [Christian] citizens. ... And this was the year 1084–5. ... And then we decided to get out of there and to stay at whatever walled city we can find, perhaps the merciful Lord would have mercy [on us], and the kind one will show kindness, and He who saves will save us[16] to keep us alive today. And he [Bishop Rüdiger of Speyer][17] accepted us with a happy face, and sent his lords and knights to escort us [into the city]. And he then gave us the outskirts of the city, and told us that he would encircle us with a wall, gates, and bolts, as a fortress to keep us safe from our enemies. And he spared us as a man spares his son.[18] And we prayed before our creator for many days.

---

[15] Isa. 33:20.

[16] Deut. 33:19.

[17] See the privilege of Rüdiger of Speyer, source 4A in this volume.

[18] Mal. 3:17.

And we were saved by the bishop Johan [during the massacre of 1096], and eleven people were killed and the rest of the community were saved, may His name be blessed and praised. And afterwards we came back to the city, each man to his own place. And those who lived in the upper neighborhood could not walk to the lower neighborhood, in the evening, morning, and noon [to pray], because of fear of the damned enemies. And so, in the upper neighborhood we prayed in the house of learning [***beit midrash***] of our Rabbi Judah son of our Rabbi Kalonymus. And those who lived in the lower neighborhood prayed there in the synagogue, and so they did for a few years.

And the entire work [of building a new synagogue, in the upper neighborhood] was completed in the month of *Elul*[19] in the year 1104. And in New Year's Eve [**Rosh haShanah**] came one of the old men and told the community: come, and we shall bring the [**Torah**] ark to the house which we have built, to its rightful place. And the elders of the community, and the *Kohanim* and *Levi'im* [decedents of the families who traditionally served in the temple], went and brought the **Torah scrolls** into the ark which was there in the synagogue with great joy. And they remained there to this day. And the next day, on New Year's Day (*Rosh haShanah*), we began to pray in it, and we continued to pray there to this day.

SOURCE: The Chronicle of Shlomo bar Shimshon. In: Eva A. Haverkamp, ed., *Hebräische Berichte über die Judenverfolgungen während des Ersten Kreuzzugs* (Hanover: Hahnsche Buchhandlung, Monumenta Germaniae Historica and Israel Academy of Sciences, 2005), 491–93.

Tz. B.

Further Reading

Chazan, Robert. *In the Year 1096: The First Crusade and the Jews*. Philadelphia: The Jewish Publication Society, 1996.

Transier, Werner. "Speyer: The Jewish Community in the Middle Ages." In *The Jews of Europe in the Middle Ages (Tenth to Fifteenth Centuries)*, ed. Christoph Cluse, 435–47. Turnhout: Brepols, 2004.

---

[19] All of the dates in this text are according to the Hebrew calendar. The month of *Elul* is parallel to September or October.

1D – Map of Medieval Speyer and Its Jewish Sites

Established in 1084, the Jewish community of Speyer was significantly younger than the large communities of Mainz, Worms, and Cologne. In the eleventh century, German emperors from the **Salian dynasty** rose to power and turned Speyer into a political and religious center, a process that included building a major cathedral[20] in the city. Speyer, however, was ruled not by the emperors but by the local **bishop**. The map overleaf shows two centers of Jewish settlement. The northern one, near the cemetery, is older, probably dating to 1084, and is the lower neighborhood mentioned in the Solomon son of Samson **chronicle** ("lower" meaning downstream of the Rhine river, though it appears on the upper half of the map, that is, the northern part of the city). The southern settlement (the "upper neighbourhood"), marked by the **synagogue** and the *mikveh*, became the center of the Jewish community after the persecutions of 1096, when, due to the hostility of the **crusaders** and some local Christians, the Jews decided to relocate closer to the cathedral and the bishop's palace in order to be better protected. This further demonstrates the importance of the bishop's role in enabling the stable existence of a Jewish settlement (also see the **privilege** of Rüdiger Huozmann of Speyer, source 4A).

SOURCE: Werner Transier, "Speyer: The Jewish Community in the Middle Ages," in *The Jews of Europe in the Middle Ages (Tenth to Fifteenth Centuries)*, ed. Christoph Cluse (Turnhout: Brepols, 2004), 437.

Tz. B.

Further Reading

Engels, Renate. "Topography of Jewish Speyer in the Middle Ages." In *The Jews of Europe in the Middle Ages*, exhibition catalog, 69–75. Speyer: Historisches Museum der Pfalz, 2004.

---

[20] The cathedral was the church that was the seat of the bishop.

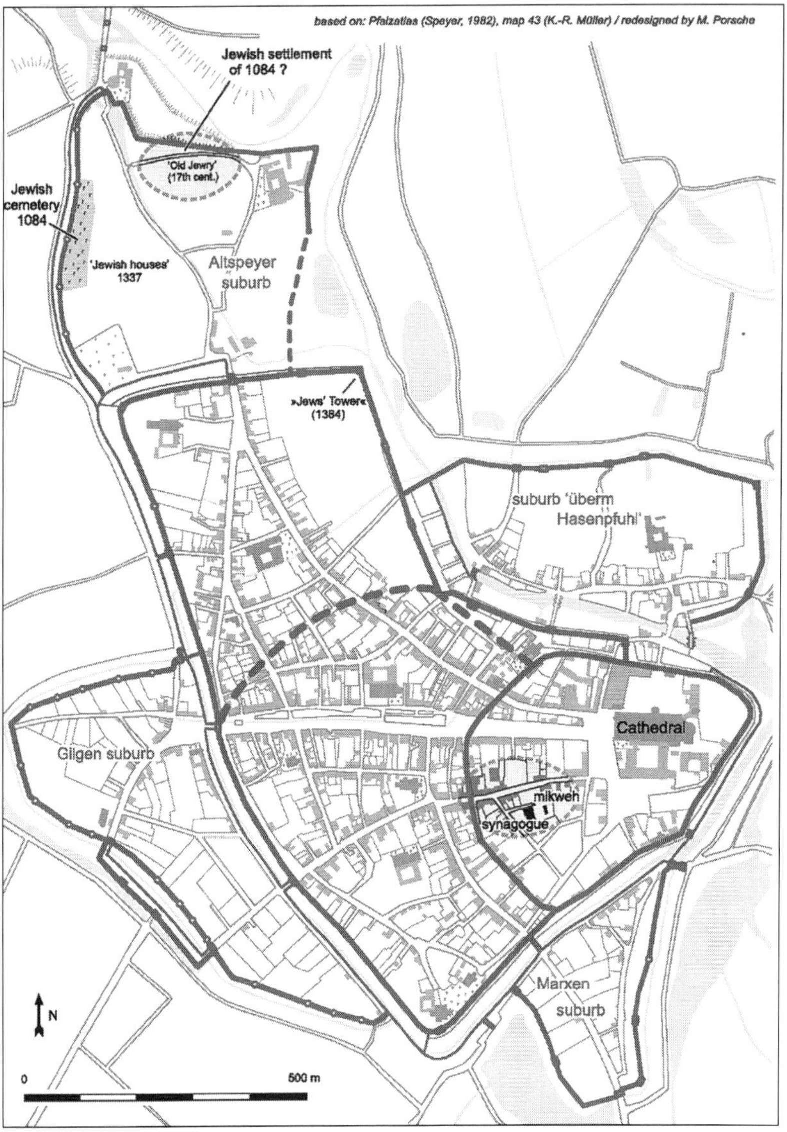

Map 3: Medieval Speyer and its Jewish sites

Figure 4: The medieval Synagogue of Speyer, © Neta Bodner

1E – The Medieval Synagogue of Speyer

Part of the remains of the medieval **synagogue** in Speyer, including some features of the original 1104 construction mentioned in the source The Establishment of the Speyer Community and its Main Synagogue (1D), have survived. Figure 4 opposite shows the eastern wall of the synagogue, the oldest one extant, and gives an idea of the size, shape, and function of the structure. The synagogue was the spiritual center of the community, where prayers as well as other religious and communal practices took place every day. The structure is rectangular in shape, and its fairly modest size, thirty-four feet wide by fifty-seven feet long (about eleven by eighteen meters), indicates that in the early twelfth century the Jewish community of Speyer was not large. Despite its modest size, the building, constructed in the Romanesque architectural style,[21] was ornate and of high quality, testifying to the great resources invested into it by the community. Attached to the eastern wall was a niche or ark in which the **Torah scrolls** were kept and towards which the worshipers (most likely) faced. In the picture it is possible to see (on the right side) a part of the women's synagogue, which was added to the structure in the thirteenth century. This indicates both that the community was growing and that in Speyer women regularly participated (or at least were present) in the communal prayers. Next to the synagogue a deep *mikveh* was built, as well as other community buildings (perhaps a small study hall, known as a *beit midrash*).

Tz. B.

Further Reading

Heberer, Pia. "The Medieval Synagogue in Speyer: Historical Building Research and Reconstruction." In *The Jews of Europe in the Middle Ages*, exhibition catalog, 77–81. Speyer: Historisches Museum der Pfalz, 2004.

Porsche, Monika. "Speyer: The Medieval Synagogue." In *The Jews of Europe in the Middle Ages (Tenth to Fifteenth Centuries)*, ed. Christoph Cluse, 421–34. Turnhout: Brepols, 2004.

---

[21] Romanesque is an architectural style which was common in Europe before the twelfth century.

1F – Marital Relations and the Laws of Penance (*Hilkhot Teshuvah*), Eleazar of Worms

Eleazar of Worms (ca. 1176–1238) wrote guidelines for people who wanted to atone for their sins, describing various penitential practices. The following source deals with the repentance of a man who had sexual relations with his wife while she was impure (*niddah*).[22] This was impermissible, as married men were supposed to wait for their wives to immerse in a **mikveh** before resuming sexual relations after their wives' monthly menstruation, or childbirth. The issue at hand was the regulation of marital sex around the laws of purity and purification.

Eleazar prescribes forty days of penance through various forms of suffering, including self-flagellation and sitting in cold water. The length of time in which the sinner should sit in cold water or in snow is the time it takes to fry an egg and eat it, considered the length of time from erection to ejaculation. The punishment, therefore, is derived from the digression—sexual contact before the necessary purification in a ritual bath.

It is noteworthy how vividly the author describes the intimate bedroom situation and the psychological impact of physical affection—the man should embrace his wife in order to show her that she is the woman of his choice and respect intimacy with clean language. The author also guides the man both to fulfill his own desire in contact with his wife (once she immerses) and also to fulfill hers, showing her love and affection.

> He who comes onto his wife while she is menstrually impure [*niddah*] needs to torture himself for forty sequential days and [he shall] flagellate [himself] every day and not eat meat and not drink wine and not eat warm food and not wash in those days. A man who comes onto [his wife's] genitals or onto his wife while she is menstrually impure needs to sit in cold water or snow for the duration of time it takes to fry an egg and eat it no less than three days and no more than forty days, and in each day he shall confess his sin whether he is thus torturing himself or not. And if he hugged his wife while she was menstrually impure or kissed her or rubbed his organ on her flesh he needs to torture himself and confess. A man is allowed to be alone with his wife in a room while she is menstrually impure … only he should not talk with her about insubstantial things. And he should

---

[22] In general, laws related to purity regulations for menstruant women. Often a term for a menstruant woman.

not hug her, nor fondle her, nor kiss her, nor eat with her, nor drink with her until she immerses in water. After her immersion he should [find ways to] make her happy: hug her and kiss her and sanctify himself by having sexual relations with her [lit. with the bed service]. He should not speak crudely or see in her anything reproachable, but rather delight in his caressing and in all sorts of hugs to fulfill his lust and her lust so that he does not think about other women except her as she is the woman of his lap and he shall show her affection and love.

SOURCE: Eleazar of Worms, *Sefer haRokeah* (Jerusalem: Yerid haSefarim, 2008), *Hilkhot Teshuva*, §14.

N. B.

Further Reading

Fishman, Talya. "The Penitential System of Hasidei Ashkenaz and the Problem of Cultural Boundaries." *Journal of Jewish Thought and Philosophy* 8 (1999): 201–29.

Kanarfogel, Ephraim. "Rabbinic Conceptions of Marriage and Matchmaking in Christian Europe." In *Entangled Histories: Knowledge, Authority, and Jewish Culture in the Thirteenth Century,* ed. Elisheva Baumgarten, Ruth Mazo Karras, and Katelyn Mesler, 23–37, 267–77. Philadelphia: University of Pennsylvania Press, 2017.

Marienberg, Evyatar. "Traditional Jewish Sexual Practices and Their Possible Impact on Jewish Fertility and Demography." *Harvard Theological Review* 106 (2013): 243–86.

1G – The Language of Prayer

This passage discusses the issue of the importance of praying in a language one understands. Traditionally all Jewish prayers are in Hebrew, but medieval Jews spoke the language of their surroundings and had only a rudimentary knowledge of Hebrew. Opposition to praying in the vernacular seems to have been widespread but there are some exceptions to this rule. This passage appears in **Sefer Hasidim**, a compilation of moral advice written primarily by Judah son of Samuel the Hasid (*Yehuda ben Shmuel heHasid*) (d. 1217) from Regensburg, Germany.

> And if someone comes to you, who does not understand the Hebrew language and he is sincere [lit. fearful of heaven] or a woman, tell them to learn the order of prayers in whatever language they understand because the most important matter concerning prayer is the heart's intention. If the heart does not understand what the mouth is saying, what good does it do for the person praying? Therefore, it is good to pray in the language one understands.
>
> SOURCE: Judah b. Samuel (d. 1217), *Sefer Hasidim*, Parma, ed. Judah Wistenetski (Frankfurt: M. A. Wahrmann, 1924), §11.

E. B.

Further Reading

Fudeman, Kirsten Anne. *Vernacular Voices: Language and Identity in Medieval French Jewish Communities*. Philadelphia: University of Pennsylvania Press, 2010.

1H – *Haroset*: A Sweet-Sour Memory of the Past

One of the ritual foods eaten at the *seder* on Passover eve, the *haroset* is a dish whose composition has varied considerably over time and place. Its essential ingredients were apples, nuts, and spices, ingredients that relate to phrases from the Song of Songs. According to the **Talmud** and its commentaries *haroset* symbolized three elements of the Exodus story: the clay used by slaves in Egypt, the apple tree under which Jewish women gave birth, and the blood of the first plague.[23] Although medieval European blood libels most often accused Jews of murdering Christian children and

---

[23] According to the Babylonian Talmud, Pesahim 116a.

using their blood for baking the unleavened bread (*matzah*) for Passover, during the fourteenth century such accusations were also made around the *haroset*.

Presented here is a recipe found written in the margins of a manuscript copied in 1470 by a scribe originating from northern France (Cod. Parma 1902), in a section devoted to the Passover **Haggadah**: the text read during the *seder*. The recipe was written in a mix of Hebrew and medieval Judeo-French, a fact indicative of the role both languages played in Jewish daily life. Vernacular language often appears within Hebrew literature when describing contemporary and local foodstuffs. Buying and making food was a key point of interaction between Jews and Christians, both with the sellers in the market and with the domestic servants in the house.

> One must put in the *haroset* fragrant spices such as spices in remembrance of the sand that is in clay [used to make bricks] and the chaff called *paillole* [straw] and *meiche* [mace], *paivre* [pepper], *gi[n] gembre* [ginger], *caneile* [cinnamon], *l'onique* [a fragrant spice], *nos nuscade* [nutmeg], *greinat* [pomegranate], *greine pardise* [cardamom], *girofle* [clove], *citoas* [zedoaries], apples, and nuts, and he who wishes to add, let him add [i.e. let him add additional ingredients if he wishes to]. There are twelve ingredients here. These represent the four cups of redemption, the four cups of poison to be given to the nations to drink, and the four cups of comfort and salvation in the messianic era and hereafter.
>
> SOURCE: Parma, Biblioteca Palatina, Cod. Parma MS 1902 fol. 90r; translated in Kirsten Anne Fudeman, *Vernacular Voices: Language and Identity in Medieval French Jewish Communities* (Philadelphia: University of Pennsylvania Press, 2010), 108–9.

A. N. C.

Further Reading

Fudeman, Kirsten Anne. *Vernacular Voices: Language and Identity in Medieval French Jewish Communities*. Philadelphia: University of Pennsylvania Press, 2010.

Weingarten, Susan. *Haroset: A Taste of Jewish History*. New Milford and London: Toby Press, 2019.

Yuval, Israel Jacob. *Two Nations in Your Womb: Perceptions of Jews and Christians in Late Antiquity and the Middle Ages*. Trans. Barbara Harshav and Jonathan Chipman. Berkeley: University of California Press, 2008.

1I – The Fate of a Match—Love Magic by Isaac of Chinon

Marriage was a central institution in medieval Jewish life: the quality and success of a match could make or break the family fortune for generations to come, and as such its success was sought using every means available—including magic. Judaism has an ancient tradition of magic that consisted of practices intended to promote health, love, financial success, and more. Evidence of these practices can be found in multiple Jewish magic books, amulets, and objects, including many examples from medieval Ashkenaz.

The text below is an example of a fortune-telling practice, aimed at deciphering the fate of a proposed match. It was found in a French manuscript from the late thirteenth century, copied not long before the expulsion from France (1306). More than 250 pages of spells, incantations, magical recipes, and rituals were carefully kept in this tiny book, about the size of a deck of cards. It belonged to a man named Isaac son of Isaac (*Yitzhak ben Yitzhak*), who lived in the city of Chinon around 1250. In this specific formula, Isaac calculates the numeric value of the bride's and groom's names using a Jewish practice called **gematria**: an alphanumeric code of assigning a numerical value to the letters of a name, word, or phrase. He then applies numerology—an understanding of the divine or mystical meaning of numbers—and astrology—the study of the movements and relative positions of celestial objects in order to decipher divine information about human affairs and terrestrial events.

In medieval Europe, the celestial sphere was considered to have a profound influence on one's fate and character. In Jewish tradition, the relationship between luck and astrological signs is even more straightforward, since the word for "luck" and "sign" is the same: *mazal*. To have good luck is to have a good astrological map or the celestial sphere on your side.

The method Isaac utilized was to sum up the numerical value of the couple's names, add sixteen to the amount, then divide the result by nine, until left with a remainder between one and nine. Each number represents a particular planet and thus a particular destiny:

> To know whether a certain man will marry a certain woman or will not, and what will be their fate if he marries her:
>
> Go and calculate his name along with hers and add to the amount

16[24] and take out[25] 9, again and again. If the reminder is 9 he won't marry her, and if he will marry her they will not succeed;

And if 1[26] – the sign of Venus, and it is good, and redemptive and prosperity will be between them;

And if 2 – the sign of Mars, bad luck, hate, fighting, and jealousy will be between them;

And if 3 – that is the hate;

And if 4 – the sign of Mercury, they will love each other, but their livelihood will be far;[27]

And if 5 – the sign of Jupiter, good and bad [will be] between them;

And if 6 – the sign of Saturn, a terrible tragedy will happen between the[m];

And if 7 they must not be together, so they will not become widowed;

And if 8 [he will marry] the daughter of an outstanding famil[y], and great love will be between them.

SOURCE: Paris, Bibliothèque nationale de France, Héb. 633, 124v.

A. S.

Further Reading

Bohak, Gideon. *Ancient Jewish Magic: A History*. New York: Cambridge University Press, 2008.

Kanarfogel, Ephraim. "Esotericism and Magic in Ashkenazic Prayer During the Tosafist Period." In *Studies in the History of Jews in Ashkenaz: Presented to Eric Zimer*, ed. Gershon Bacon, Aharon Gaimani, and Daniel Sperber, 203–15. Ramat-Gan: Bar-Ilan University Press, 2008 [Hebrew].

Saar, Ortal-Paz. *Jewish Love Magic: From Late Antiquity to the Middle Ages*. Leiden and Boston: Brill, 2017.

---

[24] The numbers are written in letters, in this case יו. For the sake of simplicity, all letters appear as numbers above since there is no direct equivalent between English and Hebrew letters.

[25] Meaning: divide by.

[26] If the reminder is 1.

[27] Meaning: financial struggle.

1J – The Monumental *Mikveh* of Friedberg

The ritual bath, ***mikveh***, is a water basin used for Jewish ritualistic purposes, in particular for purification of people or vessels. Its major use was the ritual immersion (*tevilah*) of a woman seven days after her menstruation period, in a monthly ritual required of the woman before she could resume sexual relations with her husband. Another use was the immersion of cooking vessels and eating utensils made by gentiles so that Jews may use them. Men and women also immersed in the *mikveh* before the Day of Atonement (***Yom Kippur***).

For the Jews of medieval Germany, the ritual bath was one of their major communal buildings, along with the **synagogue**. Thus, it is here that we find the deepest and most elaborate and ornate *mikveh* structures in the Jewish world, of which the ritual bath of Friedberg, in Hesse, is perhaps the most striking example. The local community was not large, and could not boast of any major scholars, but its members chose to spend a considerable sum on building their extraordinary ritual bath, work on which was completed in 1260. It was dug eighty feet (25 meters) into the ground, with eight flights of stairs leading to a large (sixteen by sixteen feet, five by five meters) basin of underground water. The experience of immersing in this unique building must have been profound, carried significant spiritual meaning, and was a major aspect of the daily life of the community.

Tz. B.

Further Reading

Cohen, Shaye J. D. "Purity, Piety, and Polemic: Medieval Rabbinic Denunciations of 'Incorrect' Purification Practices." In *Women and Water: Menstruation in Jewish Life and Law*, ed. Rahel Wasserfall, 82–100. Hanover and London: Brandeis University Press, 1999.

1J – THE MONUMENTAL *MIKVEH* OF FRIEDBERG   17

Figures 5 and 6: The Friedberg *Mikveh*, © Neta Bodner

1K – The Burial of a Man with Communal Funds

This *responsum* was written by Meir son of Barukh of Rothenburg (d. 1293),[28] one of medieval Germany's most influential and active rabbis, known for writing close to one thousand responses dealing with various halakhic matters. In this case, after receiving a small amount of money from her husband's assets upon his death, a widow faced a difficult financial decision regarding his burial. It is unclear whether the widow herself or other family members brought the case to court.

The rabbi was asked what the widow should do, since the assets granted to her following her husband's death were not sufficient to enable her to both bury him and collect her **ketubbah** (marriage contract) money. In other words, if the widow was to spend her *ketubbah* money (the money promised to her by the terms of the marriage contract) on the burial of her husband, she would not have enough money left for her own sustenance. Meir replied decisively that she may request that the costs of her husband's burial be covered by the communal funds that existed precisely for cases like these— when a community member lacked sufficient funding.

> Reuven died and did not leave enough [money] for his wife's *ketubbah*, and she didn't want to bury him using the sum he bequeathed her. And I have found in the responsum of Rav Cohen Tzedek: He who died and did not leave his wife more than a third of her *ketubbah*, and he doesn't have death shrouds [or money for] burial costs. And you asked: Who buries him—his widow or communal charity funds? Does a poor widow have to bury her husband? Where have we found that a widow must bury her husband? And even if he had left her the full *ketubbah* [sum], she does not have to pay for his burial, because she is [considered to be] a creditor and she collects her debts from him. She particularly does not need to pay if she received only a third of [the value of] her *ketubbah*, [in this case] he should be buried [using] charity, and he has no right to withdraw money from her [for his burial], and it is enough that she has lost already two thirds of her *ketubbah*, and this is the law [signed by] Meir son of Barukh.
>
> SOURCE: Meir ben Barukh of Rothenburg, *Shut Maharam b. Barukh* (Prague), vol. 1, ed. M. A. Bloch (Jerusalem: Makhon Yerushalayim, 2014), §964.

E. K.

---

[28] Born in Worms, he became the leading rabbinic authority in late thirteenth century Germany; known for his responsa and commentary on the Talmud.

Further Reading

Galinsky, Judah. "Public Charity in Medieval Germany: A Preliminary Investigation." In *Toward a Renewed Ethic of Jewish Philanthropy*, ed. Yossi Prager, 79–92. New York: Michael Scharf Publication Trust of Yeshiva University, 2010.

Tallan, Cheryl. "Medieval Jewish Widows: Their Control of Resources." *Jewish History* 5 (1991): 63–74.

1L – Mock Marriages: The Story of Nathan and Ganna

The story of Nathan and Ganna is found in a compilation of *responsa* composed by the **Tosafists**, a group of twelfth- and thirteenth-century rabbinic scholars from France and Germany.[29] The incident described in this source occurred sometime during the second half of the thirteenth century in Esslingen in the Baden-Württemberg district of southwestern Germany at the local Jewish dance hall or at a local drinking venue. During this period the vibrant Jewish community in Esslingen constituted about 5 percent of the city's population. The community had a **synagogue**, a banquet hall (also known as a wedding house, a dance hall, or a *Tanzhaus*), and a cemetery. The incident is described in a **halakhic** question sent to Meir son of Barukh of Rothenburg (d. 1293).[30] The sender sought Meir's opinion regarding the validity of the marriage enacted by the two youngsters and if Ganna had to receive a *get* (a divorce document and thus be legally divorced according to Jewish law) from Nathan. At the end of a lengthy discussion, Meir concluded that what happened between Nathan and Ganna was not a proper halakhic marriage and thus there was no need for a *get* to be issued. This source teaches us about youth culture in Ashkenaz during the Middle Ages. We learn that adolescent girls and boys socially interacted with each other, and that, not surprisingly, drinking together and behaving foolishly and irresponsibly could at times lead to trouble.

> An incident occurred in Esslingen when young men and young women sat down to drink. And there was a young man there called Nathan. And the crowd mocked him, and each one of them told him: "Nathan I want to marry you." And there was a young woman there, and she also told

---

[29] The source can also be found in a fifteenth-century halakhic manuscript, New York, Jewish Theological Seminary MS 6532, fol. 209v.

[30] See source 1K.

him so in mockery: "Nathan, marry me." And the young man was silent and left the place, and brought a ring that he had received as a gift, and reentered the room and joined them. He sat with them for a short while, and then he stood up and said loudly: "Listen all of you, Ms. Ganna told me to marry her, and so I will," and he threw the ring and said "Let her be consecrated to me according to the law of Moses[31] and Israel, you are witnesses."[32] And the young woman was frightened, silent, and did not utter a word. And when he threw the ring, the witnesses did not see if it fell on her lap or not. But nonetheless she shook her clothes, in the case that the ring fell on her, so she could remove it from her. And thereafter the young man Nathan gave everyone half a measure of wine to drink, and she also drank with them.

SOURCE: *Teshuvot Ba'alei HaTosafot*, ed. Irving Agus (New York: Talpioth, 1954), 165, §85.

E. L.

Further Reading

McSheffrey, Shannon. *Marriage, Sex and Civic Culture in Late Medieval London.* Philadelphia: University of Pennsylvania Press, 2006.

Newman, Paul B. *Growing Up in the Middle Ages.* Jefferson: McFarland & Company, 2007.

Sheehan, Michael MacMahon. *Marriage, Family and Law in Medieval Europe: Collected Studies.* Toronto: University of Toronto Press, 1997.

---

[31] A term that generally refers to the Hebrew bible and more particularly to Jewish law (*halakhah*).

[32] Engagement or marriage requires two witnesses to validate the ritual according to Jewish law.

Figure 7: Yiddish in the Worms *Mahzor*

1M – The Beginnings of Yiddish in Worms

The short sentence below was written in 1272 or 1273 within the initial letters of a Jewish prayer in the Worms *Mahzor* (a prayer book used by Jews on High Holidays; see Figure 7). It is a blessing on the person who carried this (very heavy) prayer book to the **synagogue**. The Jews of medieval Germany spoke the local dialects of their Christian neighbors and over time adapted them to their religious and everyday needs. This eventually evolved into a separate language, **Yiddish**, which was based on a combination of Hebrew and the various German dialects, with most Jews in the German Empire speaking both Yiddish and German. The sentence below is one of the earliest traces of the Yiddish language. See sources 5O and 5P below for early Yiddish literature.

> A joyful day be granted him who bears this holiday prayer book [*mahazor* = *mahzor*] into the synagogue [*bes haKneses* = *beit haKneset*]

SOURCE: Jerusalem, The National Library of Israel, MS Heb. 781 = 4°, vol. 1, fol. 92v.

A. L.

Further Reading

Frakes, Jerold C., ed. *Early Yidddish Texts, 1100–1750*, 3–4, no. 2. Oxford: Oxford University Press, 2004.

Röll, Walter. "Das älteste jüdisch-deutsche Sprachdenkmal: Ein Verspaar im Wormser Machsor von 1272/73." *Zeitschrift für Mundartforschung* 33 (1966): 127–38.

Timm, Erika. "The Early History of the Yiddish Language." In *The Jews of Europe in the Middle Ages (Tenth to Fifteenth Centuries)*, ed. Christoph Cluse, 353–64. Turnhout: Brepols, 2004.

1N – R. Yom Tov's Suicide

This story is preserved in a manuscript detailing the customs of mourning compiled by the thirteenth-century legal authority Meir of Rothenburg.[33] The story tells of the suicide, funeral, and subsequent eulogizing of Yom Tov of England. Initially, Moshe, Yom Tov's father, was not willing to participate in the preparation of his son's body for burial because he had committed suicide. After the funeral, Yom Tov appeared to his father in a dream, explaining that he committed suicide to avoid idol worship (i.e. worship of Christian symbols). This act of **piety** led Moshe and his students to reconsider their initial reaction to Yom Tov's suicide. The text sheds light on many significant aspects of everyday life in medieval England. It details, for example, the technicalities of preparing a corpse for burial and transporting it to a cemetery. It depicts the continued presence of the deceased in the lives of the living as well as contemporary understandings of demonic possession. Finally, the text demonstrates that stories traveled between locales across medieval Europe, and that **pietism** was a phenomenon that existed beyond the confines of Ashkenaz.

> A story. In England there was a wealthy and senior scholar named R. Yom Tov. On the eve of **Shavuot**[34] he took his belt and hanged himself. His father, R. Moshe, did not leave his room or shed a tear, and he continued his studies as if nothing had befallen him, for he said that his son was a suicide. R. Shemaya ben Samuel asked me whether I had ever seen such a case, and, without knowing the background to his question, I said "somewhere in [the **talmudic**] tractate *Semakhot* there was a similar case." And we saw that our father and teacher the rabbi would not take a position, and ignorant, unfeeling slaves were taking care of his [Yom Tov's] body. And we did not touch him. Only a few of us scholars carried his coffin along with the slaves, and they carried him by cart to the cemetery in London, with the rabbi and the entire **yeshiva** walking behind the coffin. That night I saw him in my dream, and he was very beautiful—more than he had been in life—and many others saw him that night. [He said] he had reached abundant light, and his place in that World was immediately assured. And the rabbi also saw something. On the eighth of *Sivan*[35] [we

---

[33] Paris, Bibliothèque Nationale, MS Heb. 1408.

[34] The Jewish Pentecost.

[35] A month in the Jewish calendar, roughly parallel to May.

returned] to London and eulogized him greatly. But that young man was a *hasid* and God-fearing—I never saw anyone like him in any of the communities—truthful and I saw in him all the holy and pure qualities. Afterwards it emerged that he had judged himself harshly, and he was also somewhat disturbed [literally: slightly possessed by a demon], for there are those who [commit suicide] for their own benefit, hoping to secure absolution from their sins in a moment, and not from love of God, and he would say that the demon was showing him a crucifix and pressing him to worship idols. It is better if a person does penance [*teshuvah*] in this world, with suffering and flagellation and canes, and then he can serve God with all his heart and soul, and father children who grow up to be good and wonderful, and then he can be renewed like Job [biblical figure].

> SOURCE: Akiva Dov and Yaakov Aharon Landa, *Sefer Hilkhot Semakhot ha-Shalem*[36] (Jerusalem: Akiva Joseph, 1976), 104–5, §89; Avraham Grossman, *Hakhme Tsarfat haRishonim: Korotehem, Darkam beHanhagat haTsibur, Yetsiratam haRuhanit* (Jerusalem: Magnes Press, 1997), 503–4.

M. F.

Further Reading

Baumgarten, Elisheva. *Practicing Piety in Medieval Ashkenaz: Men, Women, and Everyday Religious Observance*. Philadelphia: University of Pennsylvania Press, 2014.

Kupfer, Ephraim. "A Contribution to the Chronicles of the Family of R. Moses b. Yom Tov 'the Noble' of London." *Tarbitz* 40 (1971): 385–87 [Hebrew].

Roth, Pinchas. "Regional Boundaries and Medieval Halakhah: Rabbinic Responsa from Catalonia to Southern France in the Thirteenth and Fourteenth Centuries." *Jewish Quarterly Review* 105 (2015): 72–98.

---

[36] A set of religious laws concerning the period of mourning.

10 – Remembering Pietism in Ashkenaz from Spain

This will, written by Judah Asheri, is a long and complex document detailing many aspects of his life and the activities of his family. It is notable for the details it provides about everyday life in thirteenth- and early fourteenth century Ashkenaz and the differences between life in Ashkenaz and Spain, including the unusually emotive detail with which it describes the family's desperate escape from Ashkenaz several years previously. In addition, the document provides insight into the understanding of the relationship between the dead and the living in medieval Ashkenaz. It depicts the relationship between Judah's grandfather, Yehiel son of Asher, and his friend Solomon haCohen both after his death, as they have an exchange during his funeral, and also after his burial. It seems that the dead could play an active role in the lives of their still-living friends and relatives. Both familial relationships and friendships survived death and were of benefit to the deceased and to the living.

> I left Germany at the age of thirteen, and when fifteen I came to Toledo, in the new moon of *Iyar*[37] in the year 1305.
>
> My grandfather, Rabbi Yehiel son of Asher, was born in the year 1210 [in Germany]. When he was ten years old, he had a firm friend in R. Solomon haCohen. They entered into a pact that each should share the other's rewards, whether religious or secular. They held to this agreement all their days and were unique in their generation for saintliness and benevolence. Now on the eve of Day of Atonement [**Yom Kippur**] in the year 1264, early in the night, the candle of my grandfather went out in the **synagogue**. For it was customary in Germany to kindle a wax candle for every male in the synagogue, on the eve of the Fast, and the candle was of a size to burn the whole day and night. Later [during the middle of the feast of Tabernacles, **Sukkot**] my grandfather died, and great honor was shown unto him at his death, people from neighboring places attending his funeral. Now it is the practice in Germany to set the coffin on a stone appointed for the purpose near the cemetery, and to open it to see whether the body has been dislocated by the jolting of the coffin. When they did this to him, R. Solomon haCohen approached up to four cubits, and said in the presence of the assembly "In your presence I call upon him to remember our covenant." Within the coffin a look of joy lit his face,

---

[37] A month in the Jewish calendar, roughly parallel to April.

most of those present saw him smile, and I testify on the evidence of my father and grandmother that this happened.

A day came when R. Solomon haCohen was studying in his **yeshiva** in the daytime and lo my grandfather of blessed memory was seated by his side. Amazed, R. Solomon asked how he fared, and he answered, exceedingly well, and that a seat was ready at his side for his friend. "I wonder" said R. Solomon "that thou art permitted to be visible to mortals." He answered: "I have liberty to go to my house from before but I am unwilling that they should say: How this saint presides it over other righteous men." Six months after his death, at midnight on the **Sabbath** night, he appeared to his wife and said to her: "haste and rise, take your sons and daughters and remove them hence, for tomorrow all the Jews of this place will be slain. So it was decreed against the whole neighborhood, but we prayed and our petition was successful except as regards this place." She rose and obeyed, but returning to save her belongings she was killed with the congregation. She had previously rescued my lord, my father, R. Asher of blessed memory, and his brother, R. Haim, fellow disciple of R. Meir of Rothenburg, teacher of my father, who also was taught by his brother Haim.

SOURCE: Ethical will of Judah Asheri (extracts), in *Hebrew Ethical Wills*, ed. Israel Abrahams and Lawrence Fine (Philadelphia: Jewish Publication Society, 2006), 163–200.

M. F.

Further Reading

Friedman, John Block, and Kristen Mossler Figg. *Trade, Travel, and Exploration in the Middle Ages: An Encyclopedia*. London: Routledge, 2017.

Ray, Jonathan. *The Sephardic Frontier: The Reconquista and the Jewish Community in Medieval Iberia*. Ithaca: Cornell University Press, 2006.

1P – Piety Even in Death
Rabbeinu Bahya Commenting on Ashkenazi Custom

Rabbi Bahya son of Asher (1263–1340) of Spain was the student of Rabbi Solomon son of Adret who taught in thirteenth-century Barcelona. The source below is part of Bahya's commentary on the Bible. In addition to exegesis, Bahya recorded the customs (***minhagim***) and practices of contemporary Jews. Interestingly, although he lived and wrote in Spain, he mentions a notable practice of French **pietists**, namely their use of the wood from their tables to make their coffins. This is described as an act of **piety** by Bahya, meant to remind the pious every time he uses his table that his worldly possessions are immaterial and that ultimately his life will be judged by his actions. This piety is even more marked given the central place the family table occupied in medieval homes, as the locus for gathering, meals, prayer, and discussion as well as the place where study was undertaken, business transacted, and domestic rituals performed.

This source demonstrates that customs prevalent in particular local areas were sometimes known and even referenced beyond that locale. Moreover, the source illustrates that it is possible to learn about the customs of the Jews of Ashkenaz from non-Ashkenazi sources, which often identify the differences between Ashkenazi customs and their own local ones.

> It is the custom [***minhag***] of the pious in France that they make their casket [*aron*] for burial out of their table. [They do this] to show that a person will not take anything in his hand and none of his labor will accompany him, except for the charity [*tzedakah*] that he did in his life and the goodness he bestowed at his table. Therefore, the rabbis said, "One who sits at length at his table has his days and years lengthened."[38]

SOURCE: Bahya ben Asher, *Rabbenu Bahya on the Torah*, vol. 2, ed. Chaim Dov Chavel (Jerusalem: Mosad Harav Kook, 2006), 279–80.

M. F.

---

[38] Babylonian Talmud, Tractate Berakhot 54b.

Further Reading

Bar-Levav, Avriel, Andreas Lehnardt, and Stefan Reif, eds. *Death in Jewish Life: Burial and Mourning Customs Among Jews of Europe and Nearby Communities*. Berlin: De Gruyter, 2014.

Szpiech, Ryan. *Medieval Exegesis and Religious Difference: Commentary, Conflict, and Community in the Premodern Mediterranean*. New York: Fordham University Press, 2015.

1Q – Instructions to my Sons and Daughters
The Ethical Will of Eleazar

Eleazar son of Samuel the Levite died in Mainz, Germany, on the Jewish New Year (*Rosh haShanah*) in 1357. His ethical will is primarily concerned with practical aspects of everyday life rather than spiritual, theological, or theoretical aspects of **piety**. It is notable for the wide range of subjects it covers, from cleanliness and housework, to education and prayer, to gambling and financial affairs. Eleazar's approach and advice appear to be relatively consistent across all these subjects: a paragon of restraint and prudence, his attitude to eating and consumption demonstrates the focus on piety that he wanted to pass down to his children. However, the extent to which this document reflects how Eleazar, or his children, actually lived is questionable. Eleazar explicitly states that the will is prescriptive rather than descriptive, as it outlines his requests of his children rather than describing how he lived. This document is an early example of a burgeoning genre of ethical wills, which increased in number and detail during the second half of the fourteenth and during the fifteenth centuries. Despite this, its specificity and detail enable us to learn a wide range of things about daily life in medieval Ashkenaz. For example, while he forbids gambling, he permits betting in kind on specific holidays and festivals, illustrating the existence of this practice. His insistence on the activities of his daughters, not only in terms of modesty and ritual purity but also in the realms of charity and prayer, sheds light on some aspects of women's lives during this period. Moreover, that he requests that his sons avoid mixed-gender dancing and public bathing alludes to the fact that these practices were part of his Jewish community, at least for some people.

> My grandfather's testament to his children; and as it is a rule good for every God-fearer, I write it here, that all men may follow it.
>
> A worthy testament, whose ways are ways of pleasantness; proven and seemly for publishing to all the people. [...]

These are the things which my sons and daughters shall do at my request. They shall go to the house of prayer morning and evening and shall pay special regard to the prayer [*tefilah*] and the *Shema*.[39] So soon as the service is over, they shall occupy themselves a little with the **Torah**, the Psalms, or with works of charity. Their business must be conducted honestly, in their dealings both with Jew and Gentile. They must be gentle in their manners, and prompt to accede to every honorable request. They must not talk more than is necessary, by this they will be saved from slander, falsehood, and frivolity. They shall give an exact tithe of all their possessions; they shall never turn away from a poor man empty-handed, but must give him what they can, be it much or little. If he begs lodging overnight and they do not know him, let them provide him with the wherewithal to pay an inn-keeper. Thus shall they satisfy the needs of the poor in every possible way.

My daughters must obey scrupulously the rules applying to women; modesty, sanctity, and reverence should mark their married lives. They should carefully watch for the signs of the beginning of their periods and keep separate from their husbands at such times. Marital intercourse must be modest and holy, with a spirit of restraint and delicacy, in reverence and silence. They shall be very punctilious and careful with their ritual bathing, taking with them women friends of worthy character. They shall cover their eyes until they reach their home, on returning from the bath, in order not to behold anything of an unclean nature. They must respect their husbands and must be invariably amiable to them. Husbands, on their part, must honor their wives more than themselves, and treat them with tender consideration.

If they can by any means contrive it, my sons and daughters should live in communities, and not isolated from other Jews, so that their sons and daughters may learn the ways of Judaism. Even if compelled to solicit from others the money to pay a teacher, they must not let the young, of both sexes, go without instruction in the Torah.

Marry your children, O my sons and daughters, as soon as their age is ripe, to members of respectable families. Let no child of mine hunt after money by making a low match for that object; but if the family is undistinguished only on the mother's side it does not matter, for all Israel counts descent from the father's side.

Every Friday morning, they shall put themselves in careful trim for honoring the **Sabbath**, kindling the lamps while the day is still great and in winter lighting the furnace before dark, to avoid desecrating the Sabbath [by kindling fire on the Sabbath]. For due welcome to the Sabbath the women must prepare beautiful candles.

---

[39] A central part of each prayer service.

As to games of chance, I entreat my children never to engage in such pastimes. During the leisure of the festival weeks they may play for trifling stakes in kind, and the women may amuse themselves similarly on New Moons,[40] but never for money.

In their relation to women, my sons must behave modestly, avoiding mixed bathing and mixed dancing and all frivolous conversation, while my daughters ought not to speak much with strangers nor jest nor dance with them. They ought to be always at home and not gadding about. They should not stand at the door watching whatever passes. I ask, I command, that the daughters of my house be never without work to do, for idleness leads first to boredom, then to sin. But let them spin or cook or sew.

I earnestly beg my children to be tolerant and humble to all, as I was throughout my life. Should cause for dissension present itself, be slow to accept the quarrel; seek peace and pursue it with all the vigor at your command. Even if you suffer loss thereby, forbear and forgive, for God has many ways of feeding and sustaining His creatures. To the slanderer do not retaliate with counterattack; and though it be proper to rebut false accusations, yet it is most desirable to set an example of reticence. You yourselves must avoid uttering any slander, for so will you win affection. In trade be true, never grasping at what belongs to another. For by avoiding these wrongs—scandal, falsehood, money-grubbing—men will surely find tranquility and affection. And against all evils, silence is the best safeguard.

Now, my sons and daughters, eat and drink only what is necessary, as our pious parents did, refraining from heavy meals. Do not waste money on food and drink. The regular adoption of such economy in food leads to economy in expenditure generally, with a consequent reluctance to pursue after wealth, but the acquisition of a contented spirit, simplicity in diet, and many good results. Concerning such a well-ordered life it is written: "the righteous eats to the satisfaction of his desire."[41] Our teachers have said: "method in expenditure is half a sufficiency."[42] Nevertheless, accustom yourselves and your wives, your sons and your daughters, to wear nice and clean clothes, that God and man may love and honor you. In this direction do not exercise too strict a parsimony. But on no account adopt foreign fashions in dress. After the manner of your fathers order your attire, and let your cloaks be broad without buckles attached.

---

[40] The first day of each Hebrew month. This was a day on which special prayers and customs were performed.

[41] Prov. 12:25.

[42] Solomon ibn Gabirol, *Mivhar HaPninim* (*A Choice of Pearls*), ch. 1.

Be on your guard concerning vows, and cautious as to promises. The breach of one's undertakings leads to many lapses. Do not get into the habit of exclaiming "Gott!"[43] but always speak of the "Creator, blessed be He"; and in all that you propose to do, today or tomorrow, add the proviso "if the Lord wills, I shall do this thing." Thus remember God's part in your life.

Whatever happiness befall you, be it in monetary fortune or the birth of children, be it some signal deliverances or any other of the many blessings which may come to you, be not stolidly unappreciative, like dumb cattle that utter no word of gratitude. But offer praises to the Rock who has befriended you, saying: "O give thanks unto the Lord, for He is good, for His mercy endures forever. Blessed are you O Lord who are good and dispenses good." Besides thanking God for His bounties at the moment they occur, also in your regular prayers let the memory of these personal favors prompt your hearts to special fervor during the utterance of the communal thanks. When words of gratitude are used in the liturgy, pause to reflect in silence on the goodness of God to you that day. And when you make the response: "May your great Name be Blessed" call to mind your own personal experiences of the divine favor.

Be very particular to keep your houses clean and tidy. I was always scrupulous on this point, for every injurious condition and sickness and poverty are to be found in foul dwellings. Be careful over the benedictions; accept no divine gift without paying back the giver's part; and His part is man's grateful acknowledgement.

Every one of these good qualities becomes habitual to him who studies the Torah; for that study indeed leads to the formation of a noble character. Therefore, happy is he who toils in the Law! And every day one should fix himself long or short periods of Torah study, as this is the best work that man can do. Week by week read at least the set portion with the commentary of Rashi. And when your prayer is ended day by day, turn ever to the word of God, in fulfilment of the Psalmist's injunction "passing from strength to strength."[44] And O my sons and daughters, keep yourselves far from the snare of frivolous conversation which begins in tribulation and ends in destruction. Do not find yourselves in the company of these light talkers [people who gossip]. Rather, judge every man charitably and use your best efforts to detect an honorable explanation of conduct, however suspicious. Try to persuade yourselves that it was your neighbor's zeal for some good end that led him to the conduct you deplore. This is the meaning

---

[43] "God" in German.

[44] Ps. 84:8.

of the exhortation: "In righteousness you shall judge your neighbor."[45] To sum up, the fewer one's idle words the less one's risk of slander, lying, and flattery, all of those things held in utter detestation by God.

On holidays, festivals, and Sabbaths seek to make happy the poor, the unfortunate, widows, and orphans, who should always be guests at your tables; their joyous entertainment is a religious duty. Let me repeat my warning against gossip and scandal. And as you speak no scandal, so listen to none, for if there were no receivers there would be no bearers of slanderous tales; therefore the reception and credit of slander is as serious an offense as the originating of it. The less you say, the less cause you give for animosity, while "in the multitude of words there want not transgression."[46] Always be of those who see and are not seen, who hear and are not heard. Accept no invitations to banquets, except to such as are held for religious reasons: at weddings and at meals prepared for mourners, at gatherings to celebrate entry into the covenant of Abraham, or at assemblies in honor of the wise. Games of chance for money stakes, such as dicing, must be avoided. And as I have again warned you, again let me urge you to show forbearance and humility to all men, to ignore abuses leveled at you, but the indignant refutation of charges against your moral character is fully justifiable.

Be of the first ten in **Synagogue**, rising early for the purpose. Pray steadily with the congregation, giving due value to every letter and word, seeing that there are in the *Shema* 248 words, corresponding to the 248 limbs in the human body. Be careful too to let the prayer for redemption be followed immediately by the eighteen benedictions. Do not talk during the service but listen to the Precentor, and respond "Amen" at the proper time. After the morning prayer, read the chapter about *Manna*,[47] the passages associated with it, and the eleven verses [collections of scripture passages consisting of eleven verses are found in several editions of the daily liturgy] with due attention to clear enunciation. Then recite a psalm in lieu of a reading in the Torah; though it were well not to omit the later, passing, as I said above, from strength to strength, from prayer to Bible, before turning to worldly pursuits. Or if you can perform some act of loving kindness, it is accounted as equal to the study of the Law.

SOURCE: Israel Abrahms, *Jewish Ethical Wills* (Philadelphia: Jewish Publication Society of America, 1948), 207–18.

M. F.

---

[45] Lev. 19:15.

[46] Prov. 10:19.

[47] Ex. 16.

Further Reading

Bar-Levav, Avriel, Andreas Lehnardt, and Stefan Reif, eds. *Death in Jewish Life: Burial and Mourning Customs Among Jews of Europe and Nearby Communities*. Berlin: De Gruyter, 2014.

Marcus, Ivan G. *Piety and Society: The Jewish Pietists of Medieval Germany*. Leiden: Brill, 1981.

Figure 8: Jousting depicted in a Hebrew liturgical manuscript.
© The British Library Board, MS Add. 26968, fol. 339r

1R – Tournaments and Medieval Jewish Weddings

The figure opposite shows a page from a beautifully illuminated Hebrew prayer book from late fourteenth century Italy, currently in the British Library, presents a tournament scene underneath a blessing for a newly-wed couple (fol. 339r). Jousting competitions were a common form of wedding entertainment among medieval Christian nobility, so perhaps this is why the illustrator decided, or most likely was told, to draw this image under the wedding blessing. The image also reflects a known wedding custom among medieval European Jews, during which, according to rabbinic sources from the thirteenth and fourteenth centuries, some young men held pseudo jousting competitions. Here is one example from a thirteenth-century source: "Those young men who ride horses for a bridegroom and fight with each other and rip off their friend's garment or spoil his horse, they are exempt from paying compensation because they do so for the joy of the groom."[48] This custom is discussed in rabbinic literature from Spain, Provence, northern France, and Austria. And perhaps the image below is an indication that this custom was also present in some Italian Jewish communities. We also know that there were Jewish men who participated in real tournaments, as happened in Weissenfels, Germany, in 1386. Interestingly, the rabbis expressed no objection to this custom despite the fact that the young men imitated the ways of the knights. They were, however, distinctly preoccupied with how the young men dressed—and their attempt to prevent these young men from dressing like their Christian peers was meant to clarify where the social boundaries between the two groups had been drawn.

SOURCE: London, British Library, Add. 26968, f. 339r, Italy, 1383, a prayer book (*Forlì* Siddur) for the entire year, Italian rite.

E. L.

Further Reading

Shatzmiller, Joseph. *Cultural Exchange: Jews, Christians, and Art in the Medieval Marketplace*. Princeton: Princeton University Press, 2013.

Wenninger, Markus J. "Bearing and Use of Weapons by Jews in the (Late) Middle Ages." *Jewish Studies* 41 (2002): 83–92.

---

[48] **Tosafot**, *Sukkah* 45a.

2 – Living Arrangements: Family, Household, and the Home

2A – Absent Husbands and Lonely Wives

Takkanot (plural of *takkanah*) are a set of legal regulations intended to supplement Jewish law (**halakhah**). They have been an important Jewish legal framework throughout history but rose to particular prominence in the Middle Ages for several reasons. First, there was a wide range of local customs and practices in different Jewish communities across the world. In some instances, local practices sometimes led to a lack of clarity about the law in certain situations. In other cases, new circumstances required new responses. Perhaps the most famous *takkanah* was instituted in Germany by Rabbenu Gershom (Gershom son of Judah Me'or haGolah; ca. 960–1028) around the year 1000, which decreed that any man who married more than one wife should be excommunicated. This *takkanah* was approved and accepted as a binding rule in subsequent rabbinic synods of medieval Ashkenaz and is still in force today. Although monogamy was already a *de facto* reality in medieval Germany, the *takkanah* attempted to ensure that husbands who traveled to places where polygamy was still practiced would not marry a second wife, thereby making the *de facto* reality also a *de jure* reality for all German Jews.

The *takkanah* presented here was enacted by Jacob son of Meir of Ramerupt, known as Rabbenu Tam, one of the most important rabbinic scholars in northern France in the mid-twelfth century. In contrast to the example of the *takkanah* of Rabbenu Gershom, this *takkanah* explicitly addressed a set of contemporary problems that stemmed from the frequency and extent of travel in medieval Europe. Many people, especially men, traveled extensively for business and family matters during this period. Husbands occasionally took advantage of this opportunity to travel without their wives to go to distant locations and not necessarily return. The *takkanah* demonstrates that while travel was often necessary in order to conduct the business or trade that provided for the family, some men used the prominence of travel as a means to escape fraught family situations. Rabbenu Tam thus forbade a husband leaving home for a prolonged period of time while in the midst of an argument with his wife or without her explicit consent.

Takkanah of Rabbenu Tam regarding women who shall not become chained [to their husbands through abandonment, *agunot*] and shall not leave their husbands without reason [...]

We have decreed in consonance with a letter that we have received from Dreux that no one shall be permitted to leave his wife for more than eighteen months without permission of the court of the nearest city, unless he receives the consent of his wife in the presence of proper witnesses.

We have permitted the absence of eighteen months only to such as leave out of necessity to earn and provided that the husband is at peace with his wife.

No one may remain away from his wife against her will unless the Court of Seven Elders before whom the matter is taken permit the continuance of his stay. The court may give the husband permission to remain absent according to the circumstances, for example if he must collect his debts or if he is engaged in study or learning to write or he is engaged in business.

When the husband returns from his journey, he must remain at home for no less than six months before undertaking a second journey.

But in no case may one forsake his wife as the result of a quarrel or with bitter feelings, but only with the consent of the court in the manner described. Each man must send his wife the means for her livelihood every six months. He must make payment through the court for whatever debts were contracted in his absence in order to maintain his family and give his children their education in accordance with the law of the **Talmud**.[1]

One who is able to do so must before leaving on a journey give his wife sufficient means for the support of the family.

We have decreed that no one shall evade the law and leave unless he is sincerely attached to his wife, and no one may refuse to return home after being summoned by the court of the city in which his wife resides, or the court of the nearest city, if there is none in that city. He must return within six months from the time of the call.

Anyone transgressing this ordinance shall be refused hospitality and shall be excommunicated.

This decree was enacted "with a scroll of the **Torah** and the 613 commandments" and it will stand effective if approved by our masters. Rabbenu Tam wrote that it is a proper decree and in accordance with ancient custom "and we agree to it in accordance with the view of our masters in France."

---

[1] Babylonian Talmud, Ketubot 50a.

SOURCE: Louis Finkelstein, *Jewish Self-Government in the Middle Ages* (New York: Jewish Theological Seminary of America, 1924), 168–70 (edited for clarity by the author).

M. F.

Further Reading

Baumgarten, Elisheva. "Gender and Daily Life in Jewish Communities." In *The Oxford Handbook of Women and Gender in Medieval Europe*, ed. Judith M. Bennett and Ruth Karras, 213–28. Oxford: Oxford University Press, 2012.

Grossman, Avraham. *Pious and Rebellious: Jewish Women in Europe in the Middle Ages*, trans. Jonathan Chipman. Waltham: Brandeis University Press, 2004.

2B – Guests, Golden Earrings, and Domestic Fatherhood

Sometime during the twelfth century, a wedding took place in one of the Jewish communities along the Rhine river, perhaps in Mainz, and guests came from afar to celebrate with the young couple. In one household, a family hosted a man and his wife, who came from out of town to participate in the celebration. During their stay a pair of gold earrings belonging to the wife were stolen from the house. The story appears in a **halakhic** discussion originating in Mainz and sheds light on Jewish domestic spaces and the social interactions that occurred within them. It particularly discusses interactions between a father and his daughter, guests and their hosts, and Jews and their Christian maidservant.

> Reuben laid charges against Simon: "My wife and I were guests in your house, because there was a wedding in town. And you had an unmarried daughter [*bat betulah*[2]], and you convinced my wife to lend gold earrings worth three marks to your daughter to wear at the wedding, and so she did, and she [your daughter] went to the wedding, and when she returned she went to sleep in the winter room, and slept. And [while she was asleep] the gentile maidservant stole the earrings from her [your daughter's] ears and went away. Therefore, I demand that you pay me their worth." Simon replied: "It is true that your wife did me a favor, but she took in return the earrings of my daughter, and

---

[2] A virgin woman, commonly referring to an unmarried daughter.

your wife still has them. I will abide with whatever the court decides." Reuben replied: "But your earrings are worth only half a mark" (here ends Reuben's replay and begins the verdict) ... therefore, Simeon is not to be blamed [for the loss] because this is a question of ownership and although she [the daughter] was wrong as she did not put them in a safe place, he [her father, Simon] is not to be blamed ... and because he is not expected to pay for these [stolen] earrings, Reuben has to return to him [to Simon] those earrings [which were substituted for the golden earrings]."

SOURCE: Eliezer son of Nathan, *Sefer Ra'avan hu Even haEzer*, vol. 3, ed. David Deblitzky (Bnei Brak: David Deblitzky, 2012), 171–72, §458.

E. L.

Further Reading

Baskin, Judith R. "Mobility and Marriage in Two Medieval Jewish Societies." *Jewish History* 22 (2008): 223–43.

Duby, Georges. *Medieval Marriage: Two Models from Twelfth-Century France*. Baltimore: Johns Hopkins University Press, 1991.

Horowitz, Elliott, and Esther Cohen. "In Search of the Sacred: Jews, Christians, and Rituals of Marriage in the Later Middle Ages." *Journal of Medieval and Renaissance Studies* 20 (1990): 225–49.

2C – The Education of Girls

In November 1196 two Christian criminals attacked the house of Dulcia and Eleazar son of Judah of Worms. Dulcia, the mother, and her two daughters, Bellette and Hannah, were killed. Eleazar and his son Jacob survived the attack. In its aftermath Eleazar, who is best known for his work *Sefer haRokeah* (Book of the Perfumer) that provides a detailed description of medieval Jewish customs relating to daily life, wrote the following text to eulogize his murdered family.

The first part of the poem, which is not included here, describes Dulcia as a successful businesswoman, devoted wife and mother, and committed community member who clothed the poor, fed her family, and cared for her husband's students. Dulcia was also devoted in her religious practice. A God-fearing woman who was well versed in the laws of religious life, she went to the **synagogue** daily and led the women of her community in prayers. In the second part of the poem, given below, Eleazar describes his daughters and their characteristics, and in doing so teaches us about the community's educational and societal expectations and values. We can see that both daughters were taught to follow in their mother's footsteps and were trained by her to fulfill the tasks she performed daily.

> Let me relate the life of my older daughter Bellette. She was thirteen years old and as modest as a bride.
>
> She had learned all the prayers and songs from her mother, who was modest and pious, "Pleasant,"[3] and wise.
>
> The maiden followed the example of her beautiful mother; she prepared my bed and pulled off my shoes each evening.
>
> Bellette was busy about the house and spoke only truth; she served her Creator and spun, sewed, and embroidered.
>
> She was imbued with reverence and with love for her Creator; she was without any flaw. Her efforts were directed to Heaven, and she sat to listen to **Torah** from my mouth.
>
> And she was killed with her mother and with her sister on the evening of the twenty-second of *Kislev*,[4] when I was sitting peacefully at my table.
>
> Two despicable ones came and killed them before my eyes and wounded me and my students and also my son.

---

[3] Dulcia means pleasant. This is why he translates her name in this way.

[4] A month in the Jewish calendar, roughly parallel to December.

Let me tell about the life of my younger daughter [Hannah]. She recited the first part of the ***Shema*** prayer[5] every day.

She was six years old and spun and sewed and embroidered. She entertained me and she sang.

>SOURCE: Translated in Judith Baskin, *Judaism in Practice: From the Middle Ages through the Early Modern Period*, ed. Lawrence Fine (Princeton: Princeton University Press, 2002), 436–37. Appears in A. M. Haberman, *Gzerot Tzarfat veAshkenaz* (Jerusalem: Tarshish, 1946), 168.

E. B.

Further Reading

Baskin, Judith R. "Some Parallels in the Education of Medieval Jewish and Christian Women." *Jewish History* 5 (1991): 41–51.

Baskin, Judith R. "Dolce of Worms: Women Saints in Judaism." In *Women Saints in World Religions*, ed. Arvind Sharma, 39–70. Albany: State University of New York Press, 2000.

Baskin, Judith R. "Dolce of Worms: The Lives and Deaths of an Exemplary Medieval Jewish Woman and Her Daughters." In *Judaism in Practice: From the Middle Ages through the Early Modern Period*, ed. Lawrence Fine, 429–37. Princeton: Princeton University Press, 2002.

---

[5] This is the most basic prayer, recited twice a day in the morning and evening, based on Deut. 6:4.

2D – Co-habiting with Another Man's Widow

This *responsum* from Rabbi Eliezer son of Joel HaLevi of Bonn (1140–1220), one of the most prominent rabbis in late twelfth and early thirteenth century Ashkenaz, presents the case of a man and a widow who shared a house together. The relationship between the two parties is unclear, and due to a disagreement regarding the terms of their living arrangements, their case was brought to court by the man who owned the space. This story presents a rare situation in which a widow had to search for alternative living arrangements after the death of her husband. It is surprising, since the emphasis in most cases in the *responsa* literature concerning widows centers around clashes regarding the deceased husband's property. This case, on the other hand, is not focused on the inheritance or other family members. Instead, it discusses the widow's living arrangements independent of her husband's family.

After being sued, this widow was represented at court by a legal agent. The relationship between the agent and the widow is unclear, as is the reason she did not represent herself in court. This detail is worth noting, since Jewish women in medieval Ashkenaz often did so. Although there are several cases in which it is apparent that women were accompanied by a legal agent, the reasons for this are usually unknown to us.

As in many other *responsa* discussing the cases of widows and their families, many key details are missing, such as the names of the people involved, where it occurred, and other specifics. Nonetheless, this *responsum* provides a glimpse into one of the many conflicts women faced when their status changed from wife to widow, as well as the circumstances in which medieval people lived.

> Reuven sued a widow and argued: "leave my home, since I have not rented it to you, I have let you live in it out of my love for you, and now, I will not endure it anymore." Her legal agent [***apotropus***] replied: "she rented it from you for three *dinars* [Hebrew for libra/pound] annually." And we called for all witnesses to come and testify. The witnesses came and said: "the widow called for us and asked Reuven in our presence: erect a door to my room, because I have rented it from you for three *dinars* from Passover for a year, and you agreed and said it was mine. And you asked her to leave by Purim." And he [Reuven] replied: "true, I have rented it to you on the condition that you would keep it [clean] and light a fire, and that you haven't done. For that reason, I retract my offer and I do not want to rent it to you." The legal

agent replied: "you have rented her the apartment and there were no such conditions, and despite this she cleaned the house as well as she could, and she will continue to do so until Purim."

And we [R. Eliezer] think that the rental of the house has entitled her to legal possession, as is written in chapter seven of the Babylonian **Talmud**, tractate *Baba Kama*.[6] And he has even admitted [renting] it to her. … Since he had (initially) claimed that he did not rent the apartment [to her], it is as though he admits that he did not rent it under these conditions. [However], because the witnesses came and confirmed, her claim was validated. As said in the chapter on the witness's oaths in [the Babylonian Talmud, tractate] *Shevu'ot* about the one who told his friend: "give me 100 *zuzim* [pennies, the French *sous*]" etc.

SOURCE: Eliezer son of Joel of Bonn, *Sefer Ra'abiah: Hu Avi haEzri*, vol. 3, Deblitzky edition (Bnei Brak: David Deblizky, 2019), §1023.

E. K.

Further Reading

Jones, Sarah Rees. "Public and Private Space and Gender in Medieval Europe." In *The Oxford Handbook of Women and Gender in Medieval Europe,* ed. Judith M. Bennett and Ruth Mazo Karras, 246–61. Oxford: Oxford University Press, 2013.

Tallan, Cheryl. "The Position of the Jewish Medieval Widow as a Function of a Family Structure." In *The Proceedings of the World Congress of Jewish Studies* 2, no. 2 (1989): 91–98.

---

[6] Babylonian Talmud, *Baba Kama*, chapter 7, 79b.

2E – Celebrating the Sabbath at Home with Food and Song
A Song for the Sabbath Table from Northern France

With the setting of the sun on Friday evening, the **Sabbath**, a Jewish commemoration of God's creation of the world, began. Along with its numerous ritual requirements and prohibitions, the Sabbath was also a time for relaxation and enjoyment. Reproduced below from a northern French liturgical manuscript from 1204 is a depiction of what the celebration of the Sabbath might have looked like in a Jewish home. After describing the Saturday morning **synagogue** service, the scribe details the choreography and songs of the domestic lunchtime meal. Singing was an important part of Jewish culture in medieval Ashkenaz. Though also composed by famous Hebrew poets, the beautiful Hebrew table-songs found here and in other manuscripts were distinct from those recited in the synagogue liturgy and were sung almost exclusively in the home. The song (*piyut*) translated below was written by Abraham son of Ezra (1089–1164), a famous scholar born in Spain who wandered Europe teaching and writing. As residents fully immersed in the everyday realities of medieval France, Jewish ritual would frequently draw content and inspiration from the surrounding culture. Though there is no musical notation, a marginal note provides the instruction that one of the other songs in the collection should be sung to the tune of a vernacular, and likely well known, French troubadour song. In the Further Reading, you can find a citation for a modern ensemble's performance of that song in the indicated tune. What do you think these songs can tell us about how everyday Jews experienced the Sabbath? How do you think the average Jew would have related to this song that was originally written in a sophisticated Hebrew?

> After prayers, they depart from the synagogue to go home. There they recite the sanctification of the meal over a cup of wine [*Kiddush*] and say the blessing "Blessed are you, Lord our God and king of the universe, who created the fruit of the vine" and then they drink from that cup. Then they recite over two loaves of bread the blessing "Blessed are you God who brings forth bread from the earth." Afterwards, they eat half their meal and have brought before them fish and other delicacies. With these on the table, they sing the song composed by the rabbi, our teacher, Shimon the son of the rabbi, our teacher, Isaac may his memory be a blessing and then the song composed by Dunash the son of Librat and then the song composed by Rabbi Abraham son of Ezra.

This is the song composed by Abraham ibn Ezra:
If I keep the Sabbath, God shall keep me;
for it is an eternal sign between God and me.
It is forbidden to engage in business or to perform daily habits,
Even to speak about the things we need, or about matters of trade or state.
Instead, I will study God's **Torah**; I will study, and it will make me wise.
For it is an eternal sign between God and me.
On it I always find comfort for my soul.
See: My Holy One gave the first generation,
A sign, by giving them a double portion on the sixth day.
Thus may He double my food every sixth day!
For it is an eternal sign between God and me.
Engraved in the day's law is a decree to His priests,
to set the Temple's Show-Bread table before Him.
So, His sages ruled that on it fasting is forbidden
except on the Day of Atonement [*Yom Kippur*] for my sins.
For it is an eternal sign between God and me.
It is a day of honor, a day of delight,
with bread and fine wine, meat and fish.
On it those who mourn are turned around,
For it is a joyous day and it will make me joyful.
For it is an eternal sign between God and me.
Those who desecrate it by working will, in the end, be cut off.
Therefore I cleanse my heart with it as if with soap.
Evening and morning I will pray to God,
Additional and afternoon prayers also, because He will answer me.
If I keep the Sabbath, God shall keep me;
for it is an eternal sign between God and me.

SOURCE: New York, The Jewish Theological Seminary, MS 8092, 38r–v.[7]

A. E. K.

Further Reading

Francesca, Alla. Performance of "Deror Yiqra," Recorded January 20, 2014 on *Juifs et Trouvères: Jewish Songs of the Thirteenth Century in Old French and Hebrew*, Buda Musique, 2015, compact disc.

Fudeman, Kirsten A. "'They Have Ears, but Do Not Hear': Gendered Access to Hebrew and the Medieval Hebrew-French Wedding Song." *Jewish Quarterly Review* 96 (2006): 542–67.

---

[7] This translation of the poem *Ki Eshmara Shabbat* is based upon that found in *The Koren Siddur: Nusach Ashkenaz* (Jerusalem: Koren Publishers, 2015), 592. Changes have been made based upon differences in how the poem appears in the printed edition and in our manuscript.

2F – Eating and Hospitality

Until the thirteenth century, hospitality in the Middle Ages was mostly dependent on the generosity of individuals. People often hosted strangers in their homes, whether the poor of their own city or travelers from another location. In the eyes of medieval German Jews, hosting a Jew from a different city and community was a religious obligation. Medieval Hebrew literature refers to such people as guests (*ore'ah*, sing.) or lodgers (*akhsana'i*, sing.). There is also evidence from the thirteenth century of hospices owned and operated by the Jewish communities in Regensburg and Cologne. The source below is from **Sefer Hasidim**. It provides a social context for its explanation of a verse from Isaiah: "And to take the wretched poor into your home"[8] that focuses on the ethics of hospitality, connecting a person's socio-economic status to the demand to care for the needy by providing them with food and eating with them to bring them happiness and joy.

> "And to take the wretched poor into your home."[9]
>
> Hospitality to wayfarers is greater than welcoming the divine presence, as it is written: and he said "my Lord do not go on past your servant."[10] Abraham said to God, wait for me until I bring guests into my house, and no man is obligated to feed them meat and serve them wine, rather one could. He will joyfully offer bread and water. Because better a meal of vegetables where there is joy than a fattened ox served with a sullen face. And when it is mealtime, he should tell him:[11] "Sir, eat in gladness and drink your water in joy, because God knows that I would willingly and with a fervent heart give you meat, and I swear that I do not have anything more than what I give you, and on that it is said:[12] "And you offer your compassion to the hungry."
>
> SOURCE: Judah b. Samuel, *Sefer Hasidim* (Bologna, 1538), § 56.

A.N.C.

---

[8] Isa. 58:7.
[9] Isa. 58:7.
[10] Compare: Gen. 18:3.
[11] In the spirit of Ecc. 9:7.
[12] Isa. 58:10.

Further Reading

Christoph, Siegfried. "Hospitality and Status: Social Intercourse in Middle High German Arthurian Romance and Courtly Narrative." *Arthuriana* 20 (2010): 45–64.

Dudash, Susan J. "Christianian Politics, the Tavern, and Urban Revolt in Late Medieval France." In *Healing the Body Politic: The Political Thought of Christine de Pizan*, ed. Karen Green and Constant J. Mews, 35–59. Disputatio 7. Turnhout: Brepols, 2005.

Kearney, Richard and James Taylor. *Hosting the Stranger: Between Religions.* New York: Continuum, 2011.

Yuval, Israel Jacob. "Hospices and Their Guests in Jewish Medieval Germany." *Proceedings of the World Congress of Jewish Studies* 10, div. B vol. 1 (1989): 125–29 [Hebrew].

2G – The Sweetness of Learning Torah

In the passage below, Rabbi Eleazar of Worms (ca. 1176–1238), also known as *Rokeah*, describes the details of the ceremony in which young children were initiated into **Torah** learning. This source is found in Eleazar's *Sefer haRokeah* (Book of the Perfumer). There is evidence of this custom in Jewish communities outside Germany, though there are some differences in the specific aspects of how the rite was performed in descriptions from Germany, northern France, and Provence. For example, while in Germany the rite was conducted on **Shavuot**, as below, in France and Provence no time of year was specified. Instead, the age and maturity of the children were of foremost importance. However, all sources pertaining to this ritual compare a child's initiation into Torah learning with the biblical revelation at Mount Sinai.

The parallels that this ceremony drew between learning the Hebrew letters and revelation at Mount Sinai[13] were extensive, and the description of the ceremony uses biblical quotations to make those parallels explicit. It was a multi-sensory experience rich in symbolism. Taking place at dawn, a small procession of the children would make their way to the house of study, either the rabbi's house or the **synagogue**, where each letter of the Hebrew alphabet was read by the rabbi and prospective students. The child would then lick honey off the tablet on which they were written. This ceremony was followed by eating an egg and honey cake. The ceremony as

---

[13] Ex. 20.

a whole invokes the role of the rabbi as teacher and purveyor of knowledge and tradition and serves to induct the children into the long chain of Jewish legal tradition, while the repetition is indicative of early learning practices. The honey symbolizes that the words of the Torah should be as sweet for the person as the honey tastes. The two symbolic foods, the honey cake and the egg, also linked the child to the chain of traditional learning by swallowing verses of Torah and promises to commit to learning. This ceremony not only echoes the revelation of the Torah to Moses at Sinai but also hints at the utopian prophetic vision of learning Torah as ultimate fulfillment.

> It was the custom [*minhag*] of our ancestors that on **Shavuot** they sit the boys down to study because that is when the Torah was given. [We know this because of] the hint [which] is that the child should be covered and not see a dog on the days that he is taught the holy [Hebrew] letters also "neither shall the flocks and the herds graze at the foot of this mountain."[14] At dawn on *Atzeret* [i.e. *Shavuot*] the children are brought because [it is written] "as morning dawned, there was thunder, and lightning."[15] And they cover him with a cloak [and lead him] from their houses to the synagogue or to the house of the rabbi because [it is written] "and they took their places at the foot of the mountain."[16] And the child is seated in the rabbi's lap to learn as it is written "carry them in your bosom as a nurse carries an infant"[17] "I have pampered Ephraim, Taking them in My arms."[18] And the writing board [slate] is brought and the letters of the Hebrew alphabet are written on it [or a simple sentence like] he "charged us with the teaching [of Torah]"[19] "He [God] called to Moses"[20] and the rabbi reads every letter from the alphabet and the child reads after him … and the child reads after the rabbi. And a little honey is put on the slate and the child licks the honey that is on every letter with his tongue. And then people bring the child honey cakes upon which are written "The Lord God gave me a skilled tongue, to know how to speak timely

---

[14] Ex. 34:3.
[15] Ex. 19:16.
[16] Ex. 19:17.
[17] Num. 11:12.
[18] Hos. 11:3.
[19] Deut. 33:4.
[20] Lev.1:1.

48   2 – LIVING ARRANGEMENTS: FAMILY, HOUSEHOLD, AND THE HOME

words to the weary, morning by morning, He rouses, He rouses my ear to give heed to like disciples. The Lord God opened my ears, and I did not disobey, I did not run away".[21] And the rabbi reads every word of these verses, and the child reads thereafter. And after they bring him a peeled hard-boiled egg upon which is written "as He said to me, 'Mortal, feed your stomach and fill your belly with this scroll, that I give you.' I ate it, and it tasted as sweet as honey to me."[22] And the rabbi reads every word and the child thereafter, and the child is fed the cake and the egg because it is good for opening the heart. And people should not change this custom.

SOURCE: Eleazar b. Judah, *Sefer haRokeah hagadol: Hilkhot Shavuot* (Jerusalem: S. Weinfeld, 1960), §296.

M. F.

Further Reading

Baumgarten, Elisheva. *Practicing Piety in Medieval Ashkenaz: Men, Women, and Everyday Religious Observance.* Philadelphia: University of Pennsylvania Press, 2014.

Marcus, Ivan G. *Rituals of Childhood: Jewish Acculturation in Medieval Europe.* New Haven: Yale University Press, reprint 2015.

2H – Clearing Refuse in Medieval Cologne

This source is an inscribed window lintel from Cologne that directed the reader where to dispose of refuse. Dated to approximately 1266, the inscription was uncovered in 2011 during archaeological excavations of the medieval Jewish quarter of the city, in the cellar of the "Lyvermann Haus," a house situated right next to the medieval **synagogue** that belonged to the wealthiest Jewish family in Cologne at the time. The lintel, a horizontal supporting stone, was found over a sealed-up opening in the cellar wall under the house. Next to the opening, a twenty-foot-deep (6 meters) cesspit[23] was unearthed. Initially, archaeologists thought that this inscription was some sort of Jewish joke. It seemed unnecessary for there to be instructions about the disposal of excrement written in Hebrew for

---

[21] Isa. 50:4–5.

[22] Ezek. 3:3.

[23] A hole in the ground where human excrement and food waste were collected and stored.

Figure 9: Hebrew inscription at the Lyvermann house basement.
© MiQua. LVR-Jüdisches Museum im Archäologischen Quartier Köln,
City of Cologne, © Christina Kohnen

Christian servants, who were often employed by wealthy Jewish families. However, an investigation following the initial discovery revealed that the opening from the cellar to the cesspit was in fact the result of a compromise reached between the Jewish community and the local authorities. Usually, cesspits were periodically opened from above to remove the waste. However, the Lyvermann house actually bordered the synagogue courtyard, and so opening the cesspit from above would have necessitated removing excrement and other food and animal waste through the synagogue, the only way out of the synagogue courtyard. Unwilling to do this, the Jewish community successfully petitioned for this particular cesspit to have an underground access point instead.

This is the window through which excrement is removed

SOURCE: Schütte, Sven, and Marianne Gechter, eds. *Von der Ausgrabung zum Museum – Kölner Archäologie zwischen Rathaus und Praetorium: Ergebnisse und Materialien 2006–2012*. 2., second edition (Cologne: Stadt Köln, 2012), 175–76.

M. F.

Further Reading

Shyovitz, David I. *A Remembrance of His Wonders: Nature and the Supernatural in Medieval Ashkenaz*. Philadelphia: University of Pennsylvania Press, 2017.

2I – Beyond Normative Sexuality
The Story of Arloga and Her Husband Rabbi Jonah

In Vienna, during the second half of the thirteenth century, a woman left her house in a rush and went to the marketplace. There she shouted loudly that her husband, who was a local rabbi, was a heretic (*min*).[24] The reason she called him so, was because he was regularly having sex not only with his slave but also with his own son and other men. The source is found in a correspondence between Rabbi Solomon son of Aderet (1235–1310), the leading rabbinic authority in Barcelona, Spain, and Rabbi Haim son of Isaac of Vienna, active during the second half of the thirteenth century, who was the head of the rabbinic school (*yeshiva*) in Wiener Neustadt, Austria, at the time. Interestingly, the rabbis debated Arloga's exposed arms, uncovered hair, and her agitation, but remained silent concerning her accusations about her husband's sexual activities.

> Ashkenaz,[25] to Rabbi Haim the son of Rabbi Isaac of blessed memory of the city of Vienna. You said that Mistress Arloga was fighting with her husband Rabbi Jonah. And that in the midst of the fighting she burst out [of the house] and went to the market and shouted out loud that her husband was a heretic [*min*]. And that she saw him sexually engaged with his male servant and another time with his [own] son, and moreover, he was also sexually engaged with others who were her witnesses. And she went out to the market and shouted about this in the presence of many non-Jews and Jews. And while she was doing this, she took off her headcover and her arms were exposed and also a little bit [of the skin] under her arms. She also hired a non-Jew to go to the authorities, so that her husband would be burnt for this [crime].
>
> SOURCE: Shlomo ibn Aderet, *She'elot u Teshuvot haRashba*, vol. 1 (Jerusalem: Makhon Yerushalaim, 1997), §571.

E. L.

---

[24] Pl. *minim*: refers to those who held beliefs that contradicted the traditional doctrines of rabbinic Judaism. It could also refer to anyone who acted contrary to Jewish religious law.

[25] *Sic*.

Further Reading

Boswell, John. *Christianity, Social Tolerance, and Homosexuality: Gay People in Western Europe from the Beginning of the Christian Era to the Fourteenth Century*. Chicago and London: University of Chicago Press, 1980.
Dinshaw, Carolyn. *Getting Medieval. Sexualities and Communities, Pre- and Post-modern*. Durham: Duke University Press, 1999.
Fradenburg, Louise, and Carla Freccero, eds. *Premodern Sexualities*. Hoboken: Taylor and Francis, 2013.
Halperin, David M. "Is There a History of Sexuality?" *History and Theory* 28 (1989): 257–74.

2J – Late at Night in a Medieval Jewish Home
A Marriage that Went Astray

At some point during the second half of the thirteenth century a question was sent to Meir son of Barukh of Rothenburg (d. 1293)[26] asking his legal opinion regarding a husband who was convinced that his wife was sexually involved with a young man. The husband was a *cohen*, a member of a priestly family who were obligated to abide by special religious rules, among them the prohibition of having relations with a wife who had committed adultery. The story that appears in several late medieval manuscripts[27] exposes activities that took place late at night in a Jewish home in Ashkenaz. The suspected wife and her husband were part of the household of the wife's parents. Another young man lived in this household, perhaps a servant, and was the suspect in this case. Meir concluded that there was no justification to forbid the husband from having sex with his wife. Meir's decision was contrary to a prior ruling given by Hezekiah son of Jacob of Magdeburg. The story reminds us that sounds easily penetrated the wooden walls that separated the rooms in the house, and that these sounds could ignite suspicions and jealousy, especially during the quiet hours late at night.

---

[26] See source 1K.

[27] Braginsky Collection of Hebrew Manuscripts and Printed Books, Zurich, MS 345, fol. 366v (1355–1356); Paris, BnF, Hebr. 407, fol. 210 v (1418); New York, Jewish Theological Seminary Library MS 6533, fol. 210v (14–15 c.).

So goes the incident about a man, a *cohen*, who saw his wife going with a man to a secluded place. And they stayed there for a short while, although not long enough to commit adultery, and they parted because the mother of the woman came to where they were with a lit candle. Another time the *cohen* was lying in his bed at night, when people are [usually] asleep, and behind the wall he heard that they were together, and because of their breathing sounds he understood that they were engaged in a sexual act. And the *cohen* was silent. It happened again that they [the wife and her lover] were together, and he [the husband] understood from their breathing sounds that they were sexually engaged, but he did not see the actual act, only that they stayed therein together long enough to have had sexual intercourse. He put his ear on the wall and heard them breathing as people usually breathe when they are engaged in a sexual act, and due to hearing and seeing this he wanted to be granted a permission to refrain from having sex with her. And on the night of the fornication the *cohen* [i.e., the husband] saw that she was delayed [to come to bed] and [she] went to sleep late. The following morning, the *cohen* challenged his misbehaving wife for being alone with the man. And she replied: "for having sex with another man you blame me? It is me who should complain to God" [lit. the Holy Blessed One]. And she screamed: "Woe and alas [*oy va'avoy*] that you became mine." And prior to this she did not love him, and he loved her and always tried to make peace with her. And she did not listen to him and when he had sex with her she was coerced [*ba'al korhah*].

SOURCE: Meir ben Barukh of Rothenburg, *Shut Maharam b. Barukh*, vol. 2 (Jerusalem: Makhon Yerushalaim, 2014), §81.

E. L.

Further Reading

Carlebach, Elisheva. "Fallen Women and Fatherless Children: Jewish Domestic Servants in Eighteenth-Century Altona." *Jewish History* 24 (2010): 295–308.

Elliott, Dyan. *Fallen Bodies: Pollution, Sexuality, and Demonology in the Middle Ages*. Philadelphia: University of Pennsylvania Press, 1999.

Flandrin, J. L. "Repression and Change in the Sexual Life of Young People in Medieval and Early Modern Times." *Journal of Family History* 2 (1977): 196–210.

2K – The Case of Levirate Marriage (*Yibbum*) Refusal

Although found in Meir son of Barukh of Rothenburg's (d. 1293) *responsa*, this *responsum* was in fact written by his student Mordekhai son of Hillel haCohen (1250–1298), a prominent rabbi in Austria. Unlike many other *responsa*, it does not describe a case that was brought to court but rather details the actions that could be taken in a particular case. The source describes what a woman's recourse would be had she been widowed prior to having children with her deceased husband and had a brother-in-law who could perform a levirate marriage (*yibbum*)[28] (Deut. 25:5–8) but the two did not want to get married. In this instance, the childless widow and her brother-in-law had to perform *halitzah*[29] (Deut. 25:9–10; Ruth 4:1–13). If the brother-in-law refused to carry out the ceremony, the widow, with the cooperation of the court, could take extreme measures to ensure its performance and her consequent release, including corporal punishment if needed. The importance of this ceremony stems from the fact that if the woman was not released, she would become a "chained woman" (***agunah***), unable to marry another man.

> And he [R. Mordekhai] wrote: a levir [brother-in-law of a childless widow] who refuses to perform *halitzah* or *yibbum* with his sister-in-law three months after the death of her husband, must be led in whatever way possible to persuade him to cooperate with *halitzah*. For instance, [she should] pay him money she received from his brother, even grant him ownership [of property], and she should notify [the court—*beit din*] beforehand, and after the *halitzah* they will retrieve the money from him, because the authorization to beat him was given. Moreover, we have the authorization to expropriate money from him. What [money we] give him to perform the commandment [*mitzvah*] [of *halitzah*], the court has the right to retract, so to reprimand him if he violates the words of the **Torah**. If he can't be misled, he shall be bound in whipping and by words as is written in the *Mishnah*.[30] It is a commandment for the eldest [brother] to marry his deceased

---

[28] Levirate marriage is performed when a man dies childless. In such cases, the deceased man's widow and his unmarried brother are encouraged to marry each other.

[29] The biblical ceremony that releases the woman from the bonds of levirate marriage.

[30] Babylonian Talmud, Yebamot 39b.

brother's wife,[31] and if the [other] brothers refused, they [the court] should return to the eldest brother and tell him: the commandment is on you: perform *halitzah* or *yibbum*. The **Talmud** says: they return to the eldest and force him. Isaac son of Samuel the Elder said: wherever it says "force" [you can] even [beat him] with a whip, because with words alone ... a slave would not return [to his master], more so with a positive commandment[32] such as *yibbum* or *halitzah*. It is different from any other positive commandment, as it is written[33] that it is possible to beat him till his soul leaves [his body].

SOURCE: Meir ben Barukh of Rothenburg, *Shut Maharam b. Barukh*, vol. 1(Jerusalem: Makhon Yerushalaim, 2014), §492.

E. K.

Further Reading

Katz, Jacob, "Levirate Marriage (Yibbum) and Ḥalitẓah in Post-Talmudic Times." *Tarbiz* 51 (1981): 59–106 [Hebrew].

Katz, Maidi S. "The Married Woman and Her Expense Account: A Study of the Married Woman's Ownership and Use of Marital Property in Jewish Law." *Jewish Law Annual* 13 (2000): 101–41.

---

[31] Babylonian Talmud, Yebamot, 24a.

[32] A religious commandment requiring the believer to perform a certain act, rather than to avoid one. Jewish precepts are divided into positive and negative. Negative commandments require one to abstain from an action.

[33] Babylonian Talmud, Hulin, 132b.

2L – Providing Her Sustenance
Local Customs and the Daily Meal

According to Jewish law, providing his wife with alimony was one of the seven basic obligations a husband undertook when signing the marriage contract (***ketubbah***). The amount of alimony due was calculated in accordance with the economic status of the husband as well as that of the woman's natal family, and the ongoing cost of food was factored into the amount. Meals in the Middle Ages took place, usually, twice a day. Dinner, the largest meal of the day, was eaten at noon, and supper, a lighter meal mostly consisting of porridge, was eaten before sunset. Breakfast was an optional extra meal, eaten most frequently by manual laborers, as well as by the sick, the old, and young children.

The passage below, from *Sefer Etz Haim* (Book of the Tree of Life), a work written in 1287 by Jacob son of Judah Hazan of London, discusses the food and drink allotted to a woman receiving alimony. In his work Jacob combined religious law based on the *Mishneh Torah*, a code of Jewish religious law compiled by Maimonides (d. 1204, Egypt), with that from the *Sefer Mitzvot Gadol* of Moses of Coucy (thirteenth century, France), to which he also added the unique laws and customs of the "Island Jews," that is, the Jews of England. The passage below is based on the alimony law found in Maimonides's *Mishneh Torah*. It sheds light on the question of the extent to which Jews perceived themselves as a part of the towns in which they lived, and the list of foods it discusses are often regionally specific. It also demonstrates the connection of food and drink to gendered consumption, for example as relating to wine.

> This is the alimony law: Each day they allocate to her a loaf of bread and two medium-sized meals, like [for] a person who is neither sick nor gluttonous. [The bread allocated should be] as is common in their city, if a wheat bread [is common], he will give her wheat, if a barley [based bread is common] he will give barley, if rice [is common] rice [will be given]. And he will give her *parparet*[34] to eat with the bread, legumes and a vegetable, and oil for eating and lighting, and fruits.

---

[34] There is disagreement over the meaning of this term among the **Talmud**'s commentaries. According to Rashi, *parperet* means a fish or a pullet, but the **Tosafists** disagree and suggest following R. Hananel from Qairuan who explained this term as a slice of bread that one put in the bowl before adding some liquid. See: Babylonian Talmud, Brachot 42a.

If it is customary for the women to drink wine, he will give her a little wine to drink, and three meals on the **Sabbath**, and meat or fish [on the Sabbath] as is customary in her place [i.e., according to local custom]. And every week he gives her a certain sum of money for her needs, for example a coin for laundry or bathing, and that is the case for poor Jews. But if he is a rich man, everything that has been said is relative to his wealth. That means, if it is appropriate [i.e., customary for him to eat] some cooked meat [not only on the Sabbath], they [the court] force him to give it [to her]. And if he is such a poor man that he cannot provide for her needs, they [the court] force him to give her the money as a debt until he can pay.

SOURCE: Jacob son of Judah Hazan of London, *Sefer Etz Haim*, vol. 2 (Jerusalem: haRav Kook Institution, 1967), Alimony Law, 245.

A. N. C.

Further Reading

Freidenreich, David M. *Foreigners and Their Food: Constructing Otherness in Jewish, Christian, and Islamic Law.* Berkeley: University of California Press, 2011.

Henisch, Bridget Ann. *Fast and Feast: Food in Medieval Society.* University Park: Pennsylvania State University Press, 1978.

2M – The Custom of Having Sexual Relations on Sabbath Eve

This passage describes the connection between the **halakhic** requirement (*mitzvah*)[35] to light two candles on the eve of *Sabbath* and on the eve of holidays, and the custom that married couples should have sexual relations on Sabbath eve. The discussion revolves around the idea that on the Day of Atonement (***Yom Kippur***) Jews are forbidden from having intercourse, while on Sabbath eve it is recommended. It provides a rare glimpse into the intimate lives of married couples, and sheds light on the connection between halakhic requirements and personal behavior within one's family unit. This text originates from a tractate on local customs (*minhagim*) composed in the late thirteenth century by Rabbi Isaac son of Meir haLevi of Düren, in Westphalia, Germany. This is one of the first systematic tractates describing local customs, and it details many aspects of everyday life.

> And on the Day of Atonement [*Yom Kippur*] one may not light candles in the house on the table, as people do on *Sabbath*. We learn this [from the verse] "And you shall know that your tent is in peace; And you shall visit your habitation, and shall miss nothing."[36] And through exegesis we learn from this [verse] that a man needs to have a beautiful candle on *Sabbath* eve, and this [candle] is the peace of the house. And this is the time that he should call upon his wife to have intercourse (*tashmish hamitah*[37]), so he may not sin as he sees his wife adorned and yearning for him. Therefore, he needs to light two candles on *Sabbath*, so they can keep [the commandment] "be fruitful, and multiply."[38] Which is like two times the number of organs in a human being, candle and another candle,[39] a boy and a girl, as the

---

[35] A religious commandment either of biblical or rabbinic origins.

[36] Job, 5:24.

[37] Literally, "using the bed," a phrase exclusively referring to intercourse in Talmudic literature.

[38] Gen. 1:22.

[39] The sum of the *gematria* value for the Hebrew word for candle is 250, and two candles therefore equal 500. According to the Talmud (Babylonian Talmud, Beḥorot, 45a), a man's body contains 248 organs and a woman's body 252 organs. Both together also equal 500.

people of the *house of Hilel* say in the **Talmud**.[40] And also "be fruitful and multiply" in **gematria** is [equal to] two times candle.[41] And therefore, it is forbidden to light candles on the Day of Atonement, so one would not see his wife and desire her, as he is forbidden from having intercourse [on this day]. And he may not lay in the same bed with his wife. Not on the Day of Atonement, and not on *Tish'a b'Av*,[42] nor in any other time when one is not allowed to have intercourse.

SOURCE: Israel Elfenbein, "Minhagim Yeshanim mi-Dura," *Horeb* 10 (1948): 129–84, 157.

Tz. B.

Further Reading

Baumgarten, Elisheva. "Gender and Daily Life in Jewish Communities ." In *The Oxford Handbook of Women and Gender in Medieval Europe*, ed. Judith Bennett and Ruth Mazo Karras, 213–28. Oxford: Oxford University Press, 2013.

Pollack, Herman H. "An Historical Explanation of the Origin and Development of Jewish Books of Customs ('Sifre Minhagim'), 1100–1300." *Jewish Social Studies* 49 (1987): 195–216.

---

[40] Babylonian Talmud, Yebamot, 61b. Beit Hillel held that a person did not fulfill the commandment "be fruitful and multiply" until he had at least a boy and a girl.

[41] See n. 39 above. The total numeric value of the Hebrew words for "be fruitful and multiply" is also 500.

[42] The ninth day of the Hebrew month *Av* (roughly parallel to July). The major annual day of fast in the Jewish calendar.

2N – Travel on the Sabbath

This *responsum* was written in the late thirteenth century by Samuel son of Isaac. This German rabbi was presented with a case of deliberate transgression: a woman and her companion desecrated the **Sabbath** by riding after sunset on a Friday, when Jewish law prohibits traveling, because of their fear of the consequences of entering a certain city on their way. Through a representative, the woman asked the rabbi to prescribe their means of atonement for this transgression, which he then did. The source teaches us about travel habits and also exposes conventions concerning penance and rabbinic counsel.

> Once a woman was riding with a certain Jewish man through the city of Barby on a Friday.[43] This Jewish woman could not remain in that city for the Sabbath because she feared that if her presence were known, non-Jews would seize her. So she rode on to Zerbst. It became dark on the way, but they rode on to that city even though they were desecrating the Sabbath. I asked my teacher, Samuel son of Isaac, to give her instructions [on how to repent]. He replied that they should fast for forty days, but they need not be stringent and fast consecutively. Rather, they should fast on Mondays and Thursdays each week—except on the New Moon [the beginning of the Jewish month] and other festivals—until they reached [a total of] forty days. This is sufficient since they were slightly coerced.
>
> SOURCE: Simcha Emanuel, *The Responsa of Rabbi Meir of Rothenburg and his Companions* (Alon Shvut: World Union of Jewish Studies, 2014), 739, §374.

E. B.

Further Reading

Baumgarten, Elisheva. *Practicing Piety in Medieval Ashkenaz: Men, Women, and Everyday Religious Observance*. Philadelphia: University of Pennsylvania Press, 2014.

Marcus, Ivan G. *Piety and Society: The Jewish Pietists of Medieval Germany*. Leiden: Brill, 1981.

Soloveitchik, Haym. "Piety, Pietism and German Pietism: 'Sefer Hasidim I' and the Influence of Hasidei Ashkenaz." *Jewish Quarterly Review* 92 (2002): 455–93.

---

[43] South of Magdeburg, Germany.

20 – Guardianship Agreement in Hebrew and Latin

In the district court book of Rothenburg, a double entry appears in Latin and Hebrew on May 5, 1346. This unique double entry concerns legal guardianship [*apotropsut*] of two orphans. The parallel versions of the document present slightly different perspectives on the agreement. The Latin version, for example, does not state the appointment of a guardian by the Jewish community but rather stresses the orphans' consent in choosing the said guardian according to general legal formulas and practices. That being said, the majority of the document in both Hebrew and Latin is identical and details the legal terms of the guardianship, mainly the financial responsibilities of the guardian towards the orphans and future creditors. The existence of such a bilingual document also testifies to the authorization of the guardianship agreement by both the heads of the Jewish community and by the city council.

> R. Salman the scribe has become a guardian, by consent of the heads of the Rothenburg community, to Yudelin and Trudelin, the heirs of Bele of Steten. All those who give [money or property] to R. Salman by law [in the name of the heirs] or reach an agreement with him by law or by compromise regarding any of the property and businesses of Bele wife of Boker is excused from her heirs [the heirs cannot place any future claims for unresolved debts regarding property or businesses with those who have reached an agreement with their guardian]. This is so for a guardian has been assigned [to the heirs] by the heads of the Rothenburg community whom we [the heads of the community] have made liable. I [the scribe] have written this on Sunday, 14 of [the month] *Iyar*[44] and have signed Jacob b. Judah haLevi for the heads of the community.
>
> SOURCE: Theodore Kwasman, "Die mittelalterlichen jüdischen Grabsteine in Rothenburg o. d. T.," in *Zur Geschichte der mittelalterlichen jüdischen Gemeinde in Rothenburg ob der Tauber. Rabbi Meir ben Baruch von Rothenburg zum Gedenken an seinen 700. Todestag*, ed. Hilde Merz (Rothenburg: Verein Alt-Rothenburg, 1993), 115–19. D.

A. D.

Further Reading

Schultz, James A. *The Knowledge of Childhood in the German Middle Ages, 1100–1350*. Philadelphia: University of Pennsylvania Press, 1995.

---

[44] A month in the Jewish calendar, roughly parallel to April.

2P – Traveling and Friendship in the Middle Ages
The Book of Abramelin

The Book of Abramelin is a late fourteenth or early fifteenth century book of Jewish magic written in Germany by Abraham of Worms for his youngest son, Lamech, so he would have "a special treasure as his inheritance." In the book we learn of the friendship between Abraham and Samuel of Bohemia. According to the description in the book, Abraham left his hometown of Worms, and traveled to nearby Mainz to study with a well-known rabbi. There he met Samuel and they became good friends. When Abraham realized that his new friend was about to travel to the Holy Land, he felt a strong desire to travel with him and the two men promised and swore (took an oath) to travel together. In 1387 the two left Germany, getting as far as Constantinople where Samuel died and Abraham continued on his travels alone. We do not know what they promised to one another, how they managed their finances, or how they swore to keep the covenant. This type of bonding, so it seems, provided a greater sense of security while traveling and enabled travelers to maintain a sense of cultural familiarity, a shared language, and a reaffirmation of self-identity while away from home.

> Then I met Samuel from Bohemia, a young man of our religion. His demeanor and behavior showed me that he traveled on the path of God. I befriended him and he confided in me that he intended to travel to Constantinople to meet his father's brother, and from there travel on the road to the blessed land where our fathers lived. I had strong a desire to travel with him and no peace until we made an agreement, promised and swore to travel on together.[45]
>
> SOURCE: *The Book of Abramelin*, ed. George Dehn, trans. Steven Guth (Lake Worth: Ibis Press, 2006), 3.

E. L.

---

[45] *The Book of Abramelin*, 11–12.

Further Reading

Baumgärtner, Ingrid, Nirit Ben-Aryeh Debby, and Katrin Kogman-Appel, eds. *Maps and Travel in the Middle Ages and the Early Modern Period: Knowledge, Imagination, and Visual Culture.* Berlin: De Gruyter, 2018.

David, Abraham. "Jewish Travelers from Europe to the East, 12th–15th Centuries." *Miscelánea de Estudios Árabes y Hebraicos. Sección Hebreo* 62 (2013): 11–39.

Levinson, Eyal. "Eternal Love I Conceive for You: Traveling Jewish Men and Covenantal Bromances." *Mittelalter. Interdisziplinäre Forschung und Rezeptionsgeschichte* 3 (2020): 1–13.

3 – Making a Living: Money, Markets, and Professions

3A – Women as Business Partners

Medieval Jewish communities could number anywhere between a handful of families to as large as one hundred or two hundred families. The Jews were involved in many professions and crafts, and like many medieval urban dwellers often worked out of their homes. Medieval Jewish sources tell of women who were well-known businesswomen, who were successful traders and money lenders, and even of some who specialized in producing Jewish ritual items. An interesting aspect of women's involvement in business was the issue of their authority and independence. Did they take part in economic activities as independent actors or were they seen as subjects of their husbands? Could they take oaths concerning business matters in courts of law? Traditional Jewish texts such as the **Talmud** included precedents for this matter. According to the Talmud, married women were not supposed to act independently of their husbands. In fact, the Talmud in Tractate *Baba Kama*[1] forbade women from dealing with large sums of money, inferring that women would perhaps hide income from their husbands and in effect steal their money. In addition, women were not allowed to take oaths.

The source below is a twelfth-century commentary on this passage in the Talmud. It was written by Eliezer son of Nathan who lived in Mainz (d. 1170, known as Ra'avan). In this excerpt he contradicts the talmudic assumptions concerning the relationship between husband and wife and the wife's responsibility in matters of business, stating that in "our times" customs have changed and now allow for an expanded role to be played by women. Interestingly, this insistence corresponds with a period in which scholars have demonstrated that Christian women also enjoyed relative freedom as economic agents. A hundred and two hundred years later, during the thirteenth and fourteenth centuries, the roles of women in economic activities became significantly more confined for both Christian and Jewish women. As such, this source presents a twelfth-century phenomenon.

---

[1] Babylonian Talmud, *Baba Kama* (119a).

Nowadays, women are agents and vendors and negotiate and loan and borrow and repay and receive payments and make and take deposits. And if we were to say they cannot take oaths, no one will be able to make a living so [it is to their benefit to require them to take oaths] for otherwise people will refrain from doing business with them.

SOURCE: Eliezer son of Nathan, *Sefer Ra'avan hu Even haEzer*, vol. 1, Deblitzky edition (Bnei Brak, 2012), 431–32, §115.

E. B.

Further Reading

Bartlet, Suzanne. *Licoricia of Winchester: Marriage, Motherhood and Murder in the Medieval Anglo-Jewish Community.* London: Vallentine Mitchell, 2015.

Furst, Rachel. "Striving for Justice: A History of Women and Litigation in the Jewish Courts of Medieval Ashkenaz." Ph.D. Dissertation, Hebrew University of Jerusalem, 2014.

Grossman, Avraham. *Pious and Rebellious: Jewish Women in Medieval Europe.* Trans. Jonathan Chipman. Waltham: Brandeis University Press, 2004.

Goldin, Simcha. *Jewish Women in Europe in the Middle Ages: A Quiet Revolution.* Manchester: Manchester University Press, 2011.

3B – Making Kosher Cheese in Northern France

Cheese making has been around for thousands of years. In the absence of refrigeration, cheese, with its relatively long shelf life, was a popular way to consume dairy products. It was also a relatively accessible source of protein for people with limited financial means. Kosher cheese also has a long history. Due to the specialized knowledge and utensils required to produce cheese, most Jews relied on professional Christian cheesemakers rather than make it themselves. The **Talmud**, however, prohibited the eating of cheese prepared by non-Jews. To get around this prohibition, the rabbis required that the process of cheese making be supervised by a Jew.

The ***responsum*** below reveals many details about this process and how it worked. It was written by Isaac son of Samuel the Elder (known as R"I haZaken; ca. 1115–ca. 1190) from Dampierre in northern France. Isaac was a first-generation **Tosafist**, whose *responsa* appear in multiple medieval Hebrew manuscripts.

3B – MAKING KOSHER CHEESE IN NORTHERN FRANCE

Cheese was made in the home, or most probably a dairy, of a non-Jew. In order to ensure that the cheese was kosher, a Jew was supposed to be present during the milking and preparation process. Depending on the type of cheese, it could take several days for it to mature and be ready to eat, and, as the information in the source below indicates, this process also took place at the cheesemaker's dairy. In order to be able to recognize which cheeses had been supervised and were therefore kosher, the supervisor would stamp them with a special seal. One of the problems described in the source is that the Jew supervising the process forgot the seal in the cheesemaker's home and could not be sure that the cheesemaker hadn't used it to stamp other (non-kosher) cheeses so that he could sell that cheese to Jews.

> Rabbi Isaac son of Samuel was asked about many pieces of cheese that a Jew made in the house of the gentiles and had been left there for four or five days to dry out so they would not spoil when transported. And [the cheese] was signed with a seal he engraved with a wood's pattern, and they forgot the seal in the gentile's house and they were afraid that perhaps the gentile subsequently made other cheeses and stamped them with the same seal. And also there are some of them [the cheeses] on which the stamp cannot be recognized because they put the seal on the cheese when it was still soft on the first day [of maturing], and the letters [of the seal] were not absorbed, only the outline drawing of the seal on the cheese. And R. Isaac replied: concerning the cheeses you asked about, the **Torah** spares the money of Jews and you should permit [eating the cheese].
>
> SOURCE: Responsa of R. Yitzhak the Elder from Dampierre. In: Tzidkiyah b. Abraham haRofeh, *Sefer Shibbolei haLeket*, ed. Menahem Hasida (Jerusalem, 1969), vol. 2, §32.

A. N. C.

Further Reading

Adamson, Melitta Weiss. *Food in Medieval Times*. Westport: Greenwood Press, 2004.

Scully, Terence. *The Art of Cookery in the Middle Ages*. Woodbridge: Boydell Press, 1995.

3C – The Economic Importance of River Travel

The passage below is part of a ***responsum*** regarding a commercial debt, sent to a German scholar (likely Meir son of Barukh of Rothenburg (d. 1293)[2] or one of his students) in the late thirteenth or early fourteenth century. It describes a business partnership between two Jews, who wish to bring commodities from one city to a major commercial center in another city. At the suggestion of one merchant, Reuven, the other merchant, Shimon (both names are made up) agrees to switch from bringing salted fish to this other market to bringing or buying there some other unspecified product, the two thus avoiding competition with each other. In addition to issues of trade and economic activity, this passage reveals another major aspect of Jewish daily life: travel along the rivers. The said business trip was most likely a sailing operation along the Rhine (perhaps from Mainz, Worms, or Speyer to Cologne, a major marketplace). The river, which allowed for the transfer of large amounts of goods quickly and cheaply, made this kind of operation possible. This was especially true in medieval Europe, where roads were not always maintained in good shape and major commercial centers were relatively far from each other. The rivers thus served as a network of "highways" that most merchants and travelers, Jews as well as Christians, used regularly.

> [About] Reuven and Shimon, who happened to be in one city. Reuven had a ship loaded with salted fish, which [he planned] to sail to another city [in order to sell the fish]. And he came across Shimon, who wished to load another ship with fish and also sail it to the same city [to sell the fish]. [So Reuven] told [Shimon]: "what do you want now with fish? I have a ship loaded with it. I will save from it a certain amount, worth so and so marks [German silver coins], and you should go to the same marketplace, and buy there [other] commodities worth the same amount of money as I gave you in fish. And I will sell the fish, and you will sell whatever [commodities] you bring [i.e., buy], and when we meet again, each of us will have made his share, and we will divide the profits." And so they did.
>
> SOURCE: Meir ben Barukh of Rothenburg, *Shut Maharam b. Barukh*, vol. 1 (Jerusalem: Makhon Yerushalaim, 2014), §898.

Tz. B.

---

[2] See source 1K.

Further Reading

Verdon, Jean. *Travel in the Middle Ages*. Trans. George Holoch. Notre Dame: University of Notre Dame Press, 2003.

Howell, Martha C. *Commerce before Capitalism in Europe, 1300–1600*. Cambridge: Cambridge University Press, 2010.

3D – Loans between Jewish Businesswomen

The following question was sent to Meir b. Barukh of Rothenburg, the late thirteenth century German rabbi whose ***responsa*** collection is one of the most extensive to survive. In this case two women had a business agreement related to **moneylending** that went sour. Rachel lent twenty marks to Leah (both made-up names), on the agreement that the interest accrued would be divided equally. The money Rachel lent Leah was not completely her own; rather, it included sums she held for orphans and also money that was dedicated to communal needs. In return for the loan of twenty marks Leah gave Rachel goods to serve as security (i.e., pawns). Leah claimed that she had paid back all but three marks of the principal whereas Rachel claimed she owed four marks of the principal. The case becomes more complicated when Leah explains how she invested their joint money, including a loan she had given to a non-Jewish client. Leah explained that she only owed Rachel three marks of the principal because among the securities she had given Rachel one was the pawn she had received from a non-Jewish client that was worth one mark. Rachel insisted that the securities were not worth the full amount of the loan. She (Rachel) also claimed that some of the funds she had invested with Leah belonged to orphans and others had been given to her so that their profits might go to charity.

The give and take between the two women recorded in this case demonstrates that both were active and experienced businesswomen who also knew how the courts functioned. The distinction between the principal and the profit in the argument indicates that they knew the law was different as far as returning profit or principal. This source offers a unique glimpse into the everyday life of Jewish women who carried out financial transactions and their connections with non-Jewish clients.

> Leah sued Rachel and said: "I deposited my pawns with you, and I redeemed up to three marks [*zekukim*] of them and now I want my securities back."

And Rachel replied: "No [I will not return them] because your pawns are still mine [since you owe me] another eleven marks.

And this is what happened: At first, I (Rachel) lent you twenty marks. Half of them you were supposed to profit from and half of them were orphan's funds and some were deposited with me to support orphan's studies from the profits and to aid other "holy" matters (i.e., communal needs) and I was repaid everything except for the four marks that were the principal and the seven marks that were the profit that I am entitled. This is based on what you told me, that you made fourteen marks profit and that you took the seven marks that are your part.

And when you gave me the sixteen marks that were mine, your pawns were still in my possession to keep until eleven marks, four from the principal and seven from the profit, were returned to me. Now if you give me those marks, I will give you back your pawns." This was Rachel's response.

And Leah said: "You speak the truth and I owed you four marks from the principal but I gave you a pawn in return for one mark. [The pawn] was deposited with me by a non-Jew from the same funds that you lent me and those seven marks of profit that were supposed to be yours, I searched for them and did not find them. ... I only had those seven marks that I took for myself and I searched for the funds and did not know what I had or what would happen."

Rachel responded: "It is true that you gave me from the non-Jew's money but those were only worth ten dinars [half a mark], not a mark and that is why I instructed you to lend funds only in return for good [valuable] pawns and those seven marks of profit you searched for and could not find, I know you spent them on your own needs, for this and that, because you did not have any other funds to spend, because you had no funds on hand except for the profit of seven marks."

Leah responded: "What you say never occurred. [You never] told me to lend only in return for valuable pawns. And the non-Jew gave me a solid pawn and I believed him and at times he owed me ten pounds without a pawn and returned it, and I was certain he would be trustworthy now, and I did not misuse your funds. And your claim that I spent the seven marks [that were your profit] on my own needs, this never happened for I don't know what I did with them. And your claim that I gave you my pawns to hold in return for the seven marks of profit is not true because I gave you [the pawns] in return for the principal."

And we are hearing testimonies and we questioned Leah intensively about what happened with those seven marks, for two days ago she told Rachel that she made fourteen marks in profit and she should take seven of them and now she says she never profited except for those seven marks that she took.

And she [Leah] did not respond [to these inquiries], because she said: "I have no further profit except for those seven marks that I took because those were the conditions of the loan [between Rachel and Leah] that I [Leah] would take ten or twenty dinars and divide them and use them for my [Leah's] needs because we agreed that whenever I want to spend my money I could, and I put her [Rachel's] profits down as principal. And now the time to redeem the loan has come, and I cannot find any profit on the principal except for those seven marks that I took for myself, and I do not know how this happened, perhaps they were stolen."

Please instruct us, our teacher, what must Leah do because she initially told Rachel she made fourteen marks of profit—so does Leah need to give her seven marks even though she cannot find them and only has the principal and the seven marks she took for herself from her profits, especially since she took half the profits for her own needs and reinvested the other half in the principal, so do these funds count as profit or as principal if we want to have her take an oath that she misused them and if they are not considered the principal is she released from taking an oath? And also, can Rachel claim those seven marks of profit for the return of the pawns?

SOURCE: Meir son of Barukh of Rothenburg, *Shut Maharam b. Barukh*, vol. 2 (Jerusalem: Makhon Yerushalaim, 2014), §425.

E. B. and N. D.

Further Reading

Furst, Rachel. "Striving for Justice: A History of Women and Litigation in the Jewish Courts of Medieval Ashkenaz." Ph.D. Dissertation, Hebrew University of Jerusalem, 2014.

Grossman, Avraham. *Pious and Rebellious: Jewish Women in Medieval Europe*. Trans. Jonathan Chipman. Waltham: Brandeis University Press, 2004.

Soloveitchik, Haym. "Pawnbroking: A Study in Ribbit and of the Halakah in Exile." *Proceedings of the American Academy for Jewish Research* 38 (1970): 203–68.

3E – Traveling with Money on the Sabbath

The *Book of Paper* (*Sefer haNiyar*) is a compilation of Jewish laws and customs written during the second half of the thirteenth century in northern France by an anonymous author. The author copied earlier traditions which he then adapted to fit his contemporary circumstances. In the section below, he comments on a **talmudic** section discussing carrying money on the **Sabbath** which is forbidden by Jewish law (*halakhah*). The author assumes that a Jew traveling with a sum of money may be in danger and therefore suggests several methods to circumvent the talmudic prohibition, to allow him to complete his travel quickly. This reveals interesting details about the everyday reality of medieval Jewish travel, such as the methods for carrying money and the concerns of Jewish travelers. Moreover, it shows that Jews sometimes traveled long distances carrying money, probably as they were engaged in commercial or economic activity in several towns.

> A person who is on the road during nightfall [on the eve of the Sabbath] should give his wallet [*kiso*—a bag of money] to a gentile or put it on [his] horse. He can also carry it for four *amot*,[3] and put it down every four *amot*. And if he is afraid of gentiles, he can carry [the wallet] on himself and run all the way to his house. And when he reaches the front of the house, he should throw it into the house carelessly before he stands still. Therefore, our rabbi Joseph of Bossenay[4] allows, in our lands where people are often afraid of being caught on *Sabbath* [by Christians], to carry around a wallet full of coins (*ma'ot*) in the public sphere (*reshut harabim*).[5] Or [permits carrying] silver and gold and every object, even if it is forbidden on *Sabbath* (*muktze*) and hide it wherever one likes. As it was said [in the Talmud][6] there was one [method for carrying money on Sabbath] that the rabbis did not want to reveal, that is, to carry it less than four *amot* [at a time].

SOURCE: *Sefer haNiyar* (Jerusalem: Jerusalem Institute, 1994), 14–15.

Tz. B.

---

[3] A measure of distance. Four *amot* are about eight feet, or 2.4 meters.

[4] Probably Saint Martin de Bossenay, near Troyes, France. This is the only source that mentions this figure.

[5] While carrying objects through the private sphere is permitted on the Sabbath, it is forbidden in the public sphere.

[6] Babylonian Talmud, Shabbat, 153b.

Further Reading

Pollack, Herman H. "An Historical Explanation of the Origin and Development of Jewish Books of Customs ('Sifre Minhagim'), 1100–1300." *Jewish Social Studies* 49 (1987): 195–216.

Verdon, Jean. *Travel in the Middle Ages.* Trans. George Holoch. Notre Dame: University of Notre Dame Press, 2003.

3F – Stealing from Your Spouse

In this answer to a ***responsum*** sent to Meir son of Barukh of Rothenburg (d. 1293),[7] the authoritative legal sage of thirteenth-century Germany, a question was presented concerning the theft and misuse of funds. A student of Meir, Mordekhai son of Hillel, requested his opinion regarding a case in which a wife stole money from her husband. Following this initial theft, the wife gave the money to a second woman who planned to lend it with interest, in order to share the future profits created by this transaction with the wife. Interestingly, the aggrieved husband did not seek recourse against his spouse, who was the one who stole the money from him in the first place, but against the second woman who accepted the money, alleging that she knew it was stolen. The legal claim against the second woman insists that, knowing that this was stolen money, she should have returned it to the husband, the rightful owner.

> May my dear sir advise on a business of one woman named Rachel who stole from her husband one hundred marks and gave them to Leah, and Leah was to loan them with Rachel's permission for half the wage [sharing the profit from the interest accrued on the initial funds]. Leah knew that Rachel stole them [the funds] from her husband, and [that profits] would return to Rachel [the thief]. And now Reuven husband of Rachel is suing Leah for this.
>
> SOURCE: Meir ben Barukh of Rothenburg, *Shut Maharam MeRotenburg*, vol. 3 *Sefer Sini VeLikutim* (Jerusalem: Mifal Torat Hachmei Ashkenaz, 2015), §643.
>
> A. D.

---

[7] See source 1K.

Further Reading

Hoyle, Victoria. "The Bonds That Bind: Money Lending between Anglo-Jewish and Christian Women in the Plea Rolls of the Exchequer of the Jews, 1218–1280." *Journal of Medieval History* 34 (2008): 119–29.

Jordan, William C. "Women and Credit in the Middle Ages: Problems and Directions." *Journal of European Economic History* 17 (1988): 33–62.

Rokéah, Zefira Entin. "Crime and Jews in Late Thirteenth-Century England: Some Cases and Comments." *Hebrew Union College Annual* 55 (1984): 95–157.

Toch, Michael. "Economic Activities of German Jews in the Middle Ages." In *Wirtschaftsgeschichte der mittelalterlichen Juden. Fragen und Einschätzungen*, ed. Michael Toch and Elisabeth Müller-Luckner, 181–210. Munich: Oldenbourg, 2008.

3G – Conflict over the Use of a Rented Room for Business

Rabbi Haim son of Isaac of Vienna lived in the second half of the thirteenth century in Wiener Neustadt in Austria and subsequently in Mainz. In this ***responsum*** Haim is confronted with a question regarding the proper use of a rented room in a house and possible financial harm caused by its alleged misuse. The case involves two partners (Reuven and Shimon) who rented a room in a house they owned jointly to a third person (Levi). Levi started conducting business out of this room, mainly **moneylending** activities, a common practice among medieval Jews. Due to the physical layout of the house, Levi had an advantage over Reuven and Shimon, who conducted their moneylending business in a different part of the house. While describing the issue at hand, the *responsum* reveals the daily practices of lending, and the haphazard relationship between Jewish lenders and their potential Christian clients.

> Reuven and Shimon rented a house in partnership, and then rented out one room in the house to Levi, and Levi's room is situated downstairs near the gate at the entrance to the house. And now Reuven and Shimon claim that Levi is causing them damages. Because every gentile who comes to loan on interest encounters him [*pogeʾa bo*] as he enters to receive a loan, and he [Levi] does not allow any gentile to go up to them [Reuven and Shimon], and they are left with no business. Therefore, they [Reuven and Shimon] would want him [Levi] to reside upstairs with them [so that he will not attract all the

clients entering the property to seek a loan, preventing Reuven and Shimon from obtaining business]. And Levi replies, "I rented this room to reside in it, just as I have until now, and Reuven knew that it is my way to sit in my room and do business in it. Because he was initially in this house and I rented this room at first from Reuven and knowing this, I rent this room also now. And also, Shimon who became a partner with Reuven was silent then, and if he had protested at first I would have rented a room elsewhere."

SOURCE: Haim (Eliezer) b. Isaac Or Zarua, *Teshuvot Chadashot* (Jerusalem: Avitan, 2002), §172.

A. D.

Further Reading

Nicholas, David Mansfield. *The Growth of the Medieval City: From Late Antiquity to the Early Fourteenth Century.* New York: Longman, 1997.

Toch, Michael. "Economic Activities of German Jews in the Middle Ages." In *Wirtschaftsgeschichte der mittelalterlichen Juden. Fragen und Einschätzungen*, ed. Michael Toch and Elisabeth Müller-Luckner, 181–210. Munich: Oldenbourg, 2008.

Todeschini, Giacomo. "Christian Perceptions of Jewish Economic Activity in the Middle Ages." In *Wirtschaftsgeschichte der mittelalterlichen Juden. Fragen und Einschätzungen*, ed. Michael Toch and Elisabeth Müller-Luckner, 1–16. Munich: Oldenbourg, 2008.

3H – Using Your Wife's Money to Pay Your Bills

This *responsum* contains a question submitted anonymously and an answer written by the thirteenth-century German Jewish legal authority Meir son of Barukh of Rothenburg (d. 1293). Meir responds to a question about whether a man can use his wife's property to pay off his own debts, even though according to Jewish law (***halakhah***) he does not have rights to her property. While this question may have arisen from a real case, the personal details of the original case have been obscured. The participants are referred to as Reuven and Shimon, generic names for litigants that frequently feature in *responsa* literature, and the wife in question is nameless.

The source belies a range of interesting aspects of Jewish life in high medieval Ashkenaz. For example, it seems that women had some ability to transact in the market, given that the wife mentioned sold her jewelry. Meir's response also details the custom that unmarried children function as part of the economic unit of the household, even if legally their property might be considered separable from that of their parents. Perhaps most significantly, it indicates the potentially complex relationships between Jews and local civil authorities. In this instance the governor sees Reuven and Shimon completing a transaction, and he then wants to levy a tax. Meir's response is prompted by this interaction with the local authorities. This source illustrates some of the complexities of financial dealings during this period as well as the ways in which family relationships and economic ties intersected, and how these ties operated in the context of economic contact with local Christians and ruling authorities.

> And what you asked regarding Reuven and Shimon who were caught by the governor and settled [a dispute] together. The wife of one of them had money from jewelry that she had sold and her husband did not have the right to this money, is her husband obligated to use this [his wife's money] to pay his debts [bills]? [i.e., is Shimon obligated to use his wife's money to pay back Reuven?] It is clear to me that the governor wants to take from each person according to the money he has, including his wife's money, and this [case] is comparable to [the case in] the second chapter of Babylonian **Talmud**, Bava Kama,[8] ... here too if it is known that [the man] and his wife have money then the governor can come and take from them [in order to repay the original debt] in accordance with their earnings and outgoings.

---

[8] Babylonian Talmud, Baba Kama, 117b.

And even more than this, in all of our realms, it is the custom that even that which belongs to a person's unmarried sons or daughters is his from which to take [to repay a debt/bill].

And I have an additional proof that the man must give [to pay the debt/bill] from all of [the money resulting from] that [particular] transaction, and if you do not say this then he has to pay interest [on the transaction], it is clear that had he not performed the transaction with these coins he would not have been caught, just as poor people who do not have [money could not have been caught in the midst of a transaction]. And what caused him to be caught? [Because of] those coins [used during] the transaction.

Regards, Meir Ben Barukh.

SOURCE: Mordekhai b. Hillel haCohen, *Sefer Mordekhai Hashalem: Bava Kama*, ed. A. Halpern (Jerusalem: Makhon Yerushalayim, 1992), 237.

M. F.

Further Reading

Shatzmiller, Joseph. *Shylock Reconsidered: Jews, Moneylending, and Medieval Society*. Berkeley: University of California Press, 1990.

Tallen, Cheryl. "Opportunities for Medieval Northern European Jewish Widows in the Public and Domestic Spheres." In *Upon My Husband's Death: Widows in the Literature and Histories of Medieval Europe*, ed. Louise Mirrer, 115–27. Ann Arbor: University of Michigan Press, 1992.

3I – Networks of Communal Support and Trust
Who Stole the Missing Objects?

Medieval communities—both Jewish and Christian—were built upon networks of trust and accountability. Many individuals relied on their families, neighbors, and friends for everything from making a living to fulfilling their religious obligations. Not everyone was equally reliable, however. Below is a question, sent to Rabbi Asher son of Yehiel (1250–1327), which describes the networks surrounding a particular Jewish **moneylender** during a time of strife. Because the author was an Ashkenazi rabbi who moved to Toledo in the middle of his life, we cannot be certain whether this question originated in Germany or Spain, but the need to rely on others would have been the same regardless. The questioner explains that a Jewish moneylender was arrested while traveling. Hoping to protect what were likely to have been numerous pledges left unguarded in his home, he asked associates of his to go in and gather them for safekeeping. After he returned home, however, certain pledges were missing. Reuven, the moneylender, is then left to scour his various social networks trying to identify those who were worthy and those who were unworthy of his trust. We are not told anything about Shimon and Levi: why do you think Reuven trusted them in his time of need? What methods are put on display here for indicating one's trust in someone else and for validating the appropriateness of that trust?

> Question: Reuven locked his house and gave the key to Shimon before he ventured out to a city where he was arrested. As a precaution, he sent Levi a key to his chest so that he might watch over his pledges. Accordingly, Levi went with witnesses and took the contents of the box and brought them home. When Reuven returned and Levi showed him what he had recovered, Reuven asked "where is the object and money of a certain person?" Levi responded that this was all he had found in the house and his witnesses validated this claim. Reuven then went to Leah, who lives in the same house as him across the yard, and said "You were in the yard and were watching over it, tell me who entered my house?" She responded, "When you departed, you said that if I heard that something happened to you, I should watch over your property and that is what I did. When we heard you were arrested, I took your pledges from your house so that they would not be damaged. They are now in so-and-so's house." Reuven responded, "I never commanded you to do this and I never even gave you a key!

Rather, you opened up my house and entered without permission and stole all the missing items." Leah denied this and said that she only took that which was still at so-and-so's house. Advise me, is it appropriate to trust Leah's oath that she did not take any additional items since, in accordance with the rabbinic principle that we trust those who could have denied all involvement, she could have claimed she never had the items at all?

SOURCE: Asher son of Yehiel, *She'elot u-teshuvot le-Rabenu Asher ben Yeḥi'el*, ed. Yitsḥak Shelomoh Yudlov (Jerusalem: Jerusalem Institute, 1993), 440–41, §107:4.

A. E. K.

Further Reading

Shoham-Steiner, Ephraim. "'And in Most of Their Business Transactions They Rely on This': Some Reflections on Jews and Oaths in the Commercial Arena of Medieval Europe." In *On the Word of a Jew: Religion, Reliability, and the Dynamics of Trust*, ed. Nina Caputo and Mitchell B. Hart, 36–61. Bloomington: Indiana University Press, 2019.

3J – A Record of Credit Transaction between Queen Elisabeth of Germany and the Jews of Würzburg

The episcopal city of Würzburg was home to a sizable Jewish community. Established in the twelfth century, the community sustained a continued presence throughout the hardships of the Second **Crusade** (1147) and so-called **Rintfleisch Massacres** (1298) until the riots of the **Black Death** in 1349. Sources indicate that the Jews of Würzburg were involved in a broad array of trades and crafts that required everyday contacts with their Christian neighbors, such as grape picking, wine trading, butchery, baking, medicine, and **moneylending**. Specific to the case of moneylending, however, the sources from Würzburg suggest that credit and pawn transactions involved a greater diversity of Jewish–Christian contacts, as Jewish financiers often had Christian clients from more remote aristocratic and church circles.

The following source is taken from a miscellany of historical documents and **chronicles** from the regional court of Würzburg, copied in the fifteenth century. It contains fifteen documents that report some of the considerable payment obligations of secular nobility to the Jews of Würzburg, including high-ranking officials such as lords, counts, burgraves,[9] and even the queen of Germany, Elisabeth of Carinthia (1262–1312, m. King Albert I of Habsburg). This record of moneylending and the sums owed to the Jews of Würzburg by Queen Elisabeth shows that the Jews gave a loan to the queen for the sake of subsidizing her travels between Würzburg and Frankfurt in 1308. In return of payment, she ordered that the sum be deducted from the taxes payable to the Crown of the Holy Roman Empire, that is, the king. This source shows how the financial sector was a meeting point that brought, in this case, even the Jews of Würzburg and the queen of Germany together.

> By the grace of God, Our Elisabeth, Queen of Germany, declares that our Jews of Würzburg gave sixty pounds heller [a currency] for the costs of her transit between Würzburg and Frankfurt. This sum of money is to be deducted from their [the Jews'] next tax payments to Our most beloved King of Germany, and if this does not occur, this

---

[9] The official title of the ruler of a castle with its land and judicial rights.

sum is to be secured to the Jews under warranty of Our faithful chief magistrate of the citizens of Würzburg Johannes Han and five other unnamed landsmen. January 25, 1308, Würzburg.

> SOURCE: Wilhelm Füsslein, "Das Ringen um die bürgerliche Freiheit im mittelalterlichen Würzburg des 13. Jahrhunderts," *Historische Zeitschrift* 134 (1926), 304–5, no. 16.

H. T. S.

Further Reading

Müller, Karlheinz, and Christoph Cluse. "Würzburg: The World's Largest Find from a Medieval Jewish Cemetery." In *The Jews of Europe in the Middle Ages (Tenth to Fifteenth Centuries): Proceedings of the International Symposium held at Speyer, 20–25 October 2002*, ed. Christoph Cluse, 379–89. Turnhout: Brepols, 2004.

Reiner, Avraham (Rami). "The Dead as Living History: On the Publication of Die Grabsteine vom jüdischen Friedhof in Wurzburg 1147–1346." In *Death in Jewish Life: Burial and Mourning Customs Among Jews of Europe and Nearby Communities*, ed. Stefan C. Reif, Andreas Lehnardt, and Avriel Bar-Levav, 199–211. Berlin: de Gruyter, 2014.

3K – Jewish Seals on a Receipt of Debt from Zurich

The record below, a receipt of debt that was owed for a loan, was authenticated by three Jews from Zurich (although now in Switzerland, during the Middle Ages the city was part of the German Empire), who attached their personal seals to it on January 31, 1329. The document testifies to the legal and social capability of Jewish men and women to attach their own seals to records and authenticate them in their own name. In many cases they could do this without the seals of Christian officials and, as a result, gained some legal autonomy.

Receipts of debt, in particular, were sealed in this way. The brothers Moses and Gumprecht attached their seals to this document together with Susman, while the mother of the brothers, Ms. Minne, declared that she had no seal of her own. Jewish seals usually had Hebrew legends (seal inscriptions) and were often bilingual (i.e., Hebrew as well as Latin), as is the case for all three seals here. The seal images, sizes, and forms are compatible in every way to those used by Christians, particularly in Zurich and in the rest of the German Empire. Since Jews in many medieval German cities were able to acquire certain forms of citizenship, they could enjoy high social and economic status, which was, on a certain level, comparable to that of their Christian peers. During the second half of the thirteenth century Jews began to use their own seals as a device of authentication as well as a status symbol. We find such seals on **moneylending** contracts and other official documents.

> Seal 1: Hebrew *Moshe ben Menahem* ("Moses, son of Menahem"; seal image: three Jews' hats [*Judenhut*][10]), Latin S(IGILLVM) M.O.S.A. ("Seal of Moses").
>
> Seal 2: Hebrew *Mordekhai ben Menahem* ("Mordekhai, son of Menahem"; seal image: three Jews' hats [*Judenhut*]), Latin S(IGILLVM) GVMPRECHTI ("Seal of Gumprecht").
>
> Seal 3: Hebrew *Yisrael ben ha-Rabbi Shemuel, zikrono leVraha* ("Israel, son of the Rabbi Samuel, may his memory be blessed"; seal image: three concentric fishes), Latin S'(IGILLVM) SVSMA(NI) ("Seal of Susman").

SOURCE: Zürich, Staatsarchiv, C I, Nr. 277.

A. L.

Further Reading

Friedenberg, Daniel M. *Jewish Seals in Medieval Europe*. Detroit: Wayne State University Press, 1987.

Lehnertz, Andreas. "Judensiegel in Aschkenas 1 (1273–1347)." In *Corpus der Quellen zur Geschichte der Juden im spätmittelalterlichen Reich*, ed. Alfred Haverkamp and Jörg R. Müller, no. 15–17. Mainz: Akademie der Wissenschaften und Literatur, 2014..

Lehnertz, Andreas. "The Trier Archbishop's *negociator* Sealing: Two Seals Owned by Muskinus the Jew (Moshe b. Yeḥiel, *ob*. 1336 CE)." In *A Companion to Seals in the Middle Ages*, ed. Laura Whatley, 243–63. Leiden: Brill, 2019.

---

[10] This was a conical hat, often white or yellow, that adult male Jews were supposed to wear.

3L – A Receipt of Debt from Zurich

The source below is a receipt of the debts of the city of Zurich to a major Jewish **moneylending** family, issued in the year 1329. The paying of debts was concluded by returning the debt records to the debtors or, as in this case, by drawing up a separate sealed receipt record. Such moneylending business took place on a daily basis between Jews and Christians.

The document is addressed to the local nobleman John I of Habsburg, count of Klettgau (reigned 1314–1337), as well as to the urban commune of Zurich (now Switzerland but then part of the medieval German Empire). After John had paid back the whole sum he had borrowed from the Jewish family, this record was drawn up according to common practice. The Jewish moneylenders from Zurich attached their three seals for authentication and confirmation.[11] Two of the lenders were brothers (Rabbi Moses, who wrote a Jewish law (*halakhah*) commentary, and Gumprecht, that is, Mordekhai) and the third was most likely their uncle. Minne, the mother of these two brothers, was respectfully called *fro*, a medieval German title usually describing wealthy Christian women. She had declared that she had no personal seal.

This Jewish family lived in a house in the street called *Brunngasse* that was decorated with precious wall paintings, still visible today. Their house, seal usage, and learnedness point to their high social status.

> To whomever reads this record, or hears it read aloud: We, Moses and Gumprecht, Jews and brothers from Zurich, sons of the Jewish woman Ms. [*fro*] Minne, and this very Ms. [*fro*] Minne, their mother, with Susman the Jew of Zurich, announce and declare publicly: We have entirely freed the council and the citizens of Zurich in general [of any debt] and we consciously and deliberately declare them in this record free in regard to ourselves and to our heirs, whom we bind to this promise. And [we] free them [i.e., council and the citizens of Zurich] from their vow which they gave us and vowed to us about the eight hundred and eighty silver marks, which the noble lord Count John of Habsburg had to give us. Of this silver [money], seven hundred and fifty marks belonged to us, Moses and Gumprecht, and one hundred to me, the aforementioned Susman. We also had [debt] records about this from the aforementioned Count John, which were sealed with his seal and with the seal of the citizens of Zurich. To make this [record]

---

[11] For these seals and their function see source 3K.

valid and reliable, we, the aforementioned three Jews, have sealed this record publicly with our seals. And I, the aforementioned Ms. [*fro*] Minne, obligate myself to the seals of my sons since I do not have my own seal. This happened in Zurich on Tuesday before Candlemas, thirteen hundred and twenty-nine years after Christ was born.

SOURCE: Zürich, Staatsarchiv, C I, Nr. 277.

A. L.

Further Reading

Schnyder, Werner, ed. *Quellen zur Zürcher Wirtschaftsgeschichte. Von den Anfängen bis 1500,* vol. 1, 57, no. 115. Zurich and Leipzig: Rascher Verlag, 1937.

Toch, Michael, "Economic Activities of German Jews in the Middle Ages." In *Wirtschaftsgeschichte der mittelalterlichen Juden: Fragen und Einschätzungen,* ed. Michael Toch and Elisabeth Müller-Luckner, 181–210. Munich: Oldenbourg, 2008.

Figure 10: A detail from the Luxembourg coat of arms in the *Brunngasse* house. © Stadtarchäologie Zürich 1996

3M – Displays of Wealth
One Bishop's Account of a Jewish Wedding in Hereford

Wealth in the Middle Ages was not reserved for big-city dwellers alone. The southwestern English town of Hereford was enriched through its participation in the wool and leatherworking industries, in which, according to the records, the Jews of Hereford took an active part. Hereford's Jewish community traces back to the middle of the twelfth century and suddenly expanded in 1275, when the queen of England, Eleanor of Provence (d. 1291, m. King Henry III of England) expelled Jews from certain townships near Hereford, leading more Jews to resettle there. Prominent names of this Hereford community include Aaron II and Mirabelle le Blund, whose fortunes were derived from trade in wool and cloth. Some of our information about Jews in Hereford and their spectacular wealth comes from a record of wedding celebrations that took place there in August 1286.

The following source is derived from two letters found in the **register** of Richard of Swinfield (1282–1317), the **bishop** of Hereford. In them the bishop expresses his outrage upon hearing that Christians were openly invited and inclined to attend a Jewish wedding in 1286. He urges his colleague to deter this interfaith gathering by two measures: first by publicly announcing in the churches his prohibition against interfaith merriment, as well as declaring this decree loudly in the streets. On the one hand, the bishop's letters reflect ecclesiastical efforts to keep Jews and Christians apart, efforts that, to the great dismay of religious authorities, were not always effective. On the other hand, these sources tell us much about the lavish activities at this Jewish wedding, such as the games, sports, feasts, and equestrian processions that took place. They demonstrate that this Jewish family invited and entertained Christian guests at their event, indicating the wealth of some Hereford Jews, like Aaron and Mirabelle, as well as their standing within the town.

> First Letter, dated August 26, 1286:
> Regarding the wedding festivities of the Jews—To the dear son in Christ, Chancellor and Dean of Hereford, I, Richard of Swinfield [Bishop of Hereford send my greetings]. ... How great and how full of peril is the interaction between Christians and Jews! ... Although Christian charity suffers tolerantly, they [the Jews], who are by their own fault condemned to perpetual servitude, do not hesitate to hold in contempt and insult their Creator. We have learned from various reports that on Wednesday ... certain Jews of Hereford [Aaron and his family] have made preparations for a marriage feast according to

their abominable custom, to which they have invited—not secretly but rather openly—many of our Christians. They do so in order to disparage the Christian faith, of which they are the enemies, and, it can be of no doubt, to preach heresies to the simple people, thus generating scandal by their interaction. ... We therefore bid and urge you ... to make it known in all churches of the diocese that no Christian is to take part in any dinner party on Wednesday, under penalty of canonical discipline. Lest, God forbid, any should transgress through ignorance, ... have the same announced through the villages, restraining by ecclesiastical censure the defiant and willful.

Second Letter, dated September 6, 1286:

We understand, outraged by some iniquity, that certain children of wickedness and rebellion dared to take part in the impious feasts of the enemies of the Cross of Christ. ... All those who were in attendance with the Jews—eating, drinking, playing, joking, performing plays, sporting, and in any way contributing to the festivities to the disgrace of the Christian faith—are to be publicly declared excommunicated[12] on the coming [days] in all churches of the city and the suburbs. ... Their absolution is to be obtained upon completion of appropriate obligations and is subject to our discretion. But as for those that celebrated with these said enemies of Christ and honored them in nuptial procession, on horseback, in wagons and clothed in silk and cloth of gold: They are to be excommunicated unless they seek penance for this heinous deed within eight days of this decree by doing enough to serve God and the Church.

SOURCE: *Registrum Ricardi de Swinfield, Episcopi Herefordensis, A.D. 1283–1317*, ed. William W. Capes (Hereford: Wilson and Phillips, 1909), 120–21.

H. T. S.

Further Reading

Aberth, John. *Contesting the Middle Ages: Debates that are Changing our Narrative of Medieval History*. New York: Routledge, 2018.

Elukin, Jonathan. *Living Together, Living Apart: Rethinking Jewish–Christian Relations in the Middle Ages*. Princeton: Princeton University Press, 2013.

Hillaby, Joe. "Aaron le Blund and the Last Decades of the Hereford Jewry, 1253–90." *Transactions of the Woolhope Naturalists' Field Club Herefordshire* 46 (1990): 432–87.

Mundill, Robin. *England's Jewish Solution: Experiment and Expulsion, 1262–1290*. Cambridge: Cambridge University Press, 1998.

---

[12] One who was excommunicated was excluded from participating in communal activities and from contact with members of the community.

3N – Jews Assigned as Market Observers in Würzburg

During the years 1342–1343, Otto II von Wolfskeel, the **bishop** of Würzburg, assigned market observers to oversee commercial activity taking place throughout the city. Official oversight was common in commercial areas in many medieval cities, mainly in the marketplace. In a medieval city the marketplace served as the central hub for economic activity, allowing local and foreign traders to meet in a prescribed location protected by legal rights. Since local authorities had an interest in protecting the smooth and safe conduct of business in the marketplace, they instituted official oversight to ensure that no wrongdoing took place there, as well as to facilitate the exacting of taxes and tolls from those conducting business. The bishop assigned market observers for different locations throughout the city, without specifying their religion, leading to the conclusion that observers were Christians. The one exception was when assigning market observers for the Jewish street (*Judengasse*),[13] for which the bishop decreed that there would be one Jew and one Christian observer. His order, which appears below, reveals the extent of official oversight of the economic activity in the city, listing all the city spaces that were considered to be sites of official market exchange and thus requiring oversight. Among these are the actual marketplace, the city gates, and the cathedral stairs, as well as the *Judengasse*.

> The following market observers are to be ordered in the city of Würzburg: one at each city gate, one on the other main side, one on the cathedral stairs, one at the egg market, one in front of the bread hall, one at the butcher banks, one at the entrance of the *Fischergasse*, two under the cattle stalls, two at the market, one Jew and one Christian in the *Judengasse* and two supervisors beyond and two on this side of the market, which are to examine the wine measures.

SOURCE: *Archiv des Historischen Vereines von Unterfranken und Aschaffenburg*, vol. 11, ed. Georg Joseph Keller (Würzburg, 1851), 90.

A. D.

[13] In German, *Judengasse* literally means Jews' Lane. This was a street name commonly found in many cities throughout the German Empire, indicating the street where the city's Jewish population was concentrated, and often where the **synagogue** and other communal buildings were situated.

Further Reading

Howell, Martha. *Commerce before Capitalism in Europe, 1300–1600*. Cambridge: Cambridge University Press, 2010.

Masschaele, James. "The Public Space of the Marketplace in Medieval England." *Speculum* 77 (2002): 383–421.

Verlinden, Charles. "Markets and Fairs." In *The Cambridge Economic History of Europe from the Decline of the Roman Empire*, ed. M. M. Postan, E. E. Rich, and E. Miller, vol. 3, 119–54. Cambridge: Cambridge University Press, 1963.

4 – Law and Order, Disruption and Crisis

4A – The Legal Rights Granted to the Jews of Speyer

The granting of **privileges**, legal rights awarded to particular groups or individuals, was a common governance practice in medieval society. As one of a range of groups in medieval society, Jews and/or representatives of Jewish communities were also granted privileges by various sovereign authorities, whether ecclesiastical or secular. Their legal rights and obligations were defined in a document known as a privilege, copies of which were kept by both the rulers and the communities. Thus, Jews in medieval northern Europe were assigned a distinctive legal status, defined specifically for them, and their presence was dependent on the approval of rulers. The privilege was a legal instrument of protection, but also of control.

The privilege presented here is one of the earliest to survive from medieval Europe, and it was granted by **bishop** Rüdiger Huozmann of Speyer on September 13, 1084 to the first Jews who came to settle in his town. It shows that the bishop was very interested in establishing a Jewish community in Speyer, in order to promote the economic development and prestige of the city, but was also concerned about the Jewish community's relationship with the local Christians. Accordingly, the document defines in detail the terms of Jewish settlement; its location, the protections promised, and the economic commitments of the Jews.

> Whereas I have turned the villa[1] of Speyer into a city, I thought to increase infinitely the honor of our place if I should assemble there Jews as well. The assembled Jews I placed outside the commune and the habitation of the other town-dwellers, and enclosed with a wall in order that they should not be easily harassed by the insolence of the worst mob. The place of their dwelling, which I have acquired legally—the slope partly with money and partly in exchange, while the valley I received in gift from the co-heirs—that place, I say, I gave them on this condition, that they should pay annually three pounds and one-half in the money of Speyer for the common use of the brothers. I also granted them the free right to exchange gold

---

[1] In this context: a village or a small settlement.

and silver, to buy and to sell anything at their will, inside the circuit of their dwelling and from the area outside to the dock gate and in the dock gate itself. I gave them the same permission throughout the entire city. Furthermore, I gave them a burial place in hereditary right from the church's property. I also added this, that if any Jew from elsewhere should stay with them as their guest, he shall not pay there any *theloneum*.[2] Furthermore, their Archsynagogue[3] shall judge in any dispute that should occur among them and against them, just like the city tribune among the townspeople. But if, perchance, he shall not be able to give final judgment, the case shall go up before the bishop of the city or before his chamberlain. They shall perform watches, guard duty, and garrison duty around their compound only, and guard duty together with the sergeants. They shall legally have wet-nurses and hired servants from our people. Meat of slaughtered animals that they should deem unlawful for them by reason of their law's regulation, they shall legally sell to Christians, and Christians shall legally buy it. In short, out of our favor we have granted them a law that is the best law that the people of the Jews has in any city of the Teutonic kingdom.

SOURCE: Amnon Linder, *The Jews in the Legal Sources of the Early Middle Ages* (Detroit: Wayne State University Press, 1997), 400–402.

A. D. and **Tz. B.**

Further Reading

Chazan, Robert. *In the Year 1096: The First Crusade and the Jews*. Philadelphia: Jewish Publication Society, 1996.

Ray, Jonathan. "The Jew in the Text: What Christian Charters Tell Us About Medieval Jewish Society." *Medieval Encounters* 16 (2010): 243–67.

---

[2] A kind of toll.

[3] Most likely, a Jewish community leader.

4B – Imperial Privilege Granted to the Jews of Speyer

In 1084, the local **bishop** of Speyer, who was the official ruler of the city, granted the Jews of the city a **privilege**. However, Speyer was also an administrative center for the emperors of the **Salian dynasty**, a dynasty that rose to power during the eleventh century. Since Jews relied on the power of ruling authorities for their legal status, in 1090, with the support of the bishop, local Jews approached Emperor Heinrich IV[4] and petitioned him to expand and confirm the privilege the bishop had granted them six years previously. The imperial privileges granted by Heinrich later that year were linked to earlier imperial privileges and relied on pre-existing formulas. They were also reconfirmed in later imperial privileges granted to all the Jews of the German Empire until the fourteenth century. The privileges of 1090 are considered to have been more far reaching than previous privileges, and encompassed matters ranging from religious rights, such as restrictions on converting Jews to Christianity, to economic and legal regulations, allowing Jews to conduct their businesses freely and to further develop their communities.

> In the name of the Holy and Undivided Trinity. Henry the third, by divine grace Emperor Augustus of the Romans.
>
> Let it be known to all the bishops, abbots, dukes, and counts, as well as all those who are bound to the laws of our kingdom, that some Jews—Judas son of Kalonymus, David son of Meshulam, and Moses son of Guthiel, with their associates, came before our presence in Speyer and requested that we would receive and hold under our protection them with their children and all those who are seen by law to depend on them. Let the diligence of all our faithful know that we have done this. We have ordered, therefore, on the intervention and petition of Hozmann, bishop of Speyer,[5] that this royal order of ours should be conceded and given them.
>
> 1. We decree and order in this royal declaration of our highness, that henceforth no one who holds any dignity or authority under our royal authority, small or great, freeman or slave, shall presume to harass or injure them under any unjust pretext, nor dare to take from

---

[4] Emperor of the Holy Roman Empire from 1084 to 1105.
[5] See source 4A.

them anything from their properties that they possess in hereditary right, in open grounds, in houses, in gardens, in vineyards, in fields, in slaves, or in other properties, mobile and immobile. If anyone should attempt to commit any violence against them contrary to this edict, he shall be forced to pay to the treasury of our palace or to the treasury of the bishop one pound of gold and shall restore to them double what he had taken.

2. They should also have free authority to exchange their property in a lawful exchange with whomever they wish, to travel freely and undisturbed within the boundaries of our kingdom for their business and trade, to buy and to sell; and no one should demand from them *theloneum*,[6] or demand from them any public or private exaction.

3. No guests should be sent to their houses without their consent; no one should demand from them a horse for the king's or the bishop's departure or *angaria*[7] for the king's expedition.

4. If any stolen good should be discovered with them, if the Jew should say that he had bought it, he shall prove in an oath according to his law for how much he bought it, and he shall receive only this amount and restore the object to its previous owner.

5. No one shall presume to baptize their sons and daughters against their will, or if he should baptize them after they have been violently seized, or either furtively or forcefully captured, he shall pay twelve gold pounds to either the king's or the bishop's treasury. If, however, some of them should freely wish to be baptized, they shall be held for three days, in order that it should be entirely ascertained whether they forsake their law on account of the Christian religion or because of some injury done to them; and in leaving the law of their fathers they shall be relinquishing their possessions.

6. No one should remove from their service their pagan slaves under pretext of the Christian religion while baptizing them; and if he should do this, he shall pay the *bannum*,[8] that is, three silver pounds, forced by the judicial authority, and, furthermore, return the slave to his master; while the slave shall obey the orders of his master in all things with the exception, nevertheless, of the observation of the Christian faith, with whose sacraments he has

---

[6] A kind of a toll.

[7] Compulsory services.

[8] In this context, a fine for breaking the command of one's lord.

become imbued. They should be allowed to hire Christians to do their work except on holidays and Sundays: they shall not be allowed to buy a Christian slave.

7. If a Christian should have a lawsuit on some matter or a dispute against a Jew, or a Jew against a Christian, each of them, as the case might be, should assert his right according to his law and prove his case. And no one should force a Jew to the burning iron, or the hot water, or the cold water, nor flog him or put him in jail, but he shall swear according to his law after forty days; nor could he be convicted through any witnesses on any case whatever. Anyone harassing them further against this edict of ours should be forced to pay a *bannum*, that is, three silver pounds.

8. If, however, he should wound him, but not mortally, he shall compose with one pound of gold. And if the one who would kill or wound him should be a slave, his master shall either perform the said composition or hand the slave to be punished. And if anyone weighed down by his poverty could not pay, he shall be punished by the same punishment that was inflicted at the time of Henry the Emperor, our father, on the man who killed a Jew named Vivus, namely, his eyes shall be put out and his right hand cut off.

9. If Jews should have among themselves a lawsuit or a case to be determined, they shall be condemned and judged by their peers and not by others. And if it should happen that one of them, a perfidious person, should wish to hide the truth of something done among them, he shall be forced according to their law by the man who governs the **synagogue** for the bishop to confess the truth on the matter in question. Whenever difficult questions or lawsuits shall arise between them or against them, they shall be referred to the presence of the bishop in order that they should be terminated in his judgment, and their peace, in the meantime, should be assured.

10. They shall have permission, furthermore, to sell to the Christians their wine, colors, and antidotes, and (as we have said) no one should exact from them *solidi mancusi*,[9] horses, *angaria*, or any exaction, public or private.

---

[9] Type of medieval currency.

And in order that this order of concession should remain inviolate forever, we have commanded that this document be written and sealed with the impression of our seal.

> Signed by the Lord Henry the third,
> Emperor Augustus of the Romans.

> Humbert the Chancellor, acting for
> Ruthard the Arch-Chancellor ascertained.

Given on the eleventh day before the calends of March, on the 1090th year of the Lord's incarnation, the thirteenth indiction,[10] the thirty-sixth year of the reign of the Lord Henry, his sixth year of empire; done at Speyer; in Christ's name auspiciously, Amen.

> SOURCE: Amnon Linder, ed., *The Jews in the Legal Sources of the Early Middle Ages* (Detroit: Wayne State University Press, 1997), 391–96.

A. D. and **Tz. B.**

Further Reading

Haverkamp, Alfred. "Jews in the Medieval German Kingdom." In *Corpus der Quellen zur Geschichte der Juden im spätmittelalterlichen Reich*. Trier, Arye Maimon Institut für Geschichte der Juden: Universitätsbibliothek Trier, 2015.

Lotter, Friedrich. "The Scope and Effectiveness of Imperial Jewry Law in the High Middle Ages." *Jewish History* 4 (1989): 31–58.

Sapir Abulafia, Anna. *Christian–Jewish Relations, 1000–1300: Jews in the Service of Medieval Christendom*. Harlow: Pearson Education, 2011.

---

[10] A dating system based on fifteen-year cycles, which was formed in the late Roman Empire and survived in some places into the Middle Ages.

4C – The Forced Conversion of the Jews of Trier

The section below is taken from the Hebrew **chronicle** of Solomon son of Samson of Mainz, who, at some point in the 1140s, described the massacre of the Jews in 1096. During the First **Crusade**, groups of crusaders on their way to the East viciously attacked Jews, whom they considered the enemies of Christ, in several German towns. Some local citizens cooperated with the attackers while others opposed them, yet the former prevailed. Thousands of Jews were killed, others committed acts of martyrdom (***Kiddush haShem***), and many more were converted to Christianity by force. Generations of German Jews remembered these events as a major tragedy, but also viewed the martyrs and their actions with admiration, considering them to be role models.

The section below reports the gradual deterioration of the relations between the Jews and local Christians in Trier over the spring of 1096, as the crusade progressed. It focuses on the Jews' developing conflict with the local ruler, **Archbishop** Egilbert, and his men. This conflict reached its climax as the Jews were besieged in the archbishop's palace, and local Christians, with the support of the archbishop, tried to force them to convert. The text reports that several Jews were killed, or committed acts of martyrdom, while others accepted Christianity under duress. This story exemplifies the complex relations between Jews and different sovereign authorities, institutions, and groups within Christian society, especially in times of flux.

> The story of [the events in] Trier was told to me.
>
> It came to pass on the fifteenth of *Nisan*,[11] on the first day of Passover [April 10, 1096], that an apostle came to the stray ones [the crusaders] from France, an apostle of Jesus and his name was Pidron, and he was called Peter the Prelate.[12]
>
> When he came to Trier, he and the men who were with him, who were very many, [as they wished] to go on his stray path to Jerusalem, he brought with him a letter from France written by the Jews [there]: [the letter said] that in every place where he will set foot and cross paths with Jews, they should give him provisions and he would speak well about the people of Israel [in return], as he was a priest and his word carried weight. And when he came here [to Trier] our spirit flew out,

---

[11] A month in the Jewish calendar, roughly parallel to April.

[12] Solomon is referring to Peter of Amiens, known as Peter the Hermit, a priest who was one of the popular leaders of the First Crusade.

and our heart broke and we shivered [in fear] and our holiday became a day of mourning,[13] because thus far the townspeople were not talking about harming the Jewish community in any way, until these clerics have arrived. And they gave Pidor the priest [the provisions he had asked for] and he went on his way. And then came our bad neighbors, the townsmen [of Trier], and got envy of everything that happened to the other Jewish communities of Lothringia.[14] As they heard what had happened to them and what was done to them, and [that there were] many persecutions, and [the Christians] took away their wealth. So [the Jews] bribed each and every one of the townsmen. But all of this was to no avail on the day of God's wrath,[15] since the Lord in heaven had his own reason [to sentence] all of that generation to be punished, to do his will.[16]

At that time, the people of Trier's Jewish community took their **Torah scrolls** and placed them in a safe house [lit. a strong house]. But as the enemies noticed them, they went there on the next day, and broke the roof from above, and took all of the fabric and silver that wrapped the wood of the scroll, and they threw the Torah scrolls on the ground, and tore them and trampled them with their feet. And the people of the Jewish community had already fled to the **bishop**'s [palace],[17] and were not there.

Then [some of the Jews] took with them some of the bishop's men and his servants, risked their lives and went there. They found the Torah scrolls trampled, so they tore out their garments, screaming with bitter souls: "Behold, O Lord, my affliction, for the enemy hath magnified himself!"[18] Then they took the Torah scrolls, raised them from the ground, kissed them, and fled with them to the palace.

And in those days they made many fasts and mourning days, repented and performed charitable deeds, and fasted for six weeks from one day to the next, from Passover to Pentecost.[19] Every evening

---

[13] See: Lam. 5:15; Est. 9:22. Peter arrived in Trier during Passover.

[14] Modern-day northwest Germany, Belgium, and the Netherlands. In particular, Solomon is referring to the events in and around Cologne, Mainz, Worms, and Speyer.

[15] Lam. 1:12.

[16] Solomon possibly suggests here that the divine reason for the persecution was to allow the Jews to die as martyrs.

[17] Bishop Egilbert of Trier. His palace was the structure known today as the Basilica of Constantine, see picture below.

[18] Lam. 1:9.

[19] Presumably the Jews fasted only during the daytime.

they scattered away their money to the poor, and [the Christians] taxed them, four times they had to give away many dinar coins,[20] but still these many bribes were not enough, up to the point that they gave away all of their property, even from the garments which were on their bodies. Eventually they decided to give the bishop, in order to save themselves from the evil ones, everything they had. Yet nothing helped, as the Lord gave them in the hands of their enemies, and His wrath burned against them, and He hid his face from them, on the day of their judgment.

It came to pass on the first day of [the Christian] Pentecost [June 1, 1096], which was also the market day of their [local] church, that people arrived there [in Trier] from the River Rhine to the marketplace.[21] Then the righteous [Jews], the holy people, fled to the bishop's hall, which was called the palace. And the murderers came [to Trier], bragging about the killing and conversion they forced on the people of the Lord, the sacred communities.[22] And the bishop came to the vile place of Timon [meaning, the church of St. Simeon in Trier], and to safeguard the Jews.

But when the enemies heard the words of the bishop, who mentioned the Jews [i.e., ordered that they should not be harmed], they assembled together to strike the bishop. Then the bishop fled into a room within the place of idolatry [i.e., the church], and stayed there for a week. And all of the gentiles [Christians] came to the palace, where the people of the holy covenant [the Jews] were, to fight [against them] and were unable to do so. And as [the Jews] saw them, their heart was moved, as the trees of the forest are moved with the wind.[23]

When they [the besiegers] saw that they could not fight [the Jews], since the building was very strong and the width of the wall was five *amot* [around ten feet, or 2.8 meters], and [the building was] high as far as the eye can see, they went away. They thus decided to kill the bishop [who was] in the place of idolatry [church] of Timon [Simeon], and the bishop got very scared, as he was a foreigner in the city [of Trier] and had no friend or relative, so he had no power to save [the Jews]. Then the bishop came [to the Jews] to decide what should they do, and he asked them: "what would you like to do? Indeed, you see that all around you the Jews had already been killed. And I wished,

---

[20] That is, silver marks.

[21] Trier is located on the Mosel river, further east from the centers of anti-Jewish persecution on the Rhine (Mainz, Speyer, Worms, Cologne).

[22] That is, the persecution of the **Rhineland** Jews.

[23] Isa. 7:2.

as was appropriate, to keep my word to you as I promised, up to the point that I have specified, [that is] until no [other Jewish] community had survived in all of Lothringia.[24] And now see, the crusaders have come to kill me, and I am still afraid of them, and I have been running away from them for fifteen days."

And the [people] of the Jewish community said: "but was not the point that you have specified under oath that [up to which] you would keep us [safe] until the king would arrive in the kingdom?"[25] And the bishop answered and said: "even the king [the emperor] himself would not be able to save you from the marked ones [the crusaders].[26] Lose yourselves [convert] or accept the divine will." And they answered: "you should know, that even if each and every one of us had ten souls, we would give [all of] them away to sanctify His name, before we would let them [the crusades] defile [baptize] us." Then they put out their necks and said: "let us be beheaded and not betray our Lord."

As the bishop saw this, he went away with his ministers and obtained a refuge for them for four days, until after the day of the giving of the **Torah** [*Shavuot*][27] had passed, since the righteous people had asked him to do so. And [the Jews] have turned that holiday into a mourning day, as they heard that the bishop, and every [other] person who could speak up, plan an evil thing against them for no reason.

On the next day the bishop sent a messenger to [the Jews], to [ask] what shall he do and what advice should he receive, since the entire world [everyone] decided to kill him. Thus, the [Jews] thought that he wanted them to bribe him. So, they told the messenger that they will bribe [the bishop] with all of the wealth that they had. But the messenger answered and said: "the bishop does not wish this." At this point, the hands of the righteous men grew weak [i.e., they despaired].

And the heart of the bishop and his ministers turned against [the Jews] as they decided together not to kill them, but only two or three [of them], in order to scare the rest, "perhaps," [they thought] "[the

---

[24] That is, the Rhineland.

[25] By "king" the Jews referred to the emperor. Heinrich IV was a patron of the Jews in Germany (see source 4b), but in 1096 he was occupied in a military campaign in Italy, so he could not prevent the First Crusade massacres.

[26] The crusaders marked their garment with crosses.

[27] The Jewish Pentecost was on May 30 in 1096, so it seems that the text reports here a conversation which occurred before the events described above. However, the content of the conversation suggests that it took place fifteen days after the Christian Pentecost, that is, on June 15. It is difficult to determine the correct chronology in this case.

remaining Jews] will return to our false faith [i.e., will convert]." The bishop contacted them and summoned the important men of his city and his ministers with him, and they [all] came and stood in front of the gate of the hall [where the Jews were]. And in the gate was a door similar to that of an oven. The enemies stood around the palace, hundreds and thousands of them holding sharp swords, and were about to swallow the [Jews] alive, body and flesh [i.e., to kill them].

Then the commander of the army of the bishop and the ministers went into the palace and told [the Jews]: "this is what our lord the bishop said: lose yourselves [convert] or get out of his palace, for he does not wish to keep you any longer. Since many times people have tried to kill him because of you, and you cannot be saved, and your own God does not wish to save you now as he had done in the olden days. Look at the great multitude of people standing in front of the palace gate."

As they saw that the pain was so great, the righteous people came and set on the ground and cried a great cry with bitter souls, men, women, and children, and confessed their sins. Then they forced out Mister Asher son of Joseph (*Asher ben Yoseph*) *haGabbay*[28] in order to kill him, to cast fear and terror on the remaining Jews, [thinking] perhaps they would agree to accept their false faith [convert]. But Mister Asher answered and said: "Whosoever there is among you of all His people—the Lord his God be with him—let him go up.[29] And who wants to receive the Divine presence [*shkhinah*]? Here is a world filled with good things [heaven] [to be gained] in a short hour."

One boy named Meir son of Samuel answered and said: "wait for me, I want to come with you to a world that is all light [heaven], so I will sanctify with you the Name of the Sanctified, the Glorious, the Awesome One with a full heart and willing soul. And when they [Asher and Meir] came out of the gate of the palace, the [Christians] brought before them the vile thing [a crucifix] so they would bow down to it, and [Asher and Meir] threw a piece of wood at the vile thing [the crucifix]. Thus, [the Christians] then killed both these righteous men as they sanctified His Name.

In the same place was Mister Abraham son of Yom-Tov, a man of good reputation, righteous and honest and loved by the Heavens, and he used to go to the **synagogue** every morning and evening. He fell on his face and confessed his sins before the King of all kings, the Holy One blessed be He, and raised his voice and cried saying: "please O Lord, why have you forsaken your people of Israel to be mocked,

---

[28] "haGabbay" indicates that Asher carried an official position in the synagogue.
[29] 2 Chron. 36:23.

Figure 11: The Basilica of Constantine in Trier. This massive structure, built in the early fourth century by the Romans, served in the Middle Ages as the palace of the bishop of Trier, mentioned in the text. © Neta Bodner

plundered and abused, and [decided] to destroy us in the hands of the nations which are impure as a pig, who eat us, the people you have selected for yourself to be the chosen among the nations, and have raised from the earth up to the heavens? But now you have thrown down the glory of Israel from the heavens to the earth and caused many of us to die." The righteous man then completely fell on his face under the sun, and [others][30] raised him and carried him outside, where he was killed sanctifying the Name [of the Lord]. There was also a little girl there, of a good family, who sanctified the Name in holiness. After these [people] were killed, the enemies saw that those [Jews] who remained in the palace still held on to their honest [faith] as before. And their hands did not grow weak [i.e., they insisted not to convert] by what happened to the previous [Jews, who were killed]. Thus [the Christians] said to one another: "all of this is the deed of the women, who incite their husbands to keep their position [lit. keep their hands] [and] to defy the vile thing [Christianity]."

Therefore, all of the ministers came and each one held the hands of the [Jewish] women with great strength, beating and injuring them, and they led them to [the place of] idolatry [the church], in order to defile [baptize] them. Next, they [the ministers] sent [their men] to take [every] boy from the arms of his mother by force, and [the Christians] took the [boys] with them, so [the verse] will be realized: "Your sons and your daughters shall be given unto another people."[31]

[30] It is unclear whether Jews or Christians carried Abraham out of the palace.
[31] Deut. 28:32.

The women then raised their voices and cried. And three days before [the Christians] told them [the Jews][32] about this abuse, came the ministers who were in the palace and sealed off the well that was inside the palace, since they feared lest [the Jews] would throw in [the well] their sons in order to kill them. And they did not allow [Jews] to climb the walls [of the palace], so they would not throw themselves down from the walls. All night they [the Christians] had to watch [the Jews] so they would not kill each other before the morning light came. The [Christians] did all of this since they did not wish to kill [the Jews], but to catch them and force them [to convert]. And one girl was standing in front of the gate of the palace, and she stuck her neck out, saying: "anyone who wants to cut off my head, for the devotion of my Lord, should come and do so." But the gentiles did not want to touch [harm] her, as she was a very beautiful and gracious girl. But many times, they wished to take her away with them. They meant to do so, but could not, since she threw herself on the ground and pretended to be dead, and in this way stayed in the palace. Later her aunt approached her and said: "would you like to die with me in devotion of our Lord?" and she answered and said: "yes, willingly." So they went and bribed the gatekeeper and walked out [of the palace] and went to the bridge [over the Mosel river] and threw themselves into the water in devotion of the King of the world. Two girls from Cologne also did something similar. In regard to them, and others who did the same, it was said: "The Lord said, I will bring them back from Bashan[33], I will bring them back from the depths of the sea."[34] Indeed, praise be the Lord that they were [eventually] buried.

Let the Lord of vengeance avenge in our days before our eyes the poured blood of His servants,[35] and may their privilege and righteousness stand for us as credit and defend us on a day of harm.

SOURCE: The Chronicle of Solomon son of Samson. In: Eva A. Haverkamp, ed., *Hebräische Berichte über die Judenverfolgungen während des Ersten Kreuzzugs* (Hanover: Monumenta Germaniae Historica and Israel Academy of Sciences, 2005), 471–79.

Tz. B.

---

[32] Or perhaps the women—it is possible that the text continues the idea that the women were the ones who resisted the conversion.

[33] A biblical land northeast of the Holy Land. Here in the sense of a faraway place.

[34] Ps. 68:23.

[35] Ps. 79:10.

Further Reading

Chazan, Robert. "Christian and Jewish Perceptions of 1096: A Case Study of Trier." *Jewish History* 13 (1999): 9–22.

Chazan, Robert. *In the Year 1096: The First Crusade and the Jews.* Philadelphia: Jewish Publication Society, 1996.

Yuval, Israel Jacob. *Two Nations in Your Womb: Perceptions of Jews and Christians in Late Antiquity and the Middle Ages.* Trans. Barbara Harshav and Jonathan Chipman. Berkeley: University of California Press, 2008.

4D – Murder Accusations and Religious Devotion

In 1144, the body of a boy named William was found in the woods near the English town of Norwich. Local Jews were accused of murdering the boy, but since there was no clear evidence against them, the local sheriff intervened to protect them in the name of the king. Five years later, in 1149, a local monk named Thomas of Monmouth wrote a book intended to establish William as a saint. The first part of the book presents the alleged kidnap, torture, and murder of William by the Jews as an act of religious ritual attack. The Jews are depicted as inflicting on William the same injuries traditionally associated with the body of Christ, including the crucifixion itself. The act was said to have taken place during Passover, a holiday associated with the redemption of the Jews, and celebrated in parallel with Easter, commemorating the Crucifixion. The murder is explained by the alleged involvement of Jews in a conspiracy to kidnap a Christian boy every year to reenact the crucifixion on his body in order to hasten Jewish deliverance from exile. The short excerpts below, taken from the first two sections (out of seven) of Thomas's book, include some of these prominent new anti-Jewish ideas.

This Latin text clearly promotes vituperous anti-Jewish rhetoric, presenting medieval Jews as both active successors of New Testament Jews responsible for the killing of Christ, and as an actual danger to Christian children. Such rhetoric proved popular, and ritual murder accusations spread across Europe and resurfaced occasionally throughout the Middle Ages and beyond, causing persecution against Jews.[36] At the same time, it

---

[36] The most famous cases are: the boy of Blois, France, 1170; Hugh of Lincoln, England, 1255; Werner of Oberwesel, Germany, 1287; and Simon of Trent, Italy, 1475. Magda Teter, *Blood Libel: On the Trail of an Antisemitic Myth* (Cambridge: Harvard University Press, 2020), 14–99, lists seventeen known medieval cases.

seems that Thomas's major motivation was not to trigger anti-Jewish violence (which, as far as we know, did not materialize in Norwich immediately following the publication of his text), but to produce evidence for the sanctity of William. Thomas's aim was to boost the nascent cult around William, and set Norwich as a center of Christian devotion and pilgrimage. Anti-Jewish symbolism was key in achieving this aim, but most of the text focuses on miracles associated with William or his body and on describing the cult that had evolved around him. Thus, we see that anti-Jewish ideas or accusations were sometimes rooted in internal Christian interests, not directly related to tensions with local Jews. At the same time, once such ideas appeared, they could certainly transform interreligious relations for the worse and result in violence and persecution.

> Then the Jews received the boy kindly, like an innocent lamb led to the slaughter, and he was ignorant of what business was being prepared for him, and he was kept until the morrow. And so, following daybreak, which was their *pascha*[37] that year, after the appropriate chants of the day were finished in the **synagogue**, the leaders of the Jews met in the house of the aforementioned Jew, and while the boy William was eating, fearing no treachery, they suddenly seized him and humiliated him in various wretched ways. ...
>
> And when we were enquiring carefully into the affair, we found the house and in it most definite and clear signs of the affair. Moreover, there was, as rumour has it, stretched out as a cross, a post between two others and a wooden beam in the middle, attached on either side to the two other posts. And, similarly, we later discovered truly the traces made by the wounds and the chains. On the right, the right hand and foot tightly bound by chains; but on the left, the left hand and foot both pierced by a nail. And they did this with such care, of course, that if he was at any time found with nails fixed into him from this side and that, it would not be indicated that he had been killed by Jews, but rather by Christians. ...
>
> Fifth Proof (that William was killed by the Jews)
> We also interpose as an argument of faith and truth what we have heard told by Theobald, a person who was once a Jew and later one of our monks. He told us that in the ancient writings of their ancestors it was written that Jews could not achieve their freedom or ever return to the lands of their fathers without the shedding of human blood. Hence it

---

[37] That is, Passover.

was decided by them a long time ago that every year, to the shame and affront of Christ, a Christian somewhere on earth be sacrificed to the highest God, and so they take revenge for the injuries of Him, whose death is the reason for their exclusion from their fatherland and their exile as slaves in foreign lands [i.e., Christ].

Therefore, the leaders and rabbis of the Jews who dwell in Spain, at Narbonne,[38] where the seed of kings and their glory flourishes greatly, meet together, and cast lots of all the regions where Jews lived. Whichever region was chosen by lot, its capital city had to apply that lot to the other cities and towns, and the one whose name comes up will carry out that business, as decreed. In that year, however, when William, the glorious martyr of God, was killed, it so happened that the lot fell on the men of Norwich, and all the communities of the Jews of England offered their consent by letters or by messengers for the crime to be performed at Norwich.

SOURCE: Thomas of Monmouth, *The Life and Passion of William of Norwich*, ed. and trans. Miri Rubin (London: Penguin Books, 2014), 16–17, 61–62.

Tz. B.

Further Reading

Bale, Anthony. *Feeling Persecuted: Christians, Jews and Images of Violence in the Middle Ages.* London: Reaktion Books, 2010.

Langmuir, Gavin I. *Toward a Definition of Anti-Semitism.* Berkeley: University of California Press, 1990.

Tartakoff, Paola. *Conversion, Circumcision, and Ritual Murder in Medieval Europe.* Philadelphia: University of Pennsylvania Press, 2020.

Teter, Magda. *Blood Libel: On the Trail of an Antisemitic Myth.* Cambridge: Harvard University Press, 2020.

---

[38] Actually in southern France.

4E – The Attack on the Jews of York Reported in Christian Sources

William of Newburgh (1136–1198) was a canon at Newburgh in Yorkshire. Though he wrote a commentary on the biblical book the Song of Songs and several sermons, his most famous work is his five-volume **chronicle** *Historia rerum Anglicarum,* or *Historia de rebus anglicis* (History of English Affairs), which details various aspects of English history from 1066 to 1198. In this source William details the martyrdom (**Kiddush haShem**) and subsequent murder of the Jews of York at York Castle in March 1190. He describes the actors involved and the events that unfolded. Unusually for a Latin source, his description illuminates events both from the perspective of the Jews inside the castle and from the Christians threatening and attacking from the outside. He goes on to describe how the Jews who had taken refuge in the castle to escape the initial martyrdom were then executed by the mob outside despite pleading for baptism.

This source reflects the attitudes underpinning daily interactions between Jews and Christians, and the underlying political, social, and economic situation in which they lived. William's account implicitly indicates the extent to which English Jews were dependent on the monarch for safety and stability. In this instance, when neither the king nor his deputies were present, there was nothing to prevent anti-Jewish feeling from escalating into violence. Contemporaneous royal policy towards Jewish **moneylending** may have exacerbated anti-Jewish sentiment. It has been argued[39] that crusading knights were displeased that the new king, Richard I, did not forgive their debts to the Jews on ascending the throne in 1189 but rather continued his father Henry II's policy of collecting the debts owed to Jews for the benefit of the Crown.

William states that, while the city's nobility did not participate, a wide range of local people did, including people from the city and the country, as well as knights and clerics. At the end of the extract, he describes how the rioters rushed to the cathedral church to destroy the deeds of debt that were owed to the Jews. In doing so William paints a picture of the levels of popular unrest and financial resentment that seem

---

[39] Robert C. Stacey, "Crusades, Martyrdoms, and the Jews of Norman England, 1096–1190," in *Juden und Christen zur Zeit der Kreuzzüge,* ed. Alfred Haverkamp (Sigmaringen: Thorbecke, 1999), 244–47.

to have motivated the attack. He explains the theological justification for the attack—that while Jews should be subservient to Christians, in fact Christians were indebted to Jews—but then denounces this or any justification for violence against the Jews.

Chapter 9

[The attack on Clifford's Tower, where the Jews of York had taken refuge, commences]. ... Certainly, the nobility of the city and the weightier citizens were fearful of risking the king's anger and cautiously turned aside from such great frenzy. But every kind of labourer and all the city's young men with very many country folk and not a few knights came with such speed and pursued the bloodthirsty business, as if every single person was pursuing his own business and was seeking the greatest gain. There were also many clerics, among whom a certain hermit who seemed to be even more zealous than the others.

The same zeal had set everyone on fire, thinking that they were performing a great service to God if they would wipe out a people rebellious against Christ; while with blinded minds they were impervious to those words of David, indeed of the Lord, which are assuredly spoken in the person of the Saviour: "God lets me see over my enemies; slay them not, lest at any time my people forget".[40] Surely, on account of the same reason of Christian utility the perfidious Jew, the crucifier of the Lord Christ, is allowed to live among Christians by which also the shape of the Lord's cross is depicted in the church of Christ, namely to perpetuate the most salutary memory of the Lord's Passion for all the faithful, yet whereas we detest the impious action in the Jew, we truly worship the divine honour with fitting devotion in that sacred shape: consequently, Jews must certainly live among Christians for our utility, but they must serve on account of their iniquity. But the Jews living in England in the reign of Henry II, had been successful and celebrated in an inverted state of affairs over and above Christians, and on account of their great good fortune they had impudently puffed themselves up against Christ and inflicted very many burdens on Christians. For this reason in the days of the new king, their lives, which they had through the mercy of Christ, were put in peril by his just decree; nevertheless those who inflicted slaughter on them in a riot are by no means excused by the exquisite order of his judgement.

---

[40] Ps. 58(9):12.

Chapter 10

[When the Jews in the castle realize they cannot prevail against the onslaught, some of them decide to offer their lives to God rather than convert to Christianity or fall into the hands of their attackers to be killed.]

[T]hat most notorious man Josce cut the throat of his dearly beloved wife Anna with a sharpened knife; nor did he spare his own sons. And when this was also done by the other men that most wretched old man [Yom Tov of Joigny, a visiting rabbi from northern France whom William had previously described as having encouraged the Jews to martyr themselves] slit Josce's throat because he was more honourable than the others. Soon after they had all been killed together with the instigator of the error, the interior of the castle began to burn by the fire which, as has been said, had been started by those who were going to die. To be sure, those who had chosen to live did what they could to withstand the fire started by their own people so that they themselves would also be destroyed even if they were unwilling, by taking refuge in the external parts of the citadel where they would be less exposed to the flames. That irrational frenzy of rational beings against themselves is simply astonishing. But anyone who reads *History of the Jewish War* by Josephus has some understanding that that madness has come down to our time from an old custom of the Jews in the face of pending calamity. At daybreak when numerous people assembled to assault the castle, those wretched remaining Jews, perched on the ramparts, mournfully revealed the nocturnal slaughter of the others and throwing the corpses of the dead from the wall as visible proof of so great a crime they proclaimed as follows: "Behold the bodies of the wretched who inflicted death on themselves in a wicked frenzy and set fire to the inner chambers of the castle as they died in order to burn us alive because we recoiled from doing the same and preferred to throw ourselves on Christian mercy. But God has preserved us from the madness of our brothers as well as from the destruction of the fire so that we should not any longer differ from you in religion in any way. Indeed, the distress has given us understanding and we recognize the Christian truth and seek charity; we are ready to be purified by holy baptism as you are wont to demand of us and, having given up our former rituals, be united to the Church of Christ. Receive brothers out of enemies and let us live with you in the faith and peace of Christ." As they mournfully said these things, most of us both shuddered with great astonishment at the madness of the dead and pitied the survivors of the slaughter. But the leaders of the conspirators, of whom one was a certain Richard with the apt surname of Malebisse, a very violent man, were not moved by any mercy for those wretched people. They treacherously plied them with sweet words and faithfully promised them the favour they hoped for so that they would not be afraid of coming out, but as soon as they had emerged the butchers hostilely seized them and killed them, all the while they were demanding the baptism of Christ. And indeed of those who were killed by that more than brutal brutality I would have said without hesitation that, if they were sincere in their petition for baptism, they would have been by no means cheated of its effect, baptized as they were in their own blood. But whether they requested baptism falsely or not, that detestable cruelty of the murderers is unpardonable. ... The sight of those things in the city was plainly horrific and disgusting with unburied corpses of so many of the wretched lying everywhere around the castle. Once the killing had been done, the conspirators immediately made for the cathedral church and by violent insistence forced the terrified wardens to hand over the deeds of the debts, which had been stored there by the Jews, the king's usurers, by which Christians were oppressed, and they destroyed the same bonds of unholy greed in solemn flames in the middle of the church as much for their own release as for the release of many others. After this was done, those of the conspirators who had accepted the cross, went on their proposed journey ahead of any investigation; others, however, remained in the county in dread of an inquiry. Truly, such matters occurred in York at the time of our Lord's Passion, on the day before Palm Sunday [i.e., Friday night to Saturday, March 16–17]. This was *Shabbat haGadol* in the Jewish calendar [the **Sabbath** preceding Passover].

>SOURCE: William of Newburgh, "Historia Rerum Anglicarum," book IV, chs. 9 and 10. In: Richard Howlett, ed., *Chronicles of the Reigns of Stephen, Henry II, and Richard I*, Rolls Series 82.1 (London: Longman, 1884), 316–17, 320–22. Translated by Anna Sapir Abulafia in "Between Exclusion and Embrace: An Online Teaching Resource".

M. F.

Further Reading

Dobson, Richard B. *The Jewish Communities of Medieval England: The Collected Essays of R. B. Dobson*, ed. Helen Birkett. York: Borthwick Publications, 2010.

Sapir Abulafia, Anna. *Christian–Jewish Relations, 1000–1300: Jews in the Service of Medieval Christendom*. London: Routledge, 2011.

Figure 12: The Erfurt *Judeneid*. Erfurt, Municipal Archives (Stadtarchiv Erfurt), 0-0/A XLVII, no. 1

4F – The Erfurt *Judeneid*

Around the year 1200, the city of Erfurt (central Germany) released a formal record containing the Erfurt *Judeneid*, an oath formula Jews had to recite when they had to swear in different legal situations before Christians. The text was given to the city of Erfurt and its Jewish inhabitants by the **archbishop** of Mainz (**Rhineland**), who was the lord of the city as well as the lord of the local Jews. Oaths such as this one facilitated medieval business activities on a daily basis. Such oaths played a crucial role in regulating formal interactions between Jews and Christians, for example in law court cases, naturalization, or release from imprisonment. In order to make such oaths legal and accepted, they were expected to conform to local, Christian, and Jewish legal norms. This is why this text refers to biblical figures and their stories, as well as to curses from the Hebrew Bible, a source common to both Jews and Christians.

Many different *Judeneide* exist from medieval Germany. The Erfurt *Judeneid*, the oldest in the German language, was utilized to enable Jews to "cleanse" themselves from accusations in court and was sworn in a ritualized context. It therefore starts with the assertion of innocence for the accusation made against its oath taker. The very formalized and easily legible script emphasized its importance, as did the representative seal of the city of Erfurt attached to it.

The thing you have been accused of, [you swear that] you are not guilty [of it]. So help you God. The God who created heaven and earth, leaves, and grass, which have never existed before. And if you swear falsely, the earth that devoured Datan and Aviram[41] shall devour you. And if you swear falsely, the leprosy that left Naaman and befell Gehazi[42] shall befall on you. And if you swear falsely, the laws which God gave Moses on Mount Sinai, which God himself wrote with his own fingers on the stone tablets shall devour you. And if you swear falsely, all the writings which are written in the five books of Moses shall judge you. This is the Judeneid which [Arch] Bishop Conrad gave this city [of Erfurt].

SOURCE: Erfurt, Municipal Archives, 0-0/A XLVII, no. 1.

A. L.

Further Reading

Linder, Amnon. "The Jewry-Oath in Christian Europe." In *Jews in Early Christian Law: Byzantium and the Latin West, 6th–11th Centuries*, ed. John V. Tolan and Nicholas R. M. De Lange, 311–58. Turnhout: Brepols, 2014.

Ziegler, Joseph. "Reflections on the Jewry Oath in the Middle Ages." *Studies in Church History* 29 (1992): 209–20.

Ziegler, Joseph. "Oath, Jewish." In *Medieval Jewish Civilization: An Encyclopedia*, ed. Norman Roth, 483–87. New York: Routledge, 2002.

---

[41] The biblical figures Datan and Aviram conspired against Moses (Num. 16). Their punishment was that they were devoured by the earth and disappeared.

[42] The biblical figure Gehazi, a servant of the prophet Elisha, betrayed the Syrian military commander Naaman, who suffered from leprosy (2 Kings 5). His punishment was that the leprosy left Naaman and befell Gahazi.

4G – Jews in Customary Law

The *Saxon Mirror* (*Sachsenspiegel*) is one of the most influential legal texts of the Middle Ages, marking the beginning of German legal codes. Written in the 1220s by Eike von Repgow, a local juror most likely from the town of Magdeburg, the *Sachsenspiegel* is an extensive compilation of customary law (law based on local custom) for the territory of Saxony. As a compilation of legal customs, the legal codes in the *Sachsenspiegel* did not possess the status of binding legislation but were rather a description of the current legal traditions and norms in the territory. As such, they provide insight into the lives of all those living in the territory of Saxony, whether royals, peasants, women, children, or minorities, including Jews. While only a few of its 230 clauses refer to Jews, those clauses that do mention them suggest the fundamental legal norms that governed the legal relationship between Jews and Christian institutions.

> Book 2, paragraph 66
> Now hear about the old peace ordinance that the imperial power confirmed in Saxony with the agreement of the respected servants of the land. Every day and at all times, priests and religious, girls and women, and Jews shall enjoy immunity of their person and property.
>
> Book 3, paragraph 2
> Regarding priests, tonsured according to their rule, and Jews: when they carry arms in transgression of the law, they shall be compensated as laymen if they are attacked—because those who are included in the king's peace are not permitted to bear arms.[43]
>
> Book 3, paragraph 7
> A Jew need not be a Christian man's guarantor [for a loan] unless he is willing to be accountable in the Christian man's stead. If a Jew kills a Christian, or if he commits a crime against him and is seized in the act, he shall be tried the same as a Christian. In addition, if a Christian kills a Jew, he is to be sentenced for violating the king's peace against him. A Jew named Josephus earned this protection from Emperor Vespasian[44] when he cured his son Titus of gout. If a Jew buys or accepts chalices,

---

[43] This refers to immunity granted to certain groups in the royal and territorial Land-peace agreements.

[44] This comment relates to the Roman emperor during the first century CE who ruled Rome during the time of the destruction of the second temple in Jerusalem.

books, or priest's clothing in pawn for which he has no warrantor, and if it is found in his possession, he shall be tried as a thief. Whatever other items he buys openly in daylight and not behind closed doors that he can prove with two others, he retains the money he paid for it or lent upon his oath even if it has been stolen. Should his warrantor fail him, however, he loses his money.

SOURCE: Maria Dobozy, *The Saxon Mirror: A Sachsenspiegel of the Fourteenth Century*. (Philadelphia: University of Pennsylvania Press, 1999), 112, 117–18.

A. D.

Further Reading

Dobozy, Maria. *The Saxon Mirror: A Sachsenspiegel of the Fourteenth Century*. Philadelphia: University of Pennsylvania Press, 1999.

Magin, Christine. *"Wie es umb der Iuden recht stet": Der Status der Juden in Spätmittelalterlichen Deutschen Rechtsbüchern*. Göttingen: Wallstein Verlag, 1999.

4H – Jews in the Illustrations of Legal Codes

Four illustrated manuscripts of the *Saxon Mirror (Sachsenspiegel)*[45] are known to have survived, named after the libraries where they are kept today: Oldenburg, Heidelberg, Dresden, and Wolfenbüttel. In these illuminated manuscripts, the images in the legal code are closely linked to the text, with an enlarged and colored initial letter in both the text and image, allowing the reader to connect each image to its related legal clause. In this way the images provide exegetical commentary to the law, at times revealing legal practices, institutions, and norms not discussed in the text. In all the illuminated manuscripts, Jews are easily recognized by their portrayal with the Jewish hat (*Judenhut*)[46] and full beard. The image below is from the Wolfenbüttel manuscript, which was created between 1348 and 1362, and presents the best quality of illuminations of the surviving manuscripts. The illustrations below relate to book 3, paragraph 7, specifically to the punishment for those who physically harm Jews, and the prohibition on Jews from receiving church items (i.e., chalices and books) as pawns without a warrantor.

A. D.

---

[45] See more in source 4G.

[46] See source 3K.

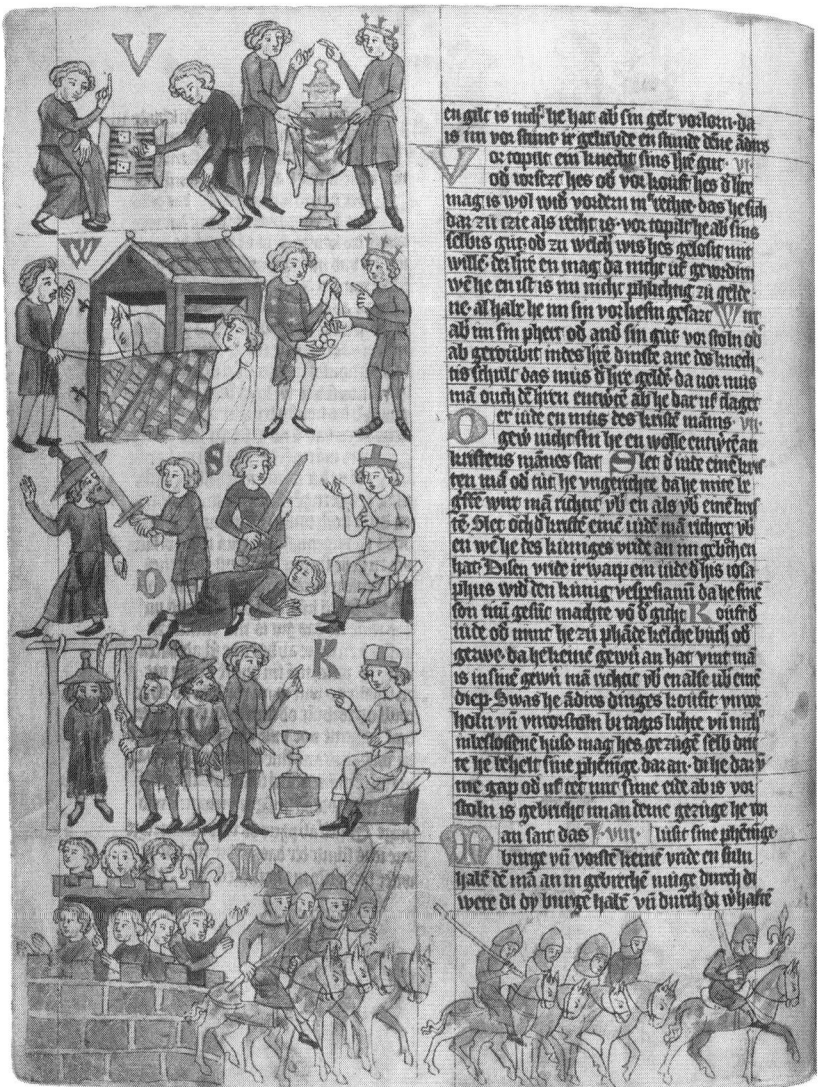

Figure 13: The *Saxon Mirror (Sachsenspiegel)*, Wolfenbüttel manuscript. *Der Sachsenspiegel und das sächsische Lehnrecht*, Cod. Guelf. 3.1 Aug. 2°; Heinemann-Nr. 1642, fol. 43v.
© Herzog August Bibliothek Wolfenbüttel: Cod. Guelf. 3.1 Aug. 2°, folio 43v

Further Reading

Caviness, Madeline H., and Charles G. Nelson. *Women and Jews in the Sachsenspiegel Picture-Books*. Turnhout: Brepols, 2018.

Dobozy, Maria. *The Saxon Mirror: A Sachsenspiegel of the Fourteenth Century*. Philadelphia: University of Pennsylvania Press, 1999.

Lipton, Sara. *Dark Mirror: The Medieval Origins of Anti-Jewish Iconography*. New York: Metropolitan Books; Henry Holt and Company, 2014.

4I – A Contract Between the City and the Jewish Community of Augsburg

In a moment of potential instability, August 23, 1298, following a wave of persecution against Jews—known as the **Rintfleisch Massacre**—the Jewish community turned to the urban commune of Augsburg (southern Germany) in the hopes of obtaining an agreement securing their protection. This contract was drawn up only weeks after the death of German emperor Adolf I (reigned 1292–1298), who, as emperor, was the traditional warrantor of freedom, but before the new emperor had been elected. In order to receive protection from the urban commune, the Jewish community promised to build part of the city wall next to the Jewish cemetery and gave their **synagogue** as a guarantee. Both parties attached their seal to confirm the agreement.

> We Benditte, son of Judlin, Michel, Lambt, brother of Aaron, Osterman, Joseph from Averde, son of Mosman, Joseph from Biberach and his son-in-law Maus, Liebaermaenin and her son Saelickman, Choewellin from Frideberch, Joseph from Mulrestat, Jaecklin, and the community of the Jews [*gemain der Juden*] in the city of Augsburg, whether they be named or not, poor and rich, announce: To all those who read the record or hear it read aloud, we declare about the grace, honor and loyalty which was given to us by the honorable councilmen and the community of the city [*gemain der stat*] of Augsburg [the following]: [1] They [the urban commune] have not caused us harm, nor have they allowed unjust force over us. [2] We trust them that they will keep their good will and their honor upon us [i.e., they will continue to protect us] with the help of our lord King Albrecht, the Roman King. We have vowed and asked and begged them [the urban commune] with our own courage and freewill to [let us] honor the city, and [act] for the city's benefit and in service of the empire. We will build a wall in front of our cemetery [*chirchof*] which is located before the city wall [and is called] "To the Holy Cross" [*zem heiligen chriuce*] by the ditch, within four years, according to the height and width which [has been/will be] told us by the modest master of the people Hartman der Langemantel and master Chunrat der Lange, who were given to us as supervisors [*phleger*]. [3] We have vowed this with loyalty by oath, our men and women, young and old, poor and rich, to master Hartman der Langemantel and master Chunrat der Lange, who represent the councilmen and the urban commune. And for this we have offered them our synagogue [*schûl*] as guarantee, and [also] everything the Jewish community [*gemain der Juden*] owns within the city justly as

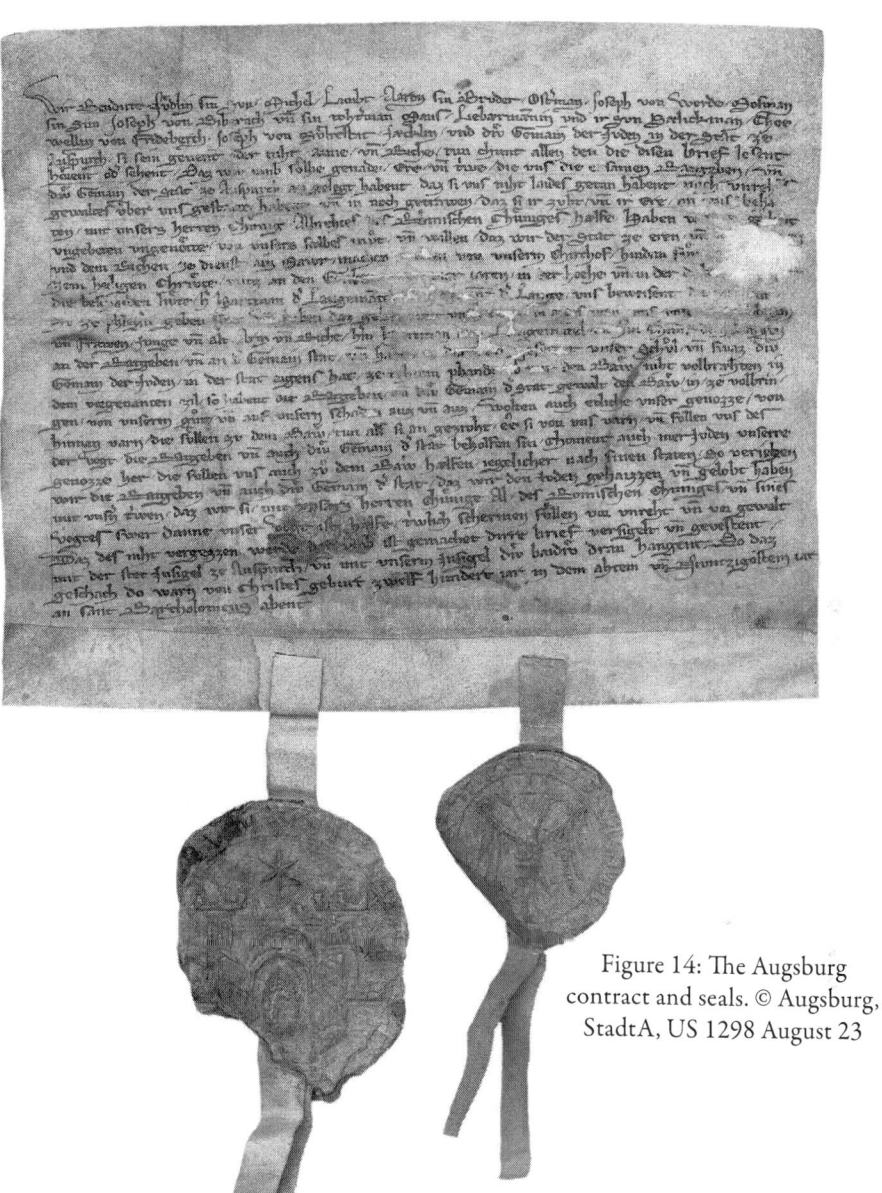

Figure 14: The Augsburg contract and seals. © Augsburg, StadtA, US 1298 August 23

pawns, in case we do not finish the construction [of the wall] within the aforementioned time. [4] In this case, the councilmen and the urban commune [*gemain der stat*] shall have the right to complete the construction by using our goods and at our complete expense. [5] Even if some of our members [*genozzen*] move away, they shall give their part for the construction as it is their duty before they move away. And the reeve [*vogt*] [of the king], the councilmen, and also the urban commune [*gemain der stat*] shall help us in this. [6] If further Jews come and become our [community] members [*genozzen*], they too shall help us with the construction, each one according to his own capacity. [7] We, the councilmen and the urban commune [*gemain der stat*] declare, that we have told and promised the Jews our loyalty: That we will protect them loyally against any wrongdoing and against violence with the help of our lord King Albrecht, Roman King, and his reeve [*vogt*], whoever will be the reeve at the time. [8] In order to not forget this, this record was written, sealed, and confirmed with the city seal of Augsburg and with our [the Jewish community's] seal, both are attached to it. This took place twelve hundred years after the birth of Christ in the ninety eighth year on Saint Bartholomeus' Eve.

Seal 1: + SIGILLVM . CIVIVM . AVGVSTENSIVM ("Seal of the Citizens of Augsburg"; seal image: a city gate with a pine tree in its midst; Seal 2: Hebrew *hotam kahal a*[spurk] ("Seal [of the Jewish] community [of] Augsburg)—Latin S(IGILLVM) IVDEORVM I(N) AVGVSTA[E] ("Seal of the [community of the] Jews in Augsburg"; seal image: a double-headed eagle with a *Judenhut*[47] between its heads).

SOURCE: Augsburg, Municipal Archives, US 1298 August 23.

A. L.

Further Reading

Meyer, Christian. *Urkundenbuch der Stadt Augsburg, vol. 1: Die Urkunden vom Jahre 1104–1346,* 129–130, no. 167. Augsburg: Butsch, 1874.

Straus, Raphael. *Regensburg and Augsburg.* Philadelphia: Jewish Publication Society of America, 1939.

---

[47] See source 3K.

4J – The Great Expulsion of the Jews of France Through the Eyes of a Christian Chronicler

On July 22, 1306 King Philippe IV (known as Philippe the Fair) of France expelled all the Jews from his kingdom. It was common for sovereigns to expel Jews, or other minorities in their lands, for different reasons. Thus, expulsions of Jewish populations were not exceptional events in the Middle Ages. The French Jews, for example, had already been expelled in 1144 and 1182. In 1306 about one hundred thousand Jews were expelled from France. Geoffrey of Paris (*Godfroy/Godfroi de Paris*, died ca. 1320) was a French chronicler and the author of the *Chronique metrique de Philippe le Bel*, which deals with the history of France from 1300 to 1316, and contains many poems narrating the history of France during this period.

One of these poems describes the expulsion of Jews from France in 1306. A segment of this poem is presented below, translated from old French. The poem, which portrays the expulsion of the Jews and the reason for this expulsion through the eyes of Geoffrey, describes how the Jews had been seized in one day due to their un-Christian behavior—especially their engagement in interest loans. But later on, the poem continues, the French king (or the French people) regretted the fact that they deprived the kingdom of lenders who were very helpful in supplying credit for business transactions.

Interestingly, Geoffrey of Paris justifies the expulsion of the Jews for religious reasons. He explains the involvement of Pope Clément V and Philippe IV in the decision to expel the Jews. On the other hand, Geoffrey reveals that Jews were an integral part of Christian business making, and that their expulsion had created a deficiency in the money market. This was perhaps the reason that the Jews expelled from France in 1306 were allowed to return in 1315, by order of Philippe's son, King Louis X.

> In the Year of 1306, in that year
> the Jews were [taken] away
> About this, I have no doubt,
> that the Jews, had no understanding
> of our Christian law [religion].
> They were seized on one day
> right on the day of Magdalaine[48]

[48] July 22.

Many [of the seized Jews] made the great prison full.
And it is certain that the true king
Philippe, and Pope Clement,
who [were responsible] for this bad remedy,
had stretched the edges of Christianity,
and removed the grain from the straw [figurative: removed an essential part]

I tell you this, Sirs, how it went,
the intention was good
but worse [came as a result].
Who shall now become a usurer,
and who will be [a usurer] in the near future?

It is better not having knowledge of
those things that poor people dread.
Because the Jews were taken wrongly
For doing too much business
that was not Christian.

SOURCE: Jean Alexandre Buchon, ed., *Chronique métrique de Godefroy de Paris: Suivie de La taille de Paris, en 1313* (Paris: Verdière, 1827), 120–24.

N. D.

Further Reading

Einbinder, Susan L. *No Place of Rest: Jewish Literature, Expulsion, and the Memory of Medieval France*. Philadelphia: University of Pennsylvania Press, 2009.

Jordan, William C. "Home Again: The Jews in the Kingdom of France, 1315–1322." In *The Stranger in Medieval Society*, ed. F. R. P. Akehurst and Stephanie Cain Van D'Elden, 27–45. Minneapolis: University of Minnesota Press, 1997.

Nahon, Gérard. "Les juifs de Paris à la veille de l'expulsion de 1306." In *Finances, Pouvoirs et Mémoire: Mélanges Offerts à Jean Favier*, ed. Jean Favier, Jean Kerhervé, and Albert Rigaudière, 27–40. Paris: Fayard, 1999.

Sibon, Juliette. *Chasser les juifs pour régner: Les expulsions par les rois de France au Moyen Âge*. Paris: Perrin, 2016.

4K – The Black Death and the Persecution of Jews

Heinrich von Herford (ca. 1300–1370) was a Dominican friar who lived in the monastery of St. Paul in Minden, Westphalia, in the German Empire. He composed a Latin **chronicle** titled *The Book of More Memorable Things* (*Liber de rebus memorabilioribus*), which he based mostly on the work of previous historians. He also inserted his own experiences, specifically in the section below describing the onset of the **Black Death** in Germany in 1349. He further depicts the subsequent persecution of local Jews. Heinrich was appalled by the anti-Jewish violence and cast doubt on the popular claim that the Jews poisoned wells to cause the plague. Still, he tried to explain the connection between the raging plague and the persecution.

> That year [1349], the Jews, including women and children, were slain by sword or fire in a cruel and inhumane manner, throughout Germany and many other provinces. This happened because of their abundant riches, which many nobles, paupers, and destitute persons sought to usurp, as did their debtors. This I think is the truth, just as [was with the things] that were said about the Templars.[49] Conversely, [the Jews were killed] due to water poisoning that they have committed, as many claimed, and as was reinforced by rumors, which were maliciously and wickedly fabricated everywhere. I do not believe this to be true. Still the plague, which raged across the world at the time, gave credibility to this rumor; it did not advance everywhere continuously, but rather, like in a game of chess, flew up from one place where it was raging, through another region which was not contaminated, to hit a third one. Sometimes it would return to the area in the middle, as if by choice. Until some places even made themselves inaccessible to guests, who were told not to pass through there, lest these guests would destroy them using poison. Also, this poison, so it was said, was scattered throughout the world by the Jews and those Christians whom they bribed. Happy and dancing the Jews hurried to be led to their death, first children, then women, and then

---

[49] The Templars were an order of crusader knights who gained enormous power, wealth, and influence. In 1307 many of the Templars in France were arrested by King Philip IV, accused of various crimes, and executed. The order was dissolved in 1312. By 1349, however, many agreed that the accusations were false, and here Heinrich meant to suggest that so were the accusations against the Jews.

those given to the flames, lest anyone would be driven against Judaism by human fragility on their part.⁵⁰ And in certain places they were burnt in different ways, in others they were broken [at the wheel], or even slaughtered like pigs in the most ferocious and barbaric manner.

SOURCE: Henricus de Hervordia, *Liber de rebus memorabilioribus sive Chronicon*, ed. Augustus Potthast (Göttingen: Dieterich, 1859), 280.

Tz. B.

Further Reading

Breuer, Mordechai. "The 'Black Death' and Antisemitism." In *Antisemitism through the Ages*, ed. Shmuel Almog, trans. Nathan H. Reisner, 139–51. Exeter: Pergamon, 1988.

Cohn, Samuel K., Jr. "The Black Death and the Burning of Jews." *Past and Present* 196 (2007): 3–36.

Horrox, Rosemary, ed. *The Black Death*. Manchester and New York: Manchester University Press, 1994.

4L – The Persecution of Jews in Nordhausen during the Black Death

This source presents a short description of the execution of the Jews of Nordhausen, which is in the region of Thuringia in the German Empire. As happened in hundreds of other communities, the Jews of this city were attacked during the first outbreak of the **Black Death** and were executed on April 28, 1349. The source describes the events from a Jewish perspective—one of the few surviving Hebrew narrative sources documenting this persecution. It presents the mass execution as a spectacle of Jewish martyrdom (**Kiddush haShem**). It was written in Hebrew by an anonymous Jew [probably from Worms] who wished to commemorate this community, perhaps as part of an annual ritual that took place on the anniversary of the execution. The text should probably be dated to the second half of the fourteenth century.⁵¹

---

⁵⁰ See the source 4K, describing the execution of Jews in Nordhausen.

⁵¹ The text was preserved, with slight variations, in two sixteenth-century manuscripts, one in Oxford and one in Frankfurt. The text below follows the Frankfurt manuscript, with some corrections based on the Oxford one.

4L – THE PERSECUTION OF JEWS IN NORDHAUSEN 119

I, Eliezer son of Samuel, may his memory be preserved for the afterlife,[52] found the story of the deed described below in an old prayer [book] of the holy community of Worms, and copied it.

The people of the community of Nordhausen sanctified the Blessed Name [of the Lord, that is, performed an act of martyrdom, *kiddush haShem*] on the third day of the week on which they read the Torah portion *Behar*.[53] And our teacher the rabbi Jacob, and his son the generous[54] Meir, may the Lord avenge their blood,[55] have asked the [Christian] townspeople to allow them [and the other Jews] to prepare themselves to sanctify the Name [i.e., for the execution]. And they [the townsmen] gave them permission. And then they took their prayer shawls [*talitot*] and shrouds,[56] men and women with joy. And here [the townspeople] dug for them a pit in the cemetery and covered it above with beams of cedar trees. And fire was lit all around [the pit]. And here the pure and righteous people wished to rent for themselves musical instruments [*mishak*] so to dance in order to serve the Lord with gladness and come into his presence with singing.[57] Then he [perhaps R. Jacob] said "O house of Jacob, come ye, let us walk in the light of the Lord."[58] And they took each other's hands, men and women, leaping and dancing with great might before the Blessed Name [of the Lord]. Our teacher the rabbi Jacob went first, and his son the generous Meir acting as the rear guard of all the camps [i.e., went last][59] so none of them would postpone death at the last minute. And they were singing and dancing into the pit. And when they were all inside the pit, Meir the generous jumped out to its edge, and walked around the pit to see whether anyone of them escaped outside. And when the [Christian] townsmen saw [this] they asked

---

[52] *Zihrono leHayei haOlam haBa*—a phrase indicating that Eliezer's father has already passed away.

[53] In addition to the standard Hebrew date, medieval Jews sometimes marked dates based on the Torah portion read in the **synagogue** on the Sabbath. The third day of the week on which the Torah portion of *beHar* was read in the year 1348–1349 corresponds to April 28.

[54] Meir probably contributed money to one of the community's institutions, earning him the title "generous."

[55] *HaShem yekom et damam*—indicating that they died as martyrs.

[56] Traditional Jewish white burial furnishings.

[57] Ps. 100:2.

[58] Isa. 2:5.

[59] Num. 10:25.

him [Meir] to save his own soul.[60] And he answered without care "for one minute your eyes are on me, and I shall be gone"[61] and went back into the pit. And [the townsmen] threw the fire on the top [of the pit], on the beams. And their [the Jews'] soul went out [of their bodies] immediately, without crying or moaning.

To all of this testified the messenger of rabbi Eleazar, the son of the rabbi Jacob, may the Lord avenge his blood, as they asked him [the messenger] to announce that none of them survived. And even one of the children did not cry or moan, even in this disaster. May their soul be bound in the bond of life[62] with the other righteous men and woman in paradise, Amen.

SOURCE: Felix Böhl, "Die hebräischen Handschriften zur Verfolgung der Juden Nordhausens und ihrem Tanz zum Tode im Jahre 1349," in *Tanz und Tod in Kunst und Literatur*, ed. Franz Link (Berlin: Duncker und Humblot, 1993), 130–31.

Tz. B.

Further Reading

Einbinder, Susan L. *Beautiful Death: Jewish Poetry and Martyrdom in Medieval France*. Princeton: Princeton University Press, 2002.

Breuer, Mordechai. "The 'Black Death' and Antisemitism." In *Antisemitism through the Ages*, ed. Shmuel Almog, trans. Nathan H. Reisner, 139–51. Exeter: Pergamon, 1988.

Horrox, Rosemary, ed. *The Black Death*. Manchester and New York: Manchester University Press, 1994.

---

[60] The context suggests that they wished Meir to convert in order to save his life, but the text does not state so explicitly.

[61] Job 7:8.

[62] The Hebrew equivalent for "may they rest in peace," according to 1 Sam. 25:29.

5 – Jews and Christians: Neighbors, Partners, Adversaries

5A – The Role of Converts in Jewish–Christian Relations

Jewish converts to Christianity were sometimes perceived as a bridge between Christians and Jews in medieval society, bringing a wealth of knowledge about Jewish practice and belief into the Christian communities. As a result, some converts attained reasonably high socio-economic status and royal patronage, and played active roles in the creation of royal and papal conversionary policies. But what kind of relationship did they have with their former coreligionists? From the Jewish point of view, conversion was indeed a threat and baptism often the epitome of betrayal. In some cases, and for various reasons, conversion was often coupled with a severe renunciation of the faith, shaping the information converts would impart and heightening existing tensions between Jews and Christians. The prominence of such former Jews in Christian circles of learning suggests their historical role in the nature of hardening Christian attitudes towards Jews and Judaism during the twelfth and thirteenth centuries.

The following source is from *Mahzor Vitry*, a compendium of Jewish liturgy and custom compiled in northern France at the start of the thirteenth century. Within the sections on the laws and practices of mourning, the author includes this tale of a convert to Christianity, who informed the king that Jewish practices of mourning involved casting spells and cursing Christians. Upon hearing this information from converts, the king then confronted the head of the Jewish community directly in demand of an explanation. And while the king and the Jewish community leader parted ways in peace and mutual understanding, the convert informant was blamed for this misunderstanding. This tale represents a best-case scenario of the many surviving Latin and Hebrew records of converts from Judaism informing Christian officials of Jewish knowledge and practice to the detriment of the community. It demonstrates the direct access converts had, in this case, to the king of France, and the general ease with which medieval rulers, emperors, and other royals moved about the city. While Jewish–royal relations are often characterized as antagonistic, this source gives the impression that monarchies and the Jews were not always in conflict but could and did meet on occasion to air their grievances or misgivings without messengers, informants, or court personnel.

In addition, this source provides an example of Jewish mourning customs that some Jews were reluctant to practice, for fear of how they would be perceived by their Christian neighbors.

> Once, the converts [to Christianity] of Paris informed the king that all Jews [lit. of Israel] throw dirt behind them when they return from the cemetery. And that the Jews do this to perform magic and to cause the death of non-Jews. This was slander. And it happened to Rabbi Moshe ben Rabbi Yehiel ben Rabbi Mattitya the Great of Paris that [the king] said to him: "What is this terrible deed that I heard, about you performing magic for the death of non-Jews?" He [Rabbi Moshe] said "My king, this is not the practice among the Jews, rather we believe in the resurrection of the dead, as it is written "may they sprout up in the city like the grass of the fields."[1] When we tear the weeds and throw them to the dead, we believe that the dead will be just like the weeds that dry in the earth and bloom again. Even though they die, God will revive the dead in the future. Hearing this, he [the king] said: "If this is so, your practice is wise and lovely. This is indeed beautiful and good faith, as you are holy to the Lord your God. Cursed are the informants on you that do not know your faith well, for this applies to all mankind." After the Rabbi returned from the company of the king in peace, he told his community. They praised God and said "The king's heart is in the hand of God; He directs it like a watercourse wherever he pleases"[2] and "God will do what He deems right."[3] Blessed is the scroll and its secrets to the God-fearing person and what he says depends on God.[4] In praise of God, I added this event in Paris, France, to this book [*Mahzor Vitry*], in order to get a feeling for this leader and in order to discover that many avoid practicing this custom due to the fear that the Gentiles will suspect them of witchcraft. And if they [the Jews] know how to reply, then "a wise man's talk brings him favor."[5]
>
> SOURCE: Simha of Vitry, *Mahzor Vitry*, vol. 3, ed. Aryeh Goldschmidt (Jerusalem: Makhon Otzar haPoskim, 2009), 670.

H. T. S.

---

[1] Ps. 72:16.

[2] Prov. 21:1.

[3] 2 Sam. 10:12.

[4] Prov. 16:1.

[5] Ecc. 10:12.

Further Reading

Cohen, Jeremy. "The Mentality of the Medieval Jewish Apostate: Peter Alfonsi, Hermann of Cologne and Pablo Christiani." In *Jewish Apostasy in the Modern World*, ed. Todd M. Endelman and Jeffrey Gurock, 20–47. New York: Lynne Rienner, 1987.

Elukin, Jonathan. "From Jew to Christian? Conversion and Immutability in Medieval Europe." In *Varieties of Religious Conversion in the Middle Ages*, ed. James Muldoon, 171–89. Gainesville: University Press of Florida, 1997.

Kanarfogel, Ephraim. "Changing Attitudes toward Apostates in Tosafist Literature, Late Twelfth–Early Thirteenth Centuries." In *New Perspectives on Jewish–Christian Relations*, ed. Elisheva Carlebach and Jacob J. Schacter, 297–327. Leiden: Brill, 2012.

Yuval, Israel J. *Two Nations in Your Womb: Perceptions of Jews and Christians in Late Antiquity and the Middle Ages*, trans. Barbara Harshav and Jonathan Chipman. Berkeley: University of California Press, 2008.

5B – The Exchequer of the Jews in Twelfth-Century England

The first Jews came to England in the late eleventh century, shortly after the Norman Conquest in 1066. Over the course of the next two centuries, particularly as a result of the advance of commerce, taxes collected from the Jews of England consistently contributed to royal revenue. A distinct department was created within the Great Exchequer (a court that dealt with matters of equity in medieval England and Wales) for the management of Jewish capital. The first Exchequer of the Jews[6] was established in order to handle the extensive assets and inheritance of Aaron of Lincoln (d. 1186), a financier and one of the wealthiest Jews in Norman England in the twelfth century. His wealth had drawn the attention of the treasurer to the Jewish revenues from interest loans and the potential royal revenues that might arise from taxing them.

The following document is a translation of an ordinance, issued in 1194, which marks the beginning of a new policy concerning the Jews, one that ultimately led to the establishment of the Exchequer of the Jews of the thirteenth century. It determines the rules according to which Jewish **moneylending** was to be conducted and documented in the royal **regis-**

---

[6] A division of the court Exchequer at Westminster, which recorded and regulated the taxes and the law-cases of the Jews of England.

ters, that are an important source for understanding interactions and relationships between Jews and Christians in England. This specific ordinance explains the way transactions were made, the way they were recorded, the people involved in editing, recording, and securing them, and the manner in which they were maintained.

> All the debts, pledges, mortgages, lands, houses, rents, and possessions of the Jews shall be registered. The Jew who shall conceal any of these shall forfeit to the King his body and the thing concealed, and likewise all his possessions and chattels, neither shall it be lawful to the Jew to recover the thing concealed.
>
> Likewise six or seven places shall be provided in which they shall make all their contracts, and there shall be appointed two lawyers that are Christians and two lawyers that are Jews, and two legal registrars, and before them and the clerks of William of the Church of St. Mary's and William of Chimilli, shall their contracts be made.
>
> And charters shall be made of their contracts by way of indenture. And one part of the indenture shall remain with the Jew, sealed with the seal of him, to whom the money is lent, and the other part shall remain in the common chest: wherein there shall be three locks and keys, whereof the two Christians shall keep one key, and the two Jews another, and the clerks of William of the Church of St. Mary and of William of Chimilli shall keep the third. And moreover, there shall be three seals to it, and those who keep the seals shall put the seals thereto.
>
> Moreover the clerks of the said William and William shall keep a roll of the transcripts of all the charters, and as the charters shall be altered so let the roll be likewise. For every charter there shall be three pence paid, one moiety thereof by the Jews and the other moiety by him to whom the money is lent; whereof the two writers shall have twopence and the keeper of the roll the third.
>
> And from henceforth no contract shall be made with, nor payment made to, the Jews, nor any alteration made in the charters, except before the said persons or the greater part of them, if all of them cannot be present. And the aforesaid two Christians shall have one roll of the debts or receipts of the payments which from henceforth are to be made to the Jews, and the two Jews one and the keeper of the roll one.

Moreover every Jew shall swear on his Roll, that all his debts and pledges and rents, and all his goods and his possessions, he shall cause to be enrolled, and that he shall conceal nothing as is aforesaid. And if he shall know that anyone shall conceal anything he shall secretly reveal it to the Justices sent to them, and that they shall detect and shew unto them all falsifiers or forgers of the charters and clippers of money, where or when they shall know them, and likewise all false charters.

SOURCE: Roger de Hoveden, "Ordinance of the Jews," in The Jews of Angevin England: Documents and Records, ed. Joseph Jacobs (London: D. Nutt, 1893), 156–59.

N. D.

Further Reading

Hoyle, Victoria. "The Bonds That Bind: Money Lending between Anglo-Jewish and Christian Women in the Plea Rolls of the Exchequer of the Jews, 1218–1280." *Journal of Medieval History* 34 (2008): 119–29.

Mundill, Robin R. "Lumbard and Son: The Businesses and Debtors of Two Jewish Moneylenders in Late Thirteenth-Century England." *Jewish Quarterly Review* 82 (1991): 137–70.

Stacey, Robert C. "The Massacres of 1189–90 and the Origins of the Jewish Exchequer, 1186–1226." In *Christians and Jews in Angevin England*, ed. Sarah Rees Jones and Sethina Watson, 106–24. York: York Medieval Press, 2013.

Tallan, Cheryl. "Structures of Power Available to Two Jewish Women in Thirteenth-Century England." *Proceedings of the World Congress of Jewish Studies* 12, section 2 (1997): 85–90.

5C – Conversion to Judaism: Acceptance and Status

Conversion to Judaism also occurred in the Middle Ages, albeit with far less frequency. Unlike sweeping Church sentiments that anyone could and should convert to Christianity, the acceptance of Christians into Judaism was selective and only permitted if one's motivations were proven to be sincere. The ceremony for Jewish conversion was strict and serious, beginning with a long process of learning the faith and a warning about the difficulties involved in Jewish affiliation and practice, and culminating in circumcision and ritual immersion. While they may not have always enjoyed equal status within the Jewish community, converts to Judaism do appear to have been integrated and welcomed into communal life.

One example involving converted men can be found in the memorial book of the German city of Nürnberg (*Nürnberg Memorbuch*) from 1296. Memorial books typically contained records of the Jewish community including the names of members who died per city. Among the names were those who had been killed or martyred in persecution for committing themselves to the Jewish faith by martyrdom (**Kiddush haShem**). The memorial book of Nürnberg is the oldest surviving example and records Jewish martyrdom from a variety of cities between the years 1096 and 1392. Among the names of the martyrs of the city of Weissenburg (Germany), we find three examples of converts who are remembered for their martyrdom and pious death in the name of Judaism. These examples demonstrate the Jewish practice of giving converts new names—son of (*ben*) or daughter of (*bat*) Abraham—in order to designate them as the children of biblical Abraham, as biblical Abraham was seen as the first person to convert to Judaism. Additionally, these entries seem to show that at least one of these converts had come from church circles, as the "head of all the barefoot ones" may imply affiliation with the mendicant friars,[7] who made up a religious Catholic community known for adopting lifestyles of poverty and barefoot preaching. One must note, however, that the converts who died are grouped together in this entry and appear last among the names of the Jewish martyrs of Weissenburg, perhaps reflecting the status of converts in the social order of the medieval Jewish community.

---

[7] A monk who relies on charity for his survival. Medieval mendicant religious orders adopted a lifestyle of poverty, traveling, and living in poor urban neighborhoods.

Rabbi Abraham son of Abraham (our Father) of France—who was the head of all the barefoot ones, became disgusted with the idols and took shelter in the shadow of the Eternal One—was burned [at the stake by Christians] for the [sake of the] unity of God.

Rabbi Abraham ben Abraham our Father of Augsburg—who was disgusted by the gods of the nations, cut off the heads of idols, and trusted in the Eternal One—underwent severe sufferings and was burned [at the stake by Christians] for the [sake of the] unity of God ... (December 19, 1264).

Rabbi Isaac ben Abraham our Father of Würzburg was burned [at the stake by Christians] for the [sake of the] unity of God.

SOURCE: Siegmund Salfeld, *Das Martyrlogium des Nürnberger Memorbuches* (Berlin: Simion, 1938), 20; Simha Goldin, *Apostasy and Jewish Identity in the High Middle Ages*, trans. Jonathan Chipman (Manchester: Manchester University Press, 2014), 107; Paola Tartakoff, "Martyrdom, Conversion, and Shared Cultural Repertoires in Late Medieval Europe," *Jewish Quarterly Review* 109 (2019): 500.

Another example involving converted women can be found in various versions of the *Sefer Hasidim*. This excerpt is a directive of how converts to Judaism should be viewed or thought of within Jewish communities. It refers to the marriageability of converted women and to the fact that, from the author's perspective, the virtue of devout converts outweighs their personal history. On the one hand, this teaching suggests the positive attitude of a rabbinic authority towards accepting converts in society, while, on the other hand, it possibly points to the hesitation of some members of the community to marry Jews who had converted.

Any kindhearted man who takes a kindhearted female convert [to Judaism], who comes from stocks that are modest, charitable, and pleasant in commerce: It is better to marry with their [converts'] seed than marrying [certain] Israelites, who do not possess such virtues, for the seed of the convert shall be upright and kind.

SOURCE: Judah b. Samuel (d. 1217), *Sefer Hasidim*, Parma, ed. Judah Wistenetski (Frankfurt: M. A. Wahrmann, 1924), §1097; trans. Avraham Reiner (Rami), "Tough Are the Geirim: Conversion to Judaism in Medieval Europe," *Havruta* 1 (2008): 63.

H. T. S.

Further Reading

Goldin, Simha. *Apostasy and Jewish Identity in the High Middle Ages*, trans. Jonathan Chipman. Manchester: Manchester University Press, 2014.

Marcus, Ivan G. *"Sefer Hasidim" and the Ashkenazic Book in Medieval Europe*. Philadelphia: University of Pennsylvania Press, 2018.

Reiner, Avraham (Rami). "Tough Are the Geirim: Conversion to Judaism in Medieval Europe." *Havruta* 1 (2008): 54–63 [Hebrew].

Tartakoff, Paola. "Martyrdom, Conversion, and Shared Cultural Repertoires in Late Medieval Europe." *Jewish Quarterly Review* 109 (2019): 500–533.

5D – Jews in the Law of the Church

In 1215 Pope Innocent III assembled a general council of the Western Church, known as the Fourth Lateran council,[8] which, in addition to religious officials, was also attended by representatives of secular rulers.[9] Innocent III, considered one of the most powerful of the medieval popes, convened the council to address several major issues that stood at the heart of Church policy, among them the call for a new **crusade**, the war against Christian heresy,[10] the schism with the Eastern Church, and the relations between the Church and secular rulers. While Christian–Jewish relations were not a major concern of this council, because it sought to clearly define the boundaries of Catholic orthodoxy, it ultimately had to address this topic as well. Thus, the last four decisions of the council (out of seventy), published on November 11, 1215, deal with this issue. Although Jews were not considered a part of the Church, the council sought to determine how Christian rulers, and the Christian community in general, should treat them. Two of the decisions focused on limiting the administrative and economic power of Jews, especially concerning **moneylending** (decisions 67 and 69) while two others defined clear social boundaries, not to be crossed, between them and their Christian neighbors (decisions 68 and 70). The council's decrees were a major step in consolidating the

---

[8] So called after the Lateran palace in Rome, where the council was held.

[9] Secular, meaning not an official part of the hierarchy of the Church. This phrase does not mean unreligious in the medieval context.

[10] Heresy is holding an opinion, belief, or theory that is strongly at variance with established beliefs or customs.

legal separation of Jews and Christians. However, the fact that the Church considered them necessary suggests that such separation was not practiced in every part of Europe.

> 67. The more the Christian religion refrains from the exaction of usury, the more does the Jewish perfidy become used to this practice, so that in a short time the Jews exhaust the financial strength of the Christians. Therefore, in our desire to protect the Christians in this matter, that they should not be excessively oppressed by the Jews, we order by a decree of this Synod,[11] that when in the future a Jew, under any pretext, extort heavy and immoderate usury from a Christian, all relationship with Christians shall therefore be denied him until he shall have made sufficient amends for his exorbitant exactions. The Christians, moreover, if need be, shall be compelled by ecclesiastical punishment without appeal, to abstain from such commerce. We also impose this upon the princes, not to be aroused against the Christians because of this, but rather to try to keep the Jews from this practice.
>
> We decree that by means of the same punishment the Jews shall be compelled to offer satisfaction to the churches for the tithes and offerings due them and which these churches were wont to receive from the houses and possessions of Christians before these properties had under some title or other passed into Jewish hands. Thus shall this property be conserved to the Church without any loss.
>
> 68. Whereas in certain provinces of the Church the difference in their clothes sets the Jews and Saracens[12] apart from the Christians, in certain other lands there has arisen such confusion that no differences are noticeable. Thus it sometimes happens that by mistake Christians have intercourse with Jewish or Saracen women, and Jews or Saracens with Christian women. Therefore, lest these people, under the cover of an error, find an excuse for the grave sin of such intercourse, we decree that these people (Jews and Saracens) of either sex, and in all Christian lands, and at all times, shall easily be distinguishable from the rest of the populations by the quality of their clothes; especially since such legislation is imposed upon them also by Moses.
>
> Moreover, they shall not walk out in public on the Days of Lamentation or the Sunday of Easter; for as we have heard, certain ones among them do not blush to go out on such days more than

---

[11] Synod is a Church council.

[12] Muslims.

usually ornamented, and do not fear to poke fun at the Christians who display signs of grief at the memory of the most holy Passion.

We most especially forbid anyone to dare to break forth into insults against the Redeemer. Since we cannot shut our eyes to insults heaped upon Him who washed away our sins, we decree that such presumptuous persons shall be duly restrained by fitting punishment meted out by the secular rulers, so that none dare blaspheme against Him Who was crucified for our sake.

69. Since it is quite absurd that any who blaspheme against Christ should have power over Christians, we, on account of the boldness of the transgressors, renew what the Council of Toledo[13] already has legislated with regard to this. We forbid that Jews be given preferment in public office since this offers them the pretext to vent their wrath against the Christians. Should anyone entrust them with an office of this kind, he shall be restrained from so doing by the Council of the Province (which we order to be held every year). Due warning having been given him, he shall be restrained (therefrom) by such means as the Council deems fit. These officials themselves, moreover, shall suffer the denial of all intercourse, commercial and otherwise, with Christians until they shall have turned for the use of poor Christians in accordance with the dispositions of the **bishop** of the diocese, all that they may have earned from the Christians through the office they had undertaken. Disgraced, they shall lose the office which they had so irreverently assumed. This shall apply also to pagans.[14]

70. We have heard that certain ones who had voluntarily approached the baptismal font,[15] have not completely driven out the old self in order the more perfectly to bring in the new. Since they retain remnants of their former faith, they tarnish the beauty of the Christian Religion by such a mixture. For it is written "Cursed be he who walks the earth in two ways,"[16] and even in wearing a garment one may not mix linen and wool. We decree, therefore, that such people shall in every possible manner be restrained by the prelates of the churches, from observing their old rites, so that those whom their free will brought to

---

[13] Innocent refers here to the Third Council of Toledo, which took place in Toledo, Spain, in 589, and set major limitations on the Jews of Visigoth Spain.

[14] That is, non-Christians who were not Jews or Muslims. In the early thirteenth century, some of the people of eastern Europe were not yet converted.

[15] That is, converted to Christianity.

[16] Ecclesiasticus (Ben-Sirah, in Latin), 3:28.

Figure 15: Jews wearing the badge. © London, British Library, MS Cotton Nero, D II, fol. 183v

the Christian religion shall be held to its observance by compulsion that they may be saved. For there is less evil in not recognizing the way of the Lord than in backsliding after having recognized it.

SOURCE: Solomon Grayzel, *The Church and the Jews in the XIIIth Century* (New York: Hermon, 1966), 307–11.

Decision 68 does not specify exactly how the clothing of Jews should be distinguished from their Christian neighbors, and thus secular rulers were left to implement it as they saw fit. The Jews of England were the first who were ordered to permanently wear a badge, in 1218. Other kingdoms took longer to implement this decree, and in some parts of Europe it was never adopted. The shape of the badge also changed from one place to another, as in many locations, especially France, a round circle, often yellow, was chosen. The image above presents a marginal sketch from an English manuscript, probably made in the late thirteenth century. It shows Jews carrying on their clothes the badge in its English form, designed as the traditional stone tablets. In this case, the badge sets them as a target for the violent attack of a Christian, painted to the right.

Further Reading

Cassen, Flora. *Marking the Jews in Renaissance Italy: Politics, Religion, and the Power of Symbols.* New York: Cambridge University Press, 2017.

Champagne, Marie-Thérèse, and Irven M. Resnick, eds. *Jews and Muslims under the Fourth Lateran Council: Papers Commemorating the Octocentenary of the Fourth Lateran Council (1215).* Turnhout: Brepols, 2018.

Rist, Rebecca. *Popes and Jews, 1095–1291.* Oxford: Oxford University Press, 2016.

Stow, Kenneth R. *Popes, Church, and Jews in the Middle Ages: Confrontation and Response.* Aldershot: Ashgate, 2007.

Tolan, John. "The First Imposition of a Badge on European Jews: The English Royal Mandate of 1218." In *The Character of Christian–Muslim Encounter: Essays in Honor of David Thomas*, ed. Douglas Pratt, Jon Hoover, John Davies, and John A. Chesworth, 145–66. Leiden: Brill, 2015.

Tz. B.

5E – Papal Incentives for Jewish Conversion to Christianity

By the high Middle Ages, the pressure to convert to Christianity was ever present for Jews, regardless of age, gender, or status. Church policy stipulated that conversion had to be voluntary and encouraged by peaceful means to persuade Jews to convert. Papal letters from the later twelfth and thirteenth centuries indicate that guidelines were in place to offer rewards for Jewish converts to Christianity and to eliminate as many obstacles as possible to enable them to leave their faith. One such obstacle, emphasized in the papal letters, relates to the family and the home. Families did not always convert as a unit, leaving the process of conversion a foreseeably splintering experience. Where Church law stipulated that Christians and Jews could not engage in intermarriage, could a Jew and a newly baptized Christian remain married? In the following letter, dated 1198, Pope Innocent III (d. 1216) ruled that, according to canon law,[17] the marriage of a man and a wife was not cancelled if one party later received baptism. This exception to the rule was likely intended to minimize the personal price of conversion by allowing converts to remain with their families and limiting their hardships as new Christians. Most of all, this letter indicates that continued marriages between Jews and converted Christians existed and presented problems and unresolved tensions for ecclesiastical authorities. It would seem that converts often occupied a grey area between two distinct groups that the Church, and especially Pope Innocent III, sought to separate.

> You have sought our advice concerning infidels converted to the Faith, who before their conversion had been married, in accordance with their [own] ancient laws and traditions, within the grades of consanguinity proscribed by canon law, as to whether such ought to separate after their baptism. Concerning this we respond to Your Devotion, that such marriage contracted before conversion is not to be dissolved after the baptism, since when the Lord was asked by the Jews whether it was permitted to put aside one's wife for any cause whatever, He answered them, "Those whom the Lord hath joined together let no man put asunder,"[18] thus hinting that marriage is binding among them.

---

[17] Ecclesiastic law based on papal pronouncements and council decrees.
[18] Matt. 19:3–6.

Other measures geared towards the encouragement of conversion were propagated by papal order. At the Third Lateran Council (an ecclesiastical synod) of March 5, 1179 the following decree was passed to protect the property rights of converts (later paraphrased in a letter by Pope Gregory IX in May 1236). The rationale behind this decree is also represented here, namely that to keep those who accept the Christian faith from returning to their previous communities, converts must see a notable improvement in their lives and livelihoods as Christians.

> If, moreover, with God's inspiration, anyone becomes a convert to Christianity, he shall under no condition be deprived of his property. For converts ought to be in better circumstances than they had been before accepting the Faith. If, however, any act to the contrary be found, we command the princes and the potentates in their respective places that, under pain of excommunication, they shall cause the hereditary portion and property of these converts to be restored to them intact.

SOURCE: Solomon Grayzel, *The Church and the Jews in the XIIIth Century* (New York: Hermon, 1966), 88–89, no. 2; 296–97.

H. T. S.

Further Reading

Brundage, James A. "Intermarriage between Christians and Jews in Medieval Canon Law." *Jewish History* 3, no. 1 (1988): 25–40.

Pakter, Walter. *Medieval Canon Law and the Jews*. Ebelsbach: R. Gremer, 1988.

Stow, Kenneth R. *Popes, Church, and Jews in the Middle Ages: Confrontation and Response*. Aldershot: Ashgate, 2007.

Synan, Edward A. *The Popes and the Jews in the Middle Ages*. New York: Macmillan, 1965.

5F – Jewish Women in a Christian Monastery

Jews and Christians lived on the same streets and in the same neighborhoods in medieval cities. While on the whole Jews and Christians dressed similarly, they knew how to recognize each other based on small differences related to identity symbols, clothes, and insignia worn by each other. Christian clergy and members of monastic orders were an exception to this rule as their distinctive dress was not shared by Jews.

The passage below, from ***Sefer Hasidim***, was probably written in Regensburg in the early thirteenth century by Judah son of Samuel the Hasid and describes the limited choices available to Jewish women during a time of persecution. Some were martyred; others converted out of fear with the intention to return to Judaism once the danger had passed. Those whose husbands were killed knew that a danger they faced was being coerced into marrying a Christian. As a result, they occasionally sought to join a celibate group in the hopes of avoiding this danger.

The passage shows the Jews' familiarity with different forms of Christian religiosity. They knew that two options existed: they could join a monastery and live in an enclosed institution (convent), or they could be beguines,[19] who lived in their homes and did not take religious vows but practiced a pious and celibate lifestyle, some wearing white, others wearing black. Here we can see how intimate daily knowledge manifested itself in a time of danger. Regensburg was a city in whose vicinity these multiple forms of religious life were current. The events described in this source cannot be dated to a specific time or place and are, perhaps, an invention of the author rather than a real occurrence.

> During a time of persecution, some [women] were killed and others converted with the intention of returning to Judaism when they had the opportunity, for they had converted due to fear of the sword. From among the women whose husbands were killed and those who were single, some said: "Lest the uncircumcised contaminate us." And those [women] said that they wished to become nuns [lit: priestesses; in Hebrew, *komrot*]. But the young [girls] were not sent there. Because they [the older women] said that if they escaped, they would not leave the young ones [the girls behind in the convent] with them [in other words, if the young girls were put in a convent they would

---

[19] Christian orders of lay women found in northern Europe during the thirteenth to sixteenth centuries.

not be released]. Others wore black clothes in their homes. Since they [the women who wore black] said if they would be like nuns, they would not be able to easily escape. The gentiles said to them: "Either you should be in the convent [*komriya*] or you should wear white clothes." So they wore white clothes. Because they [the Jewish women] said: "Perhaps if we are in the convent [*komriya*], we would be unable to escape." And the wise [women] among them said: "If they are contaminated against their will by way of prostitution, it is not as grave a sin as those who enter the *komriya* and are guarded for years that eat impure food and desecrate the **Sabbath** without escaping. But if the uncircumcised urge her to marry an uncircumcised man, she will not be able to escape from the husband who watches over her; so it is preferable for her to be in the convent [*komriya*] rather than becoming contaminated by the uncircumcised."

SOURCE: Judah b. Samuel (d. 1217), *Sefer Hasidim*, Parma, ed. Judah Wistenetski (Frankfurt: M. A. Wahrmann, 1924), §262.

E. B.

Further Reading

Baumgarten, Elisheva. *Practicing Piety in Medieval Ashkenaz: Men, Women, and Everyday Religious Observance.* Philadelphia: University of Pennsylvania Press, 2014.

5G – The House of Converts (*Domus Conversorum*) in Medieval London

By the thirteenth century, institutional pressures on Jews to convert to Christianity had been taken up and become the pious mission of medieval monarchies as well as the Church. In England, where an unusual wealth of sources from the medieval period survive, King Henry III founded a House for converted men and women in 1232, the House of Converts (*Domus Conversorum*), in London. This foundation was to offer a home to impoverished converts from Judaism to Christianity, that is, provide them with food and clothing as well as instruction in the Catholic faith and in useful trades. Many of those who converted were the poor of the Jewish communities and this level of accommodation, though modest, granted them refuge within the medieval city. Interestingly, it appears that converts had a strong attachment to this institution. While they were not required to live in the House of Converts, and there is no record of converts being penalized for living elsewhere, it would appear that many men and women who moved away from the House would later return to live there.

The following source survives from the close rolls[20] of Henry III in 1235. In it, the king engages in the gifting of further property, that is, buildings and lands, for the expansion of the House of Converts. This source demonstrates how, like other contemporary hospitals and charitable institutions for the needy, the House was intended to replicate the form of a monastery; it mentions the warden (*custodos domus*) and refers to its residents as brothers (*fratres*), despite the many surviving indications that women lived there as well.

> For the House of Converts of Newstreet—The king [Henry III] grants to the House, which he caused to be founded in the road called Newstreet ... of London, for the sustentation of the converted brothers from Judaism to the Catholic faith and for the help of these brothers' preservation in this House and its surroundings, the House and land, which once belonged to John Herlycun in London and which were fortified as escheat to the king, with the exception of the garden which was the property of the same John in said Newstreet and which the Lord King grants to the **bishop** of Carlisle, his council. ... He commands Richard ... and Ade son of William of the lands and

---

[20] Records of the royal chancery, conveying private orders and instructions, issued folded or "closed" by the application of the Great Seal.

aforementioned houses, as well as Jocea son of Peter, warden of the aforementioned House [of converts], to take possession of said lands and houses as a full freehold for the building of converts. Presently writ this same [letter] to and witnessed by the Sheriff of London.

SOURCE: *Close Rolls of the Reign of Henry III, 1234–1237*, ed. A. E. Stamp (London: Public Record Office, 1902), 78.

H. T. S.

Further Reading

Fogle, Lauren. *The King's Converts: Jewish Conversion in Medieval London.* Lanham: Lexington, 2018.

Stacey, Robert C. "The Conversion of Jews to Christianity in Thirteenth-Century England." *Speculum* 67 (1992): 263–83.

Tartakoff, Paola. "Of Purity, Piety, and Plunder: Jewish Converts and Poverty in Medieval Europe." In *Bastards and Believers: Converts and Conversion to and from Judaism,* ed. Theodor Dunkelgrün and Pawel Maciejko, 75–88. Philadelphia: University of Pennsylvania Press, 2020.

Tartakoff, Paola. "Testing Boundaries: Jewish Conversion and Cultural Fluidity in Medieval Europe, ca. 1200–1391." *Speculum* 90 (2015): 728–62.

5H – Medical Cooperation

Gershom son of Jacob, a thirteenth-century ritual circumcisor (*mohel*)[21] who lived in Worms, wrote a handbook for circumcisors that also described his various experiences working in the field over the years. As was often the case in these small Jewish communities, Gershom had learned the practice from his father, Jacob, and in turn, when the time came, taught it to his son (also named Jacob).

All Jewish boys were expected to undergo circumcision.[22] As the Jewish communities were small, most communities had only a few who were trained to perform the ritual and it is safe to assume that this was not

---

[21] A circumcisor performed the ritual of circumcision, usually performed on all males when the infants were eight days old.

[22] An obligatory ritual of biblical origin in which the foreskin is removed. It is customarily executed on the eighth day after the birth of a boy and his father is responsible for ensuring the ritual is performed. Any non-Jewish male who wished to convert to Judaism had to be circumcised.

their only occupation, as they would have carried out only a few circumcisions each year. This passage describes a case in which the operation was performed badly and help was sought from other local experts. Gershom sought the help of both a local Jewish midwife and a local Christian doctor. It demonstrates the range of medieval professionals that existed and cooperated within the community. The source also provides a nice example of some accepted medieval cures.

> One time he circumcised a child on the Day of Atonement [**Yom Kippur**] before the Holy Ark [*Aron haKodesh*][23] and it was a cloudy day and the candles' light also hindered him. And when he began cutting, the foreskin was pulled. ... And as soon as he realized he had botched up the job he hurried and washed him [the baby] because the blood was coming quickly and a wise woman instructed him to take a little linen and to soak it in an egg yolk and also a woman's pubic hair and to put it on the wound with ashes of a velvet cloth and a little bit of the cloth on which he had bled and a chicken feather and the bleeding would stop. ... And all that night they did not touch him at all, they just changed his soiled clothes and then next day he made oil from eggs and applied it to the wound four times each day for three consecutive days and it did not improve until he went to a non-Jewish doctor and bought a bandage that one applies on wounds ... and it healed in ten days ... and a miracle occurred to him, for the boy lived thanks to the commandment of circumcision
>
> SOURCE: *Sefer Sikhron Brit laRishonim*, ed. Avraham Glassberg (Berlin: Fischer, 1892), 142–43.

E. B.

Further Reading

Baumgarten, Elisheva. "Ask the Midwives: A Hebrew Manual on Midwifery from Medieval Germany." *Social History of Medicine* 32 (2019): 712–33.

---

[23] The **Torah scroll** was kept inside the ark, which was in the center of the **synagogue**.

51 – Punishment for Relapsed Converts in Jewish and Christian Practice

Return to Judaism post-baptism did occur, but at what cost? From the Christian perspective, returning to Judaism was considered a form of heresy, leading to royal and/or episcopal efforts to either re-acquire or prosecute the failed converts in their domain. In France, there are many sources indicating that relapsed men and women were sentenced to death by fire. The source below is from the **register** of Eudes Rigaud (1248–1275), **archbishop** of Rouen. The archbishop kept a tidy record of his travels, visitations, and activities between the years 1248 and 1269. One entry from April 1266 records the chain of events that led to the execution of an unnamed lapsed convert. The convert had been baptized on two separate occasions and, only upon the refusal of a third baptism, was sentenced to death. This suggests that a sentence to death was an extreme measure and some converts were given one, two, and in this case even three baptisms to commit themselves to the Catholic faith. As the source reads, the judgment was cast in a public space, for all the people of Rouen to see, and presided over by the episcopal authorities. While the archbishop's recounting of this case is somewhat neutral, later accounts of lapsed converts would become increasingly scathing, as the distrust of converts in Christian society continued to grow into the fourteenth century.

> On the fourteenth day before the Kalends of May [April 18], we preached near the mare-du-Parc, where the clergy and people of Rouen had been congregated in a procession. And there we passed judgment on a certain [man who had] converted from Judaism to the Catholic faith and had again reverted from the Catholic faith to Judaic depravity. He was once again baptized and once more reverted to Judaism, unwilling afterwards to be restored to the Catholic faith, although several times admonished [to do so]. And we condemned [him] as an apostate and a heretic; and then he was burned by the bailli.
>
> SOURCE: *Regestrum visitationem archiepiscopi rotomagensis. Journal des visites pastorals d'Eude Rigaud, archevêque de Rouen, MCCXLVIII–MCCLXIX*, ed. Theodose Bonnin (Rouen: A. Le Brument, 1852), 541; *The Register of Eudes of Rouen*, trans. Sydney Brown (New York: Columbia University Press, 1964), 618; Léopold V. Delisle, ed., *Recueil des Historiens des Gaules et de la France*, vol. 21 (Farnborough: Gregg, 1967), 591.

From the Jewish perspective, there were also penalties for community members who converted to Christianity only to return to the Jewish community. Some known practices of penance included fasting, limited washing, and avoidance of certain community events. The following such source survives from the penitential treatises of German Rabbi Eleazar son of Judah of Worms (d. before 1232). He wrote many influential works relating to ideal behavior for Jews who wished to live according to the most pious practices. Rabbi Eleazar rules relatively leniently in the case of returning converts that they should practice various expressions of repentance, such as abstinence from certain foods, bathing, and ritual submersion, upon which they are readmitted to the community. Rabbi Eleazar makes specific mention of the distance required in this process from clergymen and priests and their homes, lands, or houses of worship. Considering the close proximities and living quarters of Jews and Christians in medieval cities, this proscription would have been difficult to follow.

> The returning apostate must remove all signs of splendor or glory from himself and feel remorse, and fast regularly over a period of several years. He should not eat meat or drink wine, he should not bathe except a bit prior to the festivals, he should wash his head only once or twice a month. He should not go to weddings. He should not sit together with clergymen and priests, or where people are discussing the impure idolatry. He must keep away from all idolaters and derive no pleasure from them, and he may not come near to their homes or to the courtyard of a church. From the moment that he regrets what he has done and immerses himself, he is considered to be as a Jew. He must return to his Creator from all the sins that he has done and regret the pleasures that he had.
>
> SOURCE: MS Vatican 183/3, 166r–v.

H. T. S.

Further Reading

Baumgarten, Elisheva. *Practicing Piety in Medieval Ashkenaz: Men, Women, and Everyday Religious Observance.* Philadelphia: University of Pennsylvania Press, 2014.

Haverkamp, Alfred. "Baptised Jews in German Lands during the Twelfth Century." In *Jews and Christians in Twelfth Century Europe,* ed. Michael A. Signer and John Van Engen, 255–310. Notre Dame: University of Notre Dame Press, 2001.

Jordan, William C. "Archbishop Eudes Rigaud and the Jews of Normandy, 1248–1275." In *Friars and Jews in the Middle Ages and Renaissance,* ed. S. McMichael, 39–52. Leiden: Brill, 2004.

Kanarfogel, Ephraim. "Returning to the Jewish Community in Medieval Ashkenaz: History and Halakhah." In *Turim: Studies in Jewish History and Literature Presented to Dr. Bernard Lander,* ed. Michael A. Shmidman, vol. 1, 69–97. Jersey City: KTAV Publishing House: 2007.

5J – Jewish–Christian Dispute over Dearest Rachel
A Tale of Child Conversion to Christianity

The extent to which Jewish conversion to Christianity in the medieval period differed with regard to age, geographic region, gender, and social class is hard to determine. Still, some personal accounts survive that describe the individual experience, such as that of children. The following Latin source is taken from a compendium of *exempla*,[24] written by Thomas of Cantimpré (ca.1200–1272), a Dominican monk active during the second half of the thirteenth century. He entitled his work *On the Common Good as Taught by Bees* (*Bonum de apibus*) and uses the allegory of bees and the beehive to describe the ideal conduct and duties of all people within Christian society. In this *exemplum*, Thomas models the virtue of chastity after a story of conversion undertaken by a Jewish child, Rachel, from Leuven (in modern-day Belgium). Although this source is literary and its moralizing character must be kept in mind, the account can be excavated for its impressions of daily life and the tensions among Jews and Christians that it reveals. The narrative demonstrates their close proximity within the medieval city, as well as their movement within each other's more intimate spaces, like the home. It suggests the role of names and dress as prominent markers of religious identity, in those instances when language, physical appearance, and place of residence were less distinctive. Finally, this narrative speaks to the process of conversion, that is, its informalities, possible duration, aspects of resettlement, and the age at which children could be baptized without the consent of their parents. The ensuing dispute over the girl also suggests that a baptized child could have potentially remained within the home of her Jewish parents until he or she reached majority.

> On the Virtue of Chastity, Chapter 29:
> To all bees, integrity is a characteristic of the virginal body
>
> I once saw a Cistercian nun in Brabant, in whom, as a convert from Judaism, the work of the heavenly Maria, mother of Christ, gloriously shined forth. Not even after five full years in the house of her Jewish parents did she begin to know in her heart why one must differentiate between Jewish and Christian names, despite the fact

---

[24] Short tales or narratives used to emphasize a doctrine and to illustrate standards of right and wrong.

that the people of both groups have similar appearance and language. Still, she told me—and I was especially keen to hear it—that she felt a greater affinity for the Christian name than for the Jewish name; and she especially liked hearing the name of the holy Maria, when the Christians demanded things from one another or when they would tend to swear to each other [by her, Maria's, name]. ... It happened later that she and her parents moved from Cologne to Leuven, a city in Brabant. When the girl came into contact with young Christian boys in the house of a certain well-known priest, named Master Reiner, who noticed despite her name that she enjoyed coming to him often, he asked her: "Would you like to become Christian, dearest Rachel?" And she answered, "I would, if you teach me what it means to become Christian." ... And while beginning with the creation of the world, he started to expose the writings through which the faith in Christ or Christ himself could be signified. She understood these interpretations, as she told me, at six and a half years old with such a strength of mind, that it was barely necessary that the priest repeat any of his teachings. This instruction lasted for about a year and a half through a hidden door [in the home], through which the priest secretly and opportunely educated the girl. ... [One night] Rachel got up and found the priest at the appointed place. He took her in happily and went to the monastery called the Park of Women,[25] which is located about a half mile from the aforesaid city; he baptized her with the joy of all and gave her the name Catherine ... and dressed her immediately in the garments of the Order. A short time later, as soon as the father and his friends heard what happened, they tried much to their consternation to reach the territorial lord, the **archbishop** of Liège, and Pope Honorius [IV], by spending a lot of money, so that the girl, who was below the legitimate age, be given back to her parents. If she stays in her parents' home until her twelfth year, then she could be returned rightly to those of her newfound faith—as they [the Jews] thought most cunningly that the childish mind would be easily turned in the meantime, so the girl would convert back to the ancestral vows of her parents. ... The girl asked the Priest to be led to a hearing and judge. ... And it happened as she asked. When she came before the **bishop**, the clerics, and the magnates on this day near Liège, she stunned and moved the various advocates and judges

---

[25] Likely the Cistercian abbey *Vrauwenpark*, also called *le Parc-les-Dames* and *Parcum Dominarum*: founded just before 1215, roughly six miles (ten kilometers) north of Leuven. Its foundation coincides with the surge in women's monasteries in the first half of the thirteenth century.

with such an unbreakable and true argumentation, that ... all clearly said and saw that, at such a young age, the wisdom of the divine spirit prevailed.

SOURCE: Thomas of Cantimpré, *Bonum Universale de apibus*, ed. G. Colveneer (Douai: Baltazar Bellerus, 1627), book 2, 295–99.

H. T. S.

Further Reading

Burkhardt, Julia. *Von Bienen Lernen: Das Bonum Universale de Apibus des Thomas von Cantimpré als Gemeinschaftsentwurf. Analyse, Edition, Übersetung, Kommentar*. Regensburg: Schnell & Steiner Press, 2020.

Ehrman, Albert. "The Origins of the Ritual Murder Accusation and Blood Libel." *Tradition: A Journal of Orthodox Jewish Thought* 15 (1976): 83–90.

Levin, Chaviva. "Jewish Conversion to Christianity in Medieval Northern Europe Encountered and Imagined, 1100–1300." Doctoral Dissertation, New York University, 2006.

5K – Jewish Anti-Christian Polemics
A Walk through the Market

Jewish–Christian theological discussions were commonplace in the Middle Ages. Despite Church efforts to suppress them, such conversations and debates took place virtually anywhere Jews and Christians interacted. Some took place in indoor spaces, such as those in the twelfth-century Parisian schools that occurred inside the abbey of Saint Victor. Others, however, were often integrated into the many open spaces of the medieval city. This source is taken from the Book of Joseph the Zealot (*Sefer Yosef haMekanné*) a polemical tractate[26] from the late thirteenth century containing stories and arguments by Josef son of Nathan Official of northern France, who was active during the mid- to late thirteenth century. The following anecdote recounts a theological discussion between a learned Jew and a Christian that took place in the medieval market, where people of all social strata could gather round and hear. In recording the curiosity of a Christian monk, this Hebrew source calls upon many sensory aspects of

---

[26] A genre of writing containing aggressive arguments made with the intention of convincing people to position themselves either for or against any given religious affiliation.

the medieval city in constructing its anti-Christian arguments for its readers: the sight and sound of the church bells, the smell of fish, the sound of yelling merchants selling their wares, and the general feel of the bustling marketplace. Indeed, by evoking the familiar experiences of the medieval marketplace, this story would be relatable to all who read or heard it, and therefore an effective way to impart anti-Christian arguments to its Jewish audiences.

> Woe to Those who haul sin ....[27] A monk asked Rabbi Joseph Kara: "Why do you have no bells?" He said to him: "Come with me." They went together to the market, where they could hear the sellers of those fish that are called herring crying their wares. Afterwards he took him to the market for high-quality fish, and there they did not shout about their quality. He asked him: "What is the reason they do so?—The high-quality goods recommend themselves and need no shouting. That is why we have no bells!" This was told to me by my teacher and grandfather Rabbi Joseph, son of Rabbi Nathan, son of our teacher Meshullam. There is also another answer to this. It is said of the Christians: Woe to those who haul sin with cords of falsehood.[28]
>
> SOURCE: Joseph b. Nathan Official, *Sefer Yosef haMekanné*, ed. J. Rosenthal (Jerusalem: Mekize Nirdamim, 1970), 74. The translation of the source appears in Hanne Trautner-Kromann, *Shield and Sword: Jewish Polemics Against Christianity and the Christians in France and Spain from 1100–1500* (Tübingen: Mohr Siebeck, 1993), 99–100.

H. T. S.

Further Reading

Dahan, Gilbert. *The Christian Polemic against the Jews in the Middle Ages*, trans. J. Gladding. Notre Dame: University of Notre Dame Press, 2000.

Lasker, Daniel. "Joseph ben Nathan's Sefer Yosef Ha-Mekanné and the Medieval Jewish Critique of Christianity." In *Jews and Christians in Thirteenth-Century France*, ed. Elisheva Baumgarten and Judah Galinsky, 113–22. New York: Palgrave Macmillan, 2015.

---

[27] Isa. 5:18.
[28] Isa. 5:18.

5L – "The French King David"
Illumination of a Jewish Biblical King

Manuscript illustrations often express encounters between Jews and Christians in medieval Europe. A manuscript was an expensive object in the Middle Ages, usually commissioned or purchased by a wealthy person or family, and the manufacture of which involved a number of different craftsmen, such as a copyist or a writer, illuminators, colorists, and binders. The majority of illuminators were Christians. Thus, Jewish manuscripts were often illuminated by Christians, under the instructions of the Jewish owner of the manuscript, or of another Jew on his behalf.

The Northern French Miscellany, created in the second half of the thirteenth century, comprises many different texts, including the Pentateuch (The Five Books of Moses, **Torah**), the weekly readings from the prophets that followed the *parashat haShavuah*,[29] other biblical texts, songs (*piyyutim*), poems, the Passover *Haggadah*, daily prayers as well as those for the Sabbath and for various holidays, including the Jewish New Year (**Rosh haShanah**) and Day of Atonement (**Yom Kippur**), the blessings said after a meal (*Birkat haMazon*), Ethics of the Fathers (*Pirkei Avot*), the Scroll of Esther (*Megillat Esther*), legal codes and formulae for agreements concerning marriage, divorce, and business partnerships, and many more. It also contains many colorful illuminations, both in the margins and as whole-page illuminations, done in the French Gothic style by several artists associated with three major Parisian workshops.

The following illumination, from folio 117v, depicts King David playing the harp. The colors of his clothes indicate his eminent status, as does his hairstyle and crown. A comparison with other Jewish kings illuminated in this manuscript, and to kings depicted in contemporary Christian manuscripts, shows similar features, especially in iconography and gesture. King David's illumination is thus similar to a French king from the thirteenth century. The illuminators probably used model books for the illustrations—a very common technique.

---

[29] The weekly Torah portion read out loud every week in the synagogue during the Sabbath service. The portions are divided so that the entire Pentateuch was read over the course of one year.

Figure 16: David playing the harp.
© London, The British Library,
MS Add. 11639, fol. 117v

Comparing biblical scenes illuminated in the Northern French Miscellany with Jewish and Christian interpretations of the relevant texts can shed light on everyday interactions between Jews and Christians during this period. Similarities and differences of such illuminations point out the tension between Jews and Christians in ideas and conceptions, as well as implying the tension between illuminator and commissioner. Notwithstanding, the making of the manuscripts, and especially the encounter around its illumination process, reveal business interactions between Jews and Christians.

N. D.

Further Reading

Karras, Ruth Mazo. *"Thou Art the Man": The Masculinity of King David in the Christian and Jewish Middle Ages.* Philadelphia: University of Pennsylvania Press, 2021.

Offenberg, Sara. *Illuminated Piety: Pietistic Texts and Images in the North French Hebrew Miscellany.* Los Angeles: Cherub Press, 2013.

Rouse, Richard H., and Mary A. Rouse. *Manuscripts and their Makers: Commercial Book Producers in Medieval Paris, 1200–1500.* Turnhout: H. Miller, 2000.

Sed-Rajna, Gabrielle. "The Paintings of the London Miscellany: British Library Add. MS 11639." *Journal of Jewish Art* 9 (1982): 18–30.

Zirlin, Yael. "The Decoration of the Miscellany, its Iconography, and Style." In *The Northern French Hebrew Miscellany: Companion Volume to an Illuminated Manuscript from Thirteenth-Century France in Facsimile. Facsimile Edition*, ed. Jeremy Schonfield, 75–161. London: Facsimile Editions, 2003.

5M – Jews as Seen in Christian Eyes

In medieval Christian culture, Jews were often viewed ambivalently. From a theological perspective, they were the descendants of the biblical Israelites, but also of New Testament Jews who rejected Christ and were involved in (or even responsible for, according to medieval views) his crucifixion. Neither the image of Jews as Christ-killers nor their image as biblical heroes necessarily fitted with the characteristics of medieval Jews, whom Christians knew as their neighbors. The usually peaceful merchants, who rarely carried weapons and never challenged Christian rule, seemed very far from their ancestors, for better or for worse. This cultural gap may explain some of the medieval Christian distrust towards Jews, as powerful cultural images could not always be aligned with everyday realities, leaving some Christians with the notion that the Jews were something other than they seemed.

The image opposite is taken from a manuscript containing a world history written as a poem in German by the Austrian poet Rudolf von Ems, around 1254. This medieval genre narrated a history of humanity from biblical times to the days of the author, focusing on scenes he found particularly meaningful. The manuscript was copied around 1300 in Passau, Bavaria, and is lavishly designed and decorated in the Gothic style. The image shows the Israelites walking in the desert after the Exodus, following the Pillar of Fire.[30] The illustrator chose to emphasize the noble nature of biblical Jews, setting them on a golden background, wearing the finest garments, and followed by animals such as lions and oxen. At the same time, he painted them like the Jews of his own days, wearing the Jewish hat and carrying their young children. This ambivalence represents well the complex imagery of Jews in medieval Christian culture.

Tz. B.

Further Reading

Frojmovic, Eva, ed. *Imagining the Self, Imagining the Other: Visual Representation and Jewish–Christian Dynamics in the Middle Ages and Early Modern Period.* Leiden: Brill, 2002.

Lipton, Sara. *Dark Mirror: The Medieval Origins of Anti-Semitic Iconography.* New York: Metropolitan Books; Henry Holt and Company, 2014.

Rowe, Nina. *The Jew, the Cathedral and the Medieval City: Synagoga and Ecclesia in the Thirteenth Century.* Cambridge: Cambridge University Press, 2014.

---

[30] Ex. 13:21–22.

5M – JEWS AS SEEN IN CHRISTIAN EYES   149

Figure 17: The Israelites in the desert. © Munich,
Bayerische Staatsbibliothek, Cgm 6406, fol. 53v

5N – Sharing Tales
Jews and the Stories of Alexander the Great

As residents of medieval cities, Jews shared many features of the prevalent cultural setting with their Christian neighbors, in addition to their own unique cultural traditions. Stories about Alexander the Great are one such example. Alexander, the fourth-century BCE Macedonian emperor who was said to have conquered a great swathe of territory as far south as Egypt and as far east as India, was a mythical figure in antiquity, the hero of many legendary stories in Greek and Latin, and even of **talmudic** tales. Medieval Jews significantly expanded the corpus of such tales in Hebrew by translating material from Greek, Arabic, and old French. The passage below is taken from a version copied by Eleazar son of Asher haLevi somewhere in the **Rhineland** in 1325. While many of the original features of the stories were kept, they were adjusted to better fit medieval Jewish culture. One example is the inclusion into the story of a Jewish clerk named Menahem. In the passage below, Menahem serves as a medium for connecting the legendary events described and the words of Jewish sages, thus solidifying the cultural link between the Hellenic hero and the talmudic tradition. This passage deals with the legend of the Fountain of Life (or in this case, river), a motif that also appears in some of the French versions of these tales.

> They [Alexander and his army] set forth from there arriving at the land of Ofrat[31] where they found a large, unusual river, pleasant to behold. The king and his army were thirsty, but were afraid to drink its waters. The king ordered wells dug in the vicinity of the river and much water was found, and the king and his men drank. The king said: "If it pleases you, we will camp here by the waters, for by their fragrance I know they are beneficial." They agreed to do so, and camped there for ten days. On the tenth day, the king's hunter caught some birds, wrung their necks and washed them in the waters of the river. As he dipped them in and washed them in waters of the river, they returned to life and flew away. Seeing this, the king's servant quickly drank from that river and went to the king to tell him all that had happened. "Obviously, these are the waters of the Garden of Eden," said the king. "Whoever drinks from them shall live forever. Go quickly and fetch me some and I, too, shall drink." The servant hastened, cup in hand,

---

[31] Perhaps from the Hebrew word for lead.

to bring some of those waters to him, but he could not find them. He returned and told the king: "I could not find the waters of the river for the Lord has hidden them from me." The king grew angry, drew his sword, and beheaded his servant. Then the headless servant ran away and Menahem, the secretary,[32] related: "Our sages say that he is still headless in the sea where he overturns ships. When he comes to overturn ships, he is forced to flee if the passengers call out: 'Flee, flee! Your master Alexander is coming.' In this way the ships are saved."

SOURCE: Rosalie Reich, ed., *Tales of Alexander the Macedonian* (New York: Ktav, 1972), 80–81.

Tz. B.

Further Reading

Dönitz, Saskia. "Alexander the Great in Medieval Hebrew Traditions." In *A Companion to Alexander Literature in the Middle Ages*, ed. David Zuwiyya, 21–39. Leiden: Brill, 2011.

Kazis, Israel, ed. *The Book of the Gests of Alexander of Macedon: Sefer toledot Alexandros ha-Makdoni*. Cambridge: Medieval Academy of America, 1962.

50 – The Fountain of Life in a *Haggadah*

In the image overleaf, the Fountain of Life, a nominally Christian theme, has found its way into an early fifteenth century German **Haggadah**, a liturgical manuscript used annually during the ritual feast on Passover Eve (**Seder Pesah**). The ritual focuses on the story of the Exodus and on the future redemption of the Jews from their exile. In this particular manuscript, the scribe, Israel son of Meir of Heidelberg, who probably oversaw the production process, decided to include a visual depiction of the Fountain of Life. Perhaps he worked with a Christian illuminator, or perhaps he intended this image for the eyes of unknown Christian patrons. Whatever the impetus, Israel was clearly familiar with this Christian theme and was comfortable inserting it into a Jewish ritual manuscript. The image shows sick and disabled people, who, having washed in the ornate fountain, emerge healthy on the other side.

Tz. B.

---

[32] In some Hebrew versions of Alexander tales, he has a Jewish clerk named Menachem.

Figure 18: The Fountain of Life. © Universitäts- und Landesbibliothek Darmstadt, Cod. Or. 8, 58r

Further Reading

Epstein, Marc M. *The Medieval Haggadah: Art, Narrative, and Religious Imagination.* New Haven: Yale University Press, 2011.

Fraiman, Susan. "The Marginal Images of Marginal People." In *The Metamorphosis of Marginal Images: From Antiquity to Present Time*, ed. Nurith Kenaan-Kedar and Ovadiah Asher, 105–13. Tel Aviv: Tel Aviv University, 2001.

5P – Dukus Horant: A Heroic Epic in Old Yiddish

As part of their daily life, medieval Ashkenazi Jews read and heard heroic narratives, or epic poems that glorified battles, wars, honor, adventures, and romance (see also source 5N above). These narratives, associated with chivalric culture, circulated orally, or were written down either in the vernacular, in Hebrew, or in Old **Yiddish**. Some rabbis attempted to limit the popularity of these narratives and even forbade their dissemination, arguing that: "those [stories of] war written in the vernacular, it seems to rabbi Judah that it is forbidden to read them ... [not only on **Sabbath** and holidays] but also on mundane days, rabbi Isaac did not know who permitted them, as for him they were no more than nonsense and mockery".[33] Nonetheless, a range of sources show that these heroic tales were as popular among Ashkenazi Jews as they were among their Christian neighbors. This source and source 5Q illustrate the extent to which these epics were an integral part of Jewish daily life during the high and late Middle Ages.

The Dukus Horant is found in a codex dated to 1382/1383, consisting of eight Yiddish texts, and currently located at Cambridge University Library.[34] Adapted from a popular and "secular" epic tradition, it is the tale of a medieval feudal bridal-quest epic, the search for a suitable bride for a prince or king. In the surviving fragment of the poem, there are some 270 identifiable stanzas (many of them are severely damaged), and it tells how the main character called Duke Horant, a Danish nobleman, is sent on a quest to Greece by handsome, courageous, and strong sixteen-year-old King Itene. Horant's mission is to bring Princess Hilde, whom the king wishes to marry, back to Germany. Duke Horant, equipped with his courage, wisdom, and a beautiful voice, embarks on the mission together with an entourage of two hundred skillful knights. However, Hilde's father, the Greek king Hagene the Savage, refuses to give his daughter to the German king. Horant needs to enlist all his skills and wisdom to accomplish the mission. The following section comprises the opening verses of the poem translated by Jerold Frakes:

> In the German lands there was a widely famed king, a very bold warrior: Itene was his name. He was generous and handsome; he wore the crown of honor. All German lands served him mightily: Lombardy

---

[33] **Tosafot**, *Shabbat* 116b.

[34] The codex was recovered from the *geniza* of the Ben Ezra Synagogue in Fustat, Old Cairo, and brought to Cambridge University Library by Solomon Schechter in 1896.

and Apulia were in his hands; Sicily and Tuscany had no choice but to be subject to him. Denmark, where he wore the crown, was quite in his control. All Spanish lands also had to serve him well. The King of Hungary was subject to him and wore the crown by his grace. The lords of the land were all subject to him.

Three dreadful giants from the forest served him. One of them was named Witolt; he was a bold warrior. He carried a steel staff that was twelve fathoms in length, with which he had vanquished all the German lands for noble King Itene. He had a brother named Asprion; he had performed a great many marvels. And Wate of the Greeks, the marvelously bold warrior—many a hero lay dead at his hands. They served Itene, the noble ruler, as his bondsmen.

When King Itene turned sixteen years old, he was stalwart and strong, and bold in all battles. He was the most generous of men who ever won the name of king. He also had a comrade whose name was Horant. He was a mighty duke, born in Denmark. He was the most prudent of all men who ever won the name of ruler.

They had great pleasure with each other and many kinds of joy and much grand entertainment. Sometimes they went hunting with dogs in the forest. Horant said to the king: "Dear my lord, an exalted queen would befit you as wife." Youthful Itene laughed at that. He there began to blush greatly. He said: "My very dear Sir, send forth your men. We will have a grand festivity this Pentecost. Thus will we then confer about a lovely lady."

By Horant's counsel, envoys were sent out through all the German kingdoms. Right away twelve quite splendid kings came to him, each of whom [wore] a golden crown. Three dreadful giants came to him from the forest: Witolt with the Staff, his brother Asprion, and Wate the mighty lord. Quite laudably did they come there. They were well received by mighty King Itene. They were given rich gifts: magnificent clothing, war-horses, saddle-horses, silver and gold. The gentlemen were therefore all staunchly loyal to him.

SOURCE: Cambridge University Library, T.-S. 10K22, fols. 21r–42v.

E. L.

Further Reading

Baumgarten, Jean. *Introduction to Old Yiddish Literature*. Oxford: Oxford University Press, 2005.

Frakes C. Jerold, ed. *Early Yiddish Epic*. Syracuse: Syracuse University Press, 2014.

——, *The Emergence of Early Yiddish Literature: Cultural Translation in Ashkenaz*. Bloomington: Indiana University Press, 2017.

Fuks, Lajb. *The Oldest Known Literary Documents of Yiddish Literature (ca. 1382)*. Leiden: Brill, 1957.

5Q – "An Old Yiddish Knightly Tale" Etched into a Slate

Figure 19: Yiddish tale on a slate from Cologne. © Stefan Arendt; LVR-Zentrum für Medien und Bildung

In 2011, three fragments of a single slate tablet were unearthed by the archaeologists of MiQua LVR Jewish Museum in the Archaeological Quarter of Cologne. This museum is situated on the remains of the medieval Jewish quarter, which was destroyed in 1349 during the **Black Death** pogrom when a thriving Jewish community of approximately seventy-five households was destroyed. The text on this slate is the earliest **Yiddish** text known to scholars, and it was etched at an unknown date before 1349. Scholars concluded that the text is taken from a late medieval courtly *Märendichtung* (poetic tale or narrative poetry). Unfortunately, the text is too fragmented to allow any comprehensive study. However, the importance of the text goes beyond the fact that it documents the fascination with epic narrative among Yiddish-speaking Ashkenazi Jews, as Jerold Frakes argued. This finding is also a valuable source for social and cultural historians interested in medieval gender and masculinities, since it provides evidence for the place of chivalric culture and knightly masculinity within medieval Jewish communities. Although the text is generally illegible, we can still recognize many of the words and even whole sentences. It also enables a direct connection to a mid-fourteenth-century anonymous German Jew, who could write his native language in Hebrew characters. Moreover, via this archaeological finding, and the many other slate fragments found on the site, we learn of an everyday activity, that is, the use of slate tablets for a variety of daily needs.

SOURCE: MiQua LVR Jewish Museum in the Archaeological Quarter of Cologne

E. L.

Further Reading

Frakes, Jerold C. *Early Yiddish Texts, 1100–1750: With Introduction and Commentary.* Oxford: Oxford University Press, 2004.

———, *The Politics of Interpretation: Alterity and Ideology in Old Yiddish Studies.* Albany: SUNY Press, 1989.

Glossary

The references (1A, 2A) and so on, refer to the source numbers.

Agunah (pl. **agunot**)—literally meaning "a chained woman"; refers to a woman who cannot be released from her marriage. 2A, 2K

Apotropus/ut—a legal guardian of a minor. Apotropsut is the legal agreement appointing the guardian and determining the terms of the guardianship. 2D, 2O

Archbishop—a **bishop** (see below) of higher rank or office exerting authority on an ecclesiastical province in addition to his ordinary episcopal authority in his own diocese. 4C, 4F, 5I, 5J

Beit midrash—a house of study, where men study Torah. 1C, 1E

Bishop—an ordained and high-ranking member of the Christian clergy; often the administrative and spiritual leader of a diocese, an area containing several congregations. 1C, 1D, 3M, 3N, 4A, 4B, 4C, C12, 5D, 5G, 5J

Black Death—the plague that raged in Europe during the mid-fourteenth century, killing millions of Europeans. 3J, 4K, 4L, 5Q

Chronicle—a historical account describing events in a chronological sequence. 1C, 1D, 3J, 4C, 4E, 4K

Crusade—a Christian religious movement intended to free the Holy Land from the hands of the Muslims by force. Nine crusades left Europe for the East from 1095 to the end of the thirteenth century. 1D, 3J, 4C, 5D

Gematria—an alphanumeric code of assigning a numerical value to the letters of a name, word, or phrase. 1I, 2M

Haggadah—the text recited during the Passover *seder* (see below); usually copied in a separate manuscript, sometimes lavishly decorated, designed to be used during the *seder*. 1H, 5L, 5O

Halakhah—Jewish law. 2A, 3E, 3H, 3L

Ketubbah—a Jewish marriage contract. 1K, 2L

Kiddush haShem—literally the sanctification of the name of God, the term is used to refer to martyrdom; often used to refer to Jews who were killed by Christians or committed suicide to avoid forced conversion. 4C, 4E, 4L, 5C

Mikveh—a ritual bath used for purification, especially by women. 1D, 1E, 1F, 1J

Minhag (pl. **minhagim**)—Jewish custom(s). 1P, 2G, 2M

Moneylending—the practice of lending money with interest in exchange for a pledge or a promise that it will be returned. The medieval Church forbade Christians from lending money for interest and this practice became affiliated with Jews. 3D, 3G, 3I, 3J, 3K, 3L, 4E, 5B, 5D

Pietism/piety/pietist—practices performed by devout Jews who wished to take upon themselves additional obligations that were beyond those formally prescribed by Jewish law (*halakhah*); these often included deeds related to purity, charity for communal enterprises for the poor, fasting, and atonement. 1N, 1P, 1Q, 1O, 5I

Piyut (pl. **piyutim**)—traditional poetic writing often recited as part of prayer, written in Hebrew. 2E, 5L

Privilege—a legal right granted to particular groups or individuals; Jews were often awarded such rights by various medieval rulers, and these served as a basis for their legal, economic, and socio-religious rights and activities. 1D, 4A, 4B, 4C

Register—a miscellaneous collection of administrative acts and records tied to an institution. 3M, 5B, 5I

Responsum (pl. **responsa**)—responses to legal (*halakhic*) questions sent to leading rabbis and often compiled in collections. 1K, 1L, 2D, 2K, 2N, 3B, 3C, 3D, 3F, 3G, 3H

Rhineland—the geographical area surrounding the upper Rhine river in the western German Empire, including many of the major Jewish communities of the Middle Ages, like Mainz, Speyer, Worms, and Cologne. 4C, 4F, 5M

Rintfleisch Massacres—In 1298, Christian attacks on the Jews prompted by a host desecration accusation led by a man dubbed "Lord Rintfleisch." These attacks severely hurt the Jewish communities of Franconia, Bavaria, and Austria. 3J, 4I

Rosh haShanah—the Jewish New Year, celebrated over two days in the fall. 1C, 1Q, 5L

GLOSSARY   159

Sabbath—the Jewish day of rest, observed on Saturday, when all activities considered labor are prohibited. 1O, 1Q, 2E, 2L, 2M, 2N, 3E, 4E, 5F, 5L, 5P

Salian dynasty—a dynasty that included four kings of the German Empire, between 1024 and 1125, all of whom were crowned emperor. 1D, 4B

Sanctifying the Name of God—see *Kiddush haShem*

Seder (Pesah)—on the first evening of Passover, a holiday of eight days commemorating the biblical Exodus from Egypt, a ritual feast called Seder (literally, "order," that is, of the ritual) is held; all members of each household gathered for this ritual that included the recitation of the Hagaddah (see above) texts, singing, and eating. 1H, 5O

Shavuot—the feast of Pentecost, celebrated seven weeks after Passover (thus its name, lit. "weeks"). One of the three pilgrimage festivals, it marks the harvest of wheat. It also, most importantly for medieval Jews, commemorated the giving of the Torah to the Israelites at Mount Sinai. 1N, 2G, 4C

Sukkot—the Feast of Tabernacles. One of the three pilgrimage festivals, it marks the harvest season and is celebrated by eating and dwelling in a temporary shelter (a *sukkah*) and ritually waving the four species (citron fruit, date palm, myrtle, and willow). 1O

Passover Eve—see Seder.

Sefer Hasidim (Book of the Pious)—a book composed by Judah son of Samuel (the Pious) of Regensburg in the early thirteenth century, partly based on earlier material and containing teachings on pious practices of northern European Jews; see Pietism above. 1G, 2F, 5C, 5F

Synagogue—Jewish house of prayer, also serving as the communal center for Jews. 1A, 1C, 1D, 1E, 1J, 1L, 1M, 1O, 1Q, 2C, 2E, 2G, 2H, 4C, 4D, 4I, 5L

Talmud (adj. **talmudic**)—a collection of rabbinic discussions of Jewish law (*halakhah*), composed between the third and fifth centuries. It is the central text of Jewish legal thought and much of the subsequent discussions of Jewish law were based on this text. 1B, 1H, 1N, 2A, 2D, 2K, 2M, 3A, 3B, 3E, 3H, 5N

Torah—Hebrew word for Pentateuch; sometimes used in a general sense to refer to all Jewish teachings. 1C, 1Q, 2A, 2C, 2E, 2G, 2K, 3B, 4C, 5L

Torah scroll—a manuscript of the Pentateuch, used for reading portions of the Torah during prayer. 1A, 1C, 1E, 4C

Tosafot; Tosafists—literally "additions," referring to extensive commentary on the Talmud composed by a group of scholars (known as Tosafists) in northern France during the twelfth and early thirteenth centuries. 1L, 1R, 3B, 5P

Yeshiva—a rabbinic school. 1N, 1O, 2I

Yiddish—a German dialect influenced by the Hebrew and spoken by medieval German Jews. Starting in the late thirteenth century, Jews began to write in Yiddish occasionally, rather than Hebrew, using the Hebrew script. 1M, 5P, 5Q

Yom Kippur, Yom haKippurim—the Day of Atonement, considered the most holy day of the Jewish calendar, and celebrated ten days after the Jewish New Year (*Rosh haShanah*). The day is dedicated to atonement for sins and repentance, fasting, and prayer. 1J, 1O, 2E, 2M, 5H, 5L

Bibliography

Primary sources in translation

Abraham von Worms. *The Book of Abramelin*. Ed. George Dehn, trans. Steven Guth, foreword by Lon M. DuQuette. Lake Worth: Ibis Press, 2006.

Constable, Olivia Remie, and Damian Zurro, eds. *Medieval Iberia: Readings from Christian, Muslim, and Jewish Sources*. Philadelphia: University of Pennsylvania Press, 2012.

Frakes, Jerold C. *Early Yiddish Texts, 1100–1750, with Introduction and Commentary*. Oxford: Oxford University Press, 2004.

Friedenberg, Daniel M. *Jewish Seals in Medieval Europe*. Detroit: Wayne State University Press, 1987.

Grayzel, Solomon. *The Church and the Jews in the XIIIth Century*. New York: Hermon, 1966.

Horrox, Rosemary, ed. *The Black Death*. Manchester and New York: Manchester University Press, 1994.

Kazis, Israel, ed. *The Book of the Gests of Alexander of Macedon: Sefer Toledot Alexandros ha-Makdoni*. Cambridge: Medieval Academy of America, 1961.

Linder, Amnon, ed. *The Jews in the Legal Sources of the Early Middle Ages*. Detroit: Wayne State University Press, 1997.

Marcus, Jacob R. *The Jew in the Medieval World, A Source Book: 315–1791*. Cincinnati: Sinai Press, 1938.

Secondary sources

Abrahams, Israel. *Jewish Life in the Middle Ages*. London: Macmillan, 1896.

Adamson, Melitta W. *Food in Medieval Times*. Westport: Greenwood Press, 2004.

Bale, Anthony. *The Jew in the Medieval Book: English Antisemitisms, 1350–1500*. Cambridge: Cambridge University Press, 2010.

Bar-Levav, Avriel, Andreas Lehnardt, and Stefan Reif, eds. *Death in Jewish Life: Burial and Mourning Customs Among Jews of Europe and Nearby Communities*. Berlin: De Gruyter, 2014.

Baron, Salo W. *A Social and Religious History of the Jews*. 18 vols. New York: Columbia University Press, 1952–1983.

Baskin, Judith R. "Mobility and Marriage in Two Medieval Jewish Societies." *Jewish History* 22 (2008): 223–43.

Baumgarten, Elisheva. "Gender and Daily Life in Jewish Communities." In *The Oxford Handbook of Women and Gender in Medieval Europe*, ed. Judith M. Bennett and Ruth Karras, 213–28. Oxford: Oxford University Press, 2012.

Baumgarten, Elisheva. *Mothers and Children: Jewish Family Life in Medieval Europe*. Princeton: Princeton University Press, 2004.

Baumgarten, Elisheva. *Practicing Piety in Medieval Ashkenaz: Men, Women, and Everyday Religious Observance*. Philadelphia: University of Pennsylvania Press, 2014.

Baumgarten, Elisheva, Ruth Mazo Karras, and Katelyn Mesler, eds. *Entangled Histories: Knowledge, Authority, and Jewish Culture in the Thirteenth Century*. Philadelphia: University of Pennsylvania Press, 2016.

Breuer, Mordechai. "The 'Black Death' and Antisemitism." In *Antisemitism Through the Ages*, ed. Shmuel Almog, trans. Nathan H. Reisner, 139–51. Exeter: Pergamon, 1988.

Caviness, Madeline H., and Charles G. Nelson. *Women and Jews in the Sachsenspiegel Picture-Books*. Turnhout: Brepols, 2018.

Champagne, Marie-Thérèse, and Irven M. Resnick, eds. *Jews and Muslims under the Fourth Lateran Council: Papers Commemorating the Octocentenary of the Fourth Lateran Council (1215)*. Turnhout: Brepols, 2018.

Chazan, Robert. *Church, State, and Jew in the Middle Ages*. New York: Behrman House, 1980.

Chazan, Robert. *Daggers of Faith: Thirteenth-Century Christian Missionizing and Jewish Response*. Berkeley: University of California Press, 1989.

Chazan, Robert. *Fashioning Jewish Identity in Medieval Western Christendom*. Cambridge: Cambridge University Press, 2004.

Chazan, Robert. *In the Year 1096: The First Crusade and the Jews*. Philadelphia: Jewish Publication Society, 1996.

Chazan, Robert. *Medieval Jewry in Northern France*. Baltimore: Johns Hopkins University Press, 1974.

Chazan, Robert. *Reassessing Jewish Life in Medieval Europe*. New York: Cambridge University Press, 2010.

Chazan, Robert. *The Jews of Medieval Western Christendom*. Cambridge: Cambridge University Press, 2006.

Cluse, Christoph, ed. *The Jews of Europe in the Middle Ages (Tenth to Fifteenth Centuries)*. Turnhout: Brepols, 2004.

Cohn, Samuel K., Jr. "The Black Death and the Burning of Jews." *Past and Present* 196 (2007): 3–36.

Dinshaw, Carolyn. *Getting Medieval: Sexualities and Communities, Pre- and Postmodern*. Durham: Duke University Press, 1999.

Dobson, Richard B. *The Jewish Communities of Medieval England: The Collected Essays of R. B. Dobson*, ed. Helen Birkett. York: Borthwick Publications, 2010.

Dönitz, Saskia. "Alexander the Great in Medieval Hebrew Traditions." In *A Companion to Alexander Literature in the Middle Ages*, ed. David Zuwiyya, 21–39. Leiden: Brill, 2011.

Dudash, Susan J. "Christian Politics, the Tavern, and Urban Revolt in Late Medieval France." In *Healing the Body Politic: The Political Thought of Christine de Pizan*, ed. Karen Green and Constant J. Mews, 35–59. Turnhout: Brepols, 2005.
Einbinder, Susan L. *Beautiful Death: Jewish Poetry and Martyrdom in Medieval France*. Princeton: Princeton University Press, 2002.
Einbinder, Susan L. *No Place of Rest: Jewish Literature, Expulsion, and the Memory of Medieval France*. Philadelphia: University of Pennsylvania Press, 2009.
Epstein, Marc M. *The Medieval Haggadah: Art, Narrative, and Religious Imagination*. New Haven: Yale University Press, 2011.
Finkelstein, Louis. *Jewish Self-Government in the Middle Ages*. New York: Jewish Theological Seminary of America, 1924.
Flandrin, Jean-Louis. "Repression and Change in the Sexual Life of Young People in Medieval and Early Modern Times." *Journal of Family History* 2 (1977): 196–210.
Fraiman, Susan. "The Marginal Images of Marginal People." In *The Metamorphosis of Marginal Images: From Antiquity to Present Time*, ed. Nurith Kenaan-Kedar and Ovadiah Asher, 105–13. Tel Aviv: Tel Aviv University Press, 2001.
Frakes, Jerold C., ed. *Early Yiddish Texts, 1100–1750: With Introduction and Commentary*. Oxford: Oxford University Press, 2004.
Freidenreich, David M. *Foreigners and Their Food: Constructing Otherness in Jewish, Christian, and Islamic Law*. Berkeley: University of California Press, 2011.
Friedman, John B., and Kristen Mossler, eds. *Trade, Travel, and Exploration in the Middle Ages: An Encyclopedia*. New York: Garland Publishing, 2017.
Fudeman, Kirsten A. *Vernacular Voices: Language and Identity in Medieval French Jewish Communities*. Philadelphia: University of Pennsylvania Press, 2010.
Galinsky, Judah. "Public Charity in Medieval Germany: A Preliminary Investigation." In *Toward a Renewed Ethic of Jewish Philanthropy*, ed. Yossi Prager, 79–92. New York: Michael Scharf Publication Trust of Yeshiva University, 2010.
Goldy, Charlotte Newman. "A Thirteenth-Century Anglo-Jewish Woman Crossing Boundaries: Visible and Invisible." *Journal of Medieval History* 34 (2008): 130–45.
Goldy, Charlotte Newman. "Muriel, a Jew of Oxford: Using the Dramatic to Understand the Mundane in Anglo-Norman Towns." In *Writing Medieval Women's Lives*, ed. Charlotte N. Goldy and Amy F. Livingstone, 227–46. New York: Palgrave Macmillan, 2012.
Grossman, Avraham. *Pious and Rebellious: Jewish Women in Europe in the Middle Ages*, trans. Jonathan Chipman. Waltham: Brandeis University Press, 2004.

Haverkamp, Alfred. "Jews in the Medieval German Kingdom." In *Corpus der Quellen zur Geschichte der Juden im spätmittelalterlichen Reich*. Trier, Arye Maimon Institut für Geschichte der Juden: Universitätsbibliothek Trier, 2015.

Henisch, Bridget A. *Fast and Feast: Food in Medieval Society*. University Park: Pennsylvania State University Press, 1978.

Howell, Martha C. *Commerce before Capitalism in Europe, 1300–1600*. Cambridge: Cambridge University Press, 2010.

Hoyle, Victoria. "The Bonds That Bind: Money Lending between Anglo-Jewish and Christian Women in the Plea Rolls of the Exchequer of the Jews, 1218–1280." *Journal of Medieval History* 34 (2008): 119–29.

Jones, Sarah R. "Public and Private Space and Gender in Medieval Europe." In *The Oxford Handbook of Women and Gender in Medieval Europe*, ed. Judith M. Bennett and Ruth Mazo Karras, 246–61. Oxford: Oxford University Press, 2013.

Jordan, William C. "Problems of the Meat Market of Béziers, 1240–1247." *Revue des Etudes Juives* 135 (1976): 31–49.

Jordan, William C. *The French Monarchy and the Jews from Philip Augustus to the Last Capetians*. Philadelphia: University of Pennsylvania Press, 1989.

Jordan, William C. *The Great Famine: Northern Europe in the Early Fourteenth Century*. Princeton: Princeton University Press, 1996.

Jordan, William C. "Women and Credit in the Middle Ages: Problems and Directions." *Journal of European Economic History* 17 (1988): 33–62.

Kanarfogel, Ephraim. *Brothers from Afar: Rabbinic Approaches to Apostasy and Reversion in Medieval Europe*. Detroit: Wayne State University Press, 2020.

Kanarfogel, Ephraim. *Jewish Education and Society in the High Middle Ages*. Detroit: Wayne State University Press, 1992.

Kanarfogel, Ephraim. *Peering through the Lattices: Mystical, Magical, and Pietistic Dimensions in the Tosafist Period*. Detroit: Wayne State University Press, 2000.

Karras, Ruth Mazo. "Thou Art the Man": The Masculinity of David in the Christian and Jewish Middle Ages. Philadelphia: University of Pennsylvania Press, 2021.

Katz, Maidi S. "The Married Woman and Her Expense Account: A Study of the Married Woman's Ownership and Use of Marital Property in Jewish Law." *Jewish Law Annual* 13 (2000): 101–41.

Kearney, Richard, and James Taylor. *Hosting the Stranger: Between Religions*. New York: Continuum, 2011.

Krummel, Miriamne Ara. *Crafting Jewishness in Medieval England: Legally Absent, Virtually Present*. New York: Palgrave Macmillan, 2011.

Lehnertz, Andreas. "The Trier Archbishop's *negociator* Sealing: Two Seals Owned by Muskinus the Jew (Moshe b. Yeḥiel, *ob.* 1336 CE)." In *A Companion to Seals in the Middle Ages*, ed. Laura Whatley, 243–63. Leiden: Brill, 2019.

Lipton, Sara. *Dark Mirror: The Medieval Origins of Anti-Jewish Iconography*. New York: Metropolitan Books; Henry Holt and Company, 2014.
Lotter, Friedrich. "The Scope and Effectiveness of Imperial Jewry Law in the High Middle Ages." *Jewish History* 4 (1989): 31–58.
Marcus, Ivan G. *Piety and Society: The Jewish Pietists of Medieval Germany*. Leiden: Brill, 1981.
Marcus, Ivan G. *Rituals of Childhood: Jewish Acculturation in Medieval Europe*. New Haven: Yale University Press, 1996, reprint 2015.
Masschaele, James. "The Public Space of the Marketplace in Medieval England." *Speculum* 77 (2002): 383–421.
McSheffrey, Shannon. *Marriage, Sex and Civic Culture in Late Medieval London*. Philadelphia: University of Pennsylvania Press, 2006.
Metzger, Thérèse and Mendel. *Jewish Life in the Middle Ages: Illuminated Hebrew Manuscripts of the Thirteenth to the Sixteenth Centuries*. New York: Alpine Fine Arts Collection, 1982.
Mundill, Robin R. *The King's Jews: Money, Massacre and Exodus in Medieval England*. London: Continuum, 2010.
Newman, Paul B. *Growing Up in the Middle Ages*. Jefferson: McFarland & Company, 2007.
Nicholas, David M. *The Growth of the Medieval City: From Late Antiquity to the Early Fourteenth Century*. New York: Longman, 1997.
Nirenberg, David. *Communities of Violence: Persecution of Minorities in the Middle Ages*. Princeton: Princeton University Press, 1996.
Pollack, Herman H. "An Historical Explanation of the Origin and Development of Jewish Books of Customs ('Sifre Minhagim'), 1100–1300." *Jewish Social Studies* 49 (1987): 195–216.
Ray, Jonathan. "The Jew in the Text: What Christian Charters Tell Us About Medieval Jewish Society." *Medieval Encounters* 16 (2010): 243–67.
Rokéah, Zefira E. "Crime and Jews in Late Thirteenth-Century England: Some Cases and Comments." *Hebrew Union College Annual* 55 (1984): 95–157.
Roth, Norman. *Medieval Jewish Civilization: An Encyclopedia*. New York: Routledge, 2002.
Roth, Pinchas. "Regional Boundaries and Medieval Halakhah: Rabbinic Responsa from Catalonia to Southern France in the Thirteenth and Fourteenth Centuries." *Jewish Studies Quarterly Review* 105 (2015): 72–98.
Rubin, Nissan. *Time and Life Cycle in Talmud and Midrash: Socio-anthropological Perspectives*. Boston: Academic Studies Press, 2008.
Sapir Abulafia, Anna. *Christian–Jewish Relations, 1000–1300: Jews in the Service of Medieval Christendom*. Harlow: Pearson Education, 2011.
Schultz, James A. *The Knowledge of Childhood in the German Middle Ages, 1100–1350*. Philadelphia: University of Pennsylvania Press, 1995.
Scully, Terence. *The Art of Cookery in the Middle Ages*. Woodbridge: Boydell Press, 1995.

Shatzmiller, Joseph. *Cultural Exchange: Jews, Christians, and Art in the Medieval Marketplace*. Princeton: Princeton University Press, 2013.

Shatzmiller, Joseph. *Jews, Medicine, and Medieval Society*. Berkeley: University of California Press, 1994.

Shatzmiller, Joseph. *Shylock Reconsidered: Jews, Moneylending, and Medieval Society*. Berkeley: University of California Press, 1990.

Sheehan, Michael M. *Marriage, Family and Law in Medieval Europe: Collected Studies*. Toronto: University of Toronto Press, 1996, reprint 1997.

Shoham-Steiner, Ephraim. *Jews and Crime in Medieval Europe*. Detroit: Wayne State University Press, 2020.

Shoham-Steiner, Ephraim. *On the Margins of a Minority: Leprosy, Madness, and Disability among the Jews of Medieval Europe*. Detroit: Wayne State University Press, 2014.

Shoham-Steiner, Ephraim, ed. *Intricate Interfaith Networks in the Middle Ages: Quotidian Jewish–Christian Contacts*. Turnhout: Brepols, 2016.

Shyovitz, David I. *A Remembrance of His Wonders: Nature and the Supernatural in Medieval Ashkenaz*. Philadelphia: University of Pennsylvania Press, 2017.

Signer, Michael A., and John Van Engen, eds. *Jews and Christians in Twelfth-Century Europe*. Notre Dame: University of Notre Dame Press, 2011.

Skinner, Patricia, ed. *The Jews in Medieval Britain: Historical, Literary and Archeological Perspectives*. Woodbridge: Boydell, 2003.

Stacey, Robert C. "Jewish Lending and the Medieval English Economy." In *A Commercialising Economy? England 1000–1300*, ed. Richard Britnell and Bruce Campbell, 78–101. Manchester: Manchester University Press, 1994.

Stow, Kenneth R. *Alienated Minority: The Jews of Medieval Latin Europe*. Cambridge: Harvard University Press, 1992.

Stow, Kenneth R. *Popes, Church, and Jews in the Middle Ages: Confrontation and Response*. Aldershot: Ashgate, 2007.

Szpiech, Ryan. *Medieval Exegesis and Religious Difference: Commentary, Conflict, and Community in the Premodern Mediterranean*. New York: Fordham University Press, 2015.

Tallan, Cheryl. "Medieval Jewish Widows: Their Control of Resources." *Jewish History* 5 (1991): 63–74.

Tallan, Cheryl. "The Position of the Jewish Medieval Widow as a Function of a Family Structure." In *The Proceedings of the World Congress of Jewish Studies* 2, no. 2 (1989): 91–98.

Tartakoff, Paola. *Conversion, Circumcision, and Ritual Murder in Medieval Europe*. Philadelphia: University of Pennsylvania Press, 2020.

Toch, Michael. "Economic Activities of German Jews in the Middle Ages." In *Wirtschaftsgeschichte der mittelalterlichen Juden. Fragen und Einschätzungen*, ed. Michael Toch and Elisabeth Müller-Luckner, 181–210. Munich: Oldenbourg, 2008.

Toch, Michael. *Peasants and Jews in Medieval Germany: Studies in Cultural, Social and Economic History*. Aldershot: Ashgate, 2003.

Toch, Michael. *The Economic History of European Jews: Late Antiquity and Early Middle Ages*. Leiden: Brill, 2012.

Todeschini, Giacomo. "Christian Perceptions of Jewish Economic Activity in the Middle Ages." In *Wirtschaftsgeschichte der Mittelalterlichen Juden. Fragen und Einschätzungen*, ed. Michael Toch and Elisabeth Müller-Luckner, 1–16. Munich: Oldenbourg, 2008.

Verdon, Jean. *Travel in the Middle Ages*, trans. George Holoch. Notre Dame: University of Notre Dame Press, 2003.

Verlinden, Charles. "Markets and Fairs." In *The Cambridge Economic History of Europe from the Decline of the Roman Empire*, ed. Michael M. Postan, Edwin E. Rich, and Edward Miller, vol. 3, 119–54. Cambridge: Cambridge University Press, 1963.

Watt, John A. "The Jews, the Law, and the Church: The Concept of Jewish Serfdom in 13th Century England." In *The Church and Sovereignty: Studies in Church History*, ed. Diana Wood, 153–72. Oxford: Blackwell, 1991.

Weingarten, Susan. *Haroset: A Taste of Jewish History*. New Milford and London: Toby Press, 2019.

Wenninger, Markus J. "Bearing and Use of Weapons by Jews in the (Late) Middle Ages." *Jewish Studies* 41 (2002): 83–92.

Yuval, Israel J. *Two Nations in Your Womb: Perceptions of Jews and Christians in Late Antiquity and the Middle Ages*, trans. Barbara Harshav and Jonathan Chipman. Berkeley: University of California Press, 2008.

Ziegler, Joseph. "Reflections on the Jewry Oath in the Middle Ages." *Studies in Church History* 29 (1992): 209–20.

List of Contributors

Barzilay, Tzafrir (**Tz. B.**)—Introduction, Glossary, Bibliography, 1C, 1D, 1E, 1J, 2M, 3B, 3D, 4A, 4B, 4C, 4D, 4K, 4L, 5D, 5M, 5N, 5O

Baumgarten, Elisheva (**E. B.**)—Introduction, Glossary, Bibliography, 1A, 1G, 2C, 2N, 3A, 3C, 5F, 5H

Bodner, Neta (**N. B.**)— Photography, 1F

Dermer, Nureet (**N. D.**)—3C, 4J, 5B, 5L

Doron, Aviya (**A. D.**)—2O, 3E, 3F, 3M, 4A, 4B, 4G, 4H

Fenton, Miri (**M. F.**)—1N, 1O, 1P, 1Q, 2A, 2G, 2H, 3G, 4E

Kalaora, Etelle (**E. K.**)—1K, 2D, 2K

Kohn, Albert E. (**A. E. K.**)—2E, 3H

Lehnertz, Andreas (**A. L.**)—1M, 3J, 3K, 3L, 4F, 4I

Levinson, Eyal (**E. L.**)—Introduction, Glossary, Bibliography, 1L, 1R, 2B, 2I, 2J, 2P, 5P, 5Q

Namia-Cohen, Adi (**A. N. C.**)—1B, 1H, 2F, 2L

Schachter, Hannah Teddy (**H. T. S.**)—3I, 5A, 5C, 5E, 5G, 5I, 5J, 5K

Shafran, Amit (**A. S.**)—1I

Index

References include section and page numbers

Aaron of Lincoln, 5B 123
Abraham of Worms (author of *Book of Abramelin*), 2P 61
Accusations, xiv, 1H 13, 1Q 29, 2I 50, 4D 100, 4F 107, 4K 117
Agunah (pl. -ot), 2A 36, 2K 53
Albrecht I (king of the German Empire), 4I 112–14
Alexander the Great, 5N 150–51
Alimony, 2L 55
Anna, 4E 105
Apotropus, 2D 41, 2O 60
Archbishop, 4C 93, 4F 107, 5I 140, 5J 143
Architecture, 1E 8–9
Archsynagogue, 4A 88
Arloga, 2I 50
Asher son of Yehiel, 1O 24–25, 3I 76
Augsburg, 4I 112, 5C 127
Austria, 1R 33, 2I 50, 2K 53, 3G 72

Badge (to identify Jews), 5D 131
Bahya son of Asher, 1P 26
Barcelona, 1P 26, 2I 50
Baptism, 4B 90, 4C 96, 4E 103, 105–6, 5A 121, 5D 130, 5E 133, 5I 140, 5J 142
Beit midrash, 1C 6, 1E 9
Bele of Steten, 2O 60
Bellette of Worms, 2C 39–40
Bible *or* biblical, xxii, 1B 4, 1N 23, 1P 26, 1Q 31, 2G 46, 2K 53, 2M 57, 4C 99, 4E 103, 4F 107, 5C 126, 5H 138, 5L 146, 5M 148

Birth, xvii, 1A 1, 1H 12, 1Q 30, 4I 114, 5H 138
Bishop, 1C 5–6, 1D 7, 3M 83, 3N 85, 4A 87–88, 4B 89–90, 4C 93–98, 4F 107–8, 5D 130, 5G 137, 5J 143
Black Death, xiv–xv, 3J 78, 4K 117, 4L 118, 5Q 155
Blood, 1H 12, 4C 99, 4D 101, 4E 106, 4L 119–20, 5H 139
Blood libels, 1H 12
Bohemia, 2P 61
Book of Paper, 3E 70
Book of the Perfume.
  See *Sefer haRokeah*
Books, xxii, 1I 14, 4F 108, 4G 109, 4H 110, 5C 126, 5L 146. *See also specific titles or authors*
Bread, A1 2, 1B 4, 1H 13, 2E 43–44, 2F 45, 2L 55, 3N 85
Buildings, xiv, xvii, xx, xxii, 1C 5–6, 1D 7, 1E 8–9, 1J 16, 3N 85, 4C 95, 5G 137
Burial, 1K 18, 1N 22, 1O 24, 1P 26, 4A 88, 4L 118–120
Business, xiv, xviii, 1P 26, 1Q 28, 2A 35–36, 2E 44, 2O 60, 3A 63–64, 3C 66, 3D 67, 3F 71, 3G 72–73, 3L 81, 3N 85, 4B 90, 4D 101–2, 4E 104, 4F 107, 4J 115–16, 5L 146

Candles, 1O 24, 1Q 28, 2J 52, 2M 57, 5H 139
Canon law, 5D 128–32, 5E 133
Cathedral, 1D 7, 3N 85, 4E 103, 106
Cemetery, xi, 1A 3, 1D 7, 1L 19, 1N 22, 1O 24, 4I 112, 4L 119, 5A 122
Ceremony, 2G 46–47, 2K 53, 5C 126
Chalices, 4G 109, 4H 110
Charity, 1K 18, 1P 26, 1Q 27–28, 3D 67, 3M 83, 4E 105, 5C 126
Cheese, 3B 64–65
Church (building), 1D 7, 4A 88, 4C 95, 99, 4E 103–4, 106, 5A 124, 5I 141, 5K 145
Church (institution), xvi, xvii–xviii, 3J 78, 3M 83–84, 4E 103–6, 4H 110, 5C 126, 5D 128–32, 5E 133–34, 5G 137, 5K 144
Coat of arms, 3L 81–82
Cohen, 1A 2, 1K 18, 1O 24–25, 2J 51–52, 2K 53
Children, xii, xv–xvi, 1H 12, 1N 23, 1Q 27–31, 2A 36, 2G 46–48, 2K 53–54, 2L 55–56, 3H 74–75, 3M 84, 4B 89, 4C 97, 4D 100, 4G 109, 4K 117, 4L 120, 5C 126, 5H 139, 5J 142–44, 5M 148
Christ, 3M 83, 4C 93, 4D 100–102, 4E 104–6, 5D 129–30, 5J 142–43, 5M 148
Chronicle, xxi, 1C 5, 1D 7, 3J 78, 4C 93, 4E 103, 4J 115, 4K 117
Circumcision, 5C 126, 5H 138–39
Clément V (pope), 4J 115–16
Clothes, xvi, 1L 20, 1Q 29, 2C 39, 3M 84, 4G 109, 5D 129, 132, 5F 135–36, 5G 137, 5H 139, 5L 146
Coins, 2L 56, 3C 66, 3E 70, 3H 75, 4C 95
Cologne, 1D 7, 2F 45, 2H 48–49, 3C 66, 4C 94, 96, 99, 5J 143, 5Q 155–56
Commandment (religious). See *Mitzvah*
Commentary, xxii, 1B 4, 1H 12, 1P 26, 1Q 30, 2L 55, 2M 57, 3A 63, 3L 81, 4E 103, 4H 110
Communal rules. See *Takkanah*
Constantinople, 2P 61
Contracts, 1K 18, 2A 36, 2L 55, 3K 80–81, 4I 112–14, 5B 124, 5E 133
Conversion (to Christianity), 4C 93–99, 5A 121–22, 5E 133–34, 5F 135–36, 5G 137–38, 5J 142–44
Conversion (to Judaism), 5C 126–27
Council (of the Church), 5D 128–32, 5E 133–34, 5G 138
Council (Urban), 2O 60, 3L 81–82, 4I 112–14
Court (Jewish, *beit din*), 1K 18, 2A 35–37, 2B 38, 2D 41–42, 2K 53–54, 2L 55–56, 3A 63–64, 3D 67–68
Court (of law, Christian), xviii, 2O 60, 3J 78–79, 4F 107–8, 5A 121, 5B 123–24
Crafts, 2C 39–40, 3A 63–64, 3J 78
Craftsmen, xv, xvii, 5L 146–47
Credit *or* creditor, xvii, 1K 19, 1Q 31, 2O 60, 3J 78–79, 4J 115–16
Crucifixion *or* crucifix, 1N 23, 4C 97, 4D 100, 5M 148
Crusade, 1C 5, 3J 78, 4C 93–99, 5D 128
Crusaders, 1D 7, 4C 93–99, 4K 117
Custom. See *Minhag*

Daughters, 1A 1–3, 1I 15, 1O 25, 1Q 27–32, 2B 37–38, 2C 39–40, 3H 75, 4B 90, 4C 99, 5C 126, 5P 153–54
David (biblical figure), 4E 104, 5L 146–47

David son of Meshulam, 4D 89
Day of Atonement. See *Yom Kippur*
Death, xii, xvii, 1A 1–3, 1K 18, 1N 22–23, 1O 24–25, 1P 26, 1Q 27–31, 2C 39, 2D 41, 2K 53, 4D 100–102, 4E 103–6, 4I 112, 4K 117–18, 4L 118–20, 5A 122, 5C 126, 5I 140
Debt, 1K 18, 2A 36, 2L 56, 2O 60, 3C 66, 3H 74–75, 3J 78–79, 3K 79–80, 3L 81–82, 4E 103–6, 4K 117, 5B 124–25
Desecration (of the Sabbath), 1Q 28, 2E 44, 2N 59, 5F 136
Denmark, 5P 154
Devotion, xviii, 4C 93–99, 4D 100–102, 4E 104
Dinars (currency), 2D 41, 3D 67–69, 4C 95
Divorce, 1L 19, 5L 146
Duke Horant, 5P 153–54
Düren, 2M 57

Earrings, 2B 37–38
Education, 1G 12, 1Q 27–31, 2A 36, 2C 39–40, 2G 46–48, 5J 142–44
Economic activities, xvii, 3A 63–64, 3C 66, 3D 67–69, 3E 70, 3G 72–73, 3H 74–75, 3J 78–79, 3N 85, 4J 115–16, 5A 124
Economic status, xv–xvi, xvii, xx, 2F 45, 2L 55–56, 3A 63–64, 3K 79–80, 3L 81–82, 3M 83–84, 3N 85, 4A 87–88, 4B 89–90, 5A 121–22, 5D 128–30
Egilbert of Trier, 4C 93
Eleanor of Provence, 3M 83
Eleazar son of Asher haLevi, 5N 150
Eleazar son of Judah of Worms (Rokeah), 1F 10–11, 2C 39–40, 2G 46–48, 5I 141
Eleazar son of Samuel the Levite, 1Q 27–32

Eliezer son of Joel haLevi of Bonn, 2D 41–42
Eliezer son of Nathan of Mainz, 2B 37–38, 3A 63–64
Elisabeth of Carinthia (Queen of the German Empire), 3J 78–79
Emperors, 1D 7, 4B 89–92, 4C 96, 4G 109, 4I 112, 5A 121, 5N 150–51
England, xiii, xv, xxii, xxiv, 1N 22–23, 2L 55–56, 3M 83–84, 4D 100–102, 4E 103–6, 5B 123–25, 5D 131, 5G 137–38
Erfurt, 4F 107–8
Esslingen, 1L 19–20
Eudes Rigaud, 5I 140
Exchequer (of the Jews), 5B 123–25
Excrement, 2H 48–49
Exegesis *or* Exegetical, 1B 4, 1P 26, 2M 57–58, 4H 110–11. See also commentary
Exempla (sing. *exemplum*), 5J 142–44
Expulsion, xv, 1I 14, 4J 115–16

Father *or* Fatherhood, 1A 1–3, 1N 22–23, 1O 24–25, 1Q 27–32, 2B 37–38, 2P 61, 5C 126–27, 5H 138, 5J 143–44
Family, xii, xvi, xvii, xix, xx, 1I 14–15, 1K 18, 1O 24–25, 1P 26, 1Q 27–32, 2A 35–36, 2B 37–38, 2C 39–40, 2D 41–42, 2H 48–49, 2J 51–52, 2K 53–54, 2L 55, 2M 57, 2O 60, 3A 63, 3H 74–75, 3L 81, 3M 83, 4C 98, 5E 133, 5L 146
Fish, 2E 43–44, 2L 55–56, 3C 66, 3K 80, 5K 145
Frakes, Jerold, 5P 154
France, xiii, xv, xxii, 1H 13, 1I 14–15, 1L 19, 1P 26, 1R 33, 2A 35–36, 2E 43–44, 2G 46, 2L 55, 3B 64–65, 3E 70, 4C 93, 4D 100, 4E 105, 4J 115–16, 5A 121–22, 5C 127, 5D 131, 5I 140, 5K 144–45, 5L 147

Frankfurt, 3J 78, 4L 118
French (language), 1H 13, 1I 14–15, 2E 43–44, 4J 115–16, 5L 146, 5N 150
Friedberg, 1J 16–17
Food, 1B 4, 1F 10, 1H 12–13, 1Q 29, 2E 43–44, 2F 45, 2G 47, 2H 49, 2L 55–56, 3B 65, 5F 136, 5G 137, 5I 141
Fornication, 2J 52
Fountain of Life, 5N 150–51, 5O 151–52

Ganna, 1L 19–20
Gematria, 1I 14–15, 2M 58
Gender, xvi, xxiii, 1A 1–3, 1F 10–11, 1G 12, 1I 14–15, 1J 16–17, 1L 19–20, 1Q 27–31, 1R 33, 2A 35–37, 2B 37–38, 2C 39–40, 2D 41–42, 2I 50, 2J 51–52, 2K 53–54, 2L 55–56, 2M 57–58, 3A 63–64, 3D 67–69, 3F 71, 3H 74–75, 3K 79–80, 3L 81–82, 5C 127, 5E 133–34, 5F 135–36, 5H 139, 5J 142–43
German (language), 1M 21, 1Q 30, 3L 81, 3N 85, 4F 107, 5M 148, 5Q 155–56
German Empire, xi, xiii–xv, xxii, 1D 7, 1J 16, 1M 21, 1O 24, 2A 35, 2G 46, 2F 35, 3I 76, 3J 78–79, 3K 79–80, 3L 81, 3N 85, 4B 89–90, 4C 93–94, 4G 109, 4I 112, 4K 117–18, 4L 118–19, 5P 153–54
Germany. See *specific cities and areas*
Gershom son of Jacob, 5H 138–39
Gershom son of Judah (*Me'or haGolah*) 1A 1, 2A 35
Geoffrey of Paris, 4J 115–16
Get, 1L 19
Gothic, 5L 146, 5M 148
Gregory IX (pope), 5E 134
Guardian. See *Apotropus*

Guests, 1Q 31, 2B 37–38, 2F 45, 3M 83–84, 4A 88, 4B 90, 4K 117
Gumprecht son of Minne and Menahem 3K 79–80, 3L 81–82

Haim son of Isaac of Vienna, 2I 50, 3G 72
Haggadah, 1H 13, 5L 146, 5O 151–52
Halakhah or Jewish law, xviii, xxii, 1L 19–20, 2A 35, 2L 55, 2N 59, 3E 70, 3H 74, 3L 81
Halitzah, 2K 53–54
Hannah daughter of Dulcia and Eleazar of Worms, 2C 39–40
Haroset, 1H 12–13
Hebrew, xiii, xviii, xx, xxii, 1A 1–3, 1G 12, 1H 13, 1I 15, 1M 21, 1R 33, 2D 41, 2E 43–44, 2F 45, 2G 46–47, 2H 48–49, 2I 57, 2M 57–58, 2O 60, 3B 64–65, 3K 79–80, 4C 93, 4F 107, 4I 114, 4L 118–20, 5A 121, 5F 135, 5K 144–45, 5N 150, 5P 153, 5Q 156
Heinrich IV (emperor of the German Empire), 4B 89–92, 4C 96
Heinrich von Herford, 4K 117
Henry II (king of England), 4E 103–6
Henry III (king of England), 3M 83, 5G 137
Hereford, 3M 83–84
Heretics, 2I 50, 5I 140
Hezekiah son of Jacob of Magdeburg, 2J 51–52
Holidays, xvii, 1M 21, 1Q 27, 31, 2M 57, 4B 91, 4C 94, 96, 4D 100, 5L 146, 5P 153
Holy Land, 2P 61, 4C 99
Home/House, xii, xvi, 1A 2, 1B 4, 1H 13, 1O 25, 1P 26, 1Q 28–30, 2A 35–36, 2B 37–38, 2C 39–40, 2D 41–42, 2E 43–44, 2F 45, 2G 47, 2H 48–49, 2I 50, 2J 51–52,

2M 57–58, 2P 61, 3A 63–64, 3B 65, 3E 70, 3G 72–73, 3I 76–77, 3L 81, 4B 90, 4C 94, 4D 101, 5B 124, 5E 133, 5F 135–36, 5G 137–38, 5I 141, 5J 142–143, 5Q 155
Honor, 1A 2, 1O 24, 1Q 28–31, 2E 44, 3M 84, 4A 87, 4I 112, 5P 153
Honorius V (pope), 5J 143
Hospitality, 2A 36, 2F 45
House of Converts, 5G 137–38
Hungary, 5P 154
Husband, 1J 16, 1K 18, 1Q 28, 2A 35–36, 2C 39–40, 2D 41–42, 2I 50, 2J 51–52, 2K 53–54, 2L 55–56, 3A 63–64, 3F 71, 3H 74–75, 4C 98, 5F 135–36

Iconography, 5L 146–47
Illumination, 1R 33, 4H 110–11, 5L 146–47, 5O 151–52
Innocent III (pope), 5D 128–30, 5E 133–34
Inscription, xii, 2H 48–49, 3K 79–80
Intercourse, xvi, 1F 10–11, 1J 16, 1Q 28, 2I 50–51, 2J 51–52, 2M 57–58, 5D 129
Interest loans, xvii, 3D 67–69, 3F 71, 3G 72–73, 3J 78, 3K 79, 4G 109, 4J 115, 5B 123–25. *See also* Moneylending
Isaac (biblical figure), 1B 4
Isaac of Chinon, 1I 14–15
Isaac of Vienna, 2I 50, 3G 72
Isaac son of Abraham, 5C 127
Isaac son of Meir haLevi of Düren, 2M 57
Isaac son of Samuel the Elder, 2K 54, 3B 64–65, 5P 153
Israel son of Meir of Heidelberg, 5O 151–52
Italy, xiii, 1R 33, 4C 96, 4D 100

Jacob (biblical figure), 1B 4, 4L 119
Jacob of Nordhausen, 4L 118–20
Jacob son of Dulcia and Eleazar of Worms, 2C 39
Jacob son of Judah HaLevi, 2O 60
Jacob son of Judah Hazan of London, 2L 55–56
Jacob son of Meir of Ramerupt (*Rabbenu Tam*), 2A 35–36
John of Habsburg, 3L 81–82
Joseph Kara, 5K 145
Joseph of Bossenay, 3E 70
Joseph son of Nathan Official, 5K 144–45
Josephus, 4E 105, 4G 109
Judah son of Asher, 1O 24
Judah Hazan of London, 2L 55–56
Judah son of Kalonymus, 1C 6, 4D 89
Judah son of Samuel (*the pious*), 1G 12, 2F 45, 5C 127, 5F 135–36
Judah son of Yakar of Mainz, 1A 1
Judeneid, 4F 107–8

Kiddush haShem or Martyrdom, 1A 2, 4C 93–99, 4E 103–6, 4L 118–20, 5C 126–27, 5F 135–36
Ketubbah, 1K 18, 2L 55–56
King (European). *See specific monarchs*
Knights, 1C 5, 1R 32–33, 4E 103, 104, 4K 117, 5P 153, 5Q 155–56

Language, xx, xxi, xxii, xxiii, xxiv, 1F 10, 1G 12, 1H 13, 1M 21, 2P 61, 4F 107–8, 5J 142–143, 5Q 156
Latin, xviii, xx, xxii, 2O 60, 3K 79–80, 4D 100, 4E 103, 4I 114, 4K 117, 5A 121, 5D 130, 5J 142, 5N 150
Law (canon). *See* Canon law
Law (Jewish). *See Halakah*
Legal agent, 2D 41–42, 3A 63–64
Leuven, 5J 142–43
Levirate marriage. See *Yibum*
Liège, 5J 143

Literature, xii, 1H 13, 1M 21, 2F 45
Literature (rabbinic or halakhic), xxii, 1R 33, 2D 41, 2M 57, 3H 74
Liturgy, *or* liturgical, xxii, 1Q 30–31, 1R 32, 2E 43–44, 5A 121, 5O 151
Liturgical poems. See *Piyut*
Louis X (king of France), 4J 115–16
London, 1N 22–23, 2L 55–56, 5G 137–38
Love, xii, xvi, 1B 4, 1F 10–11, 1I 14–15, 1N 23, 1Q 29, 2C 39–40, 2D 41–42, 2J 51–52, 4C 97, 4E 105

Mahram. See Meir son of Barukh of Rothenburg
Mahzor Vitry, xiii, 5A 121–22
Mahzor Worms, 1M 21
Magic, 1I 14–15, 2P 61, 5A 122
Maimonides (Moses son of Maimon) 2L 55–56
Mainz, 1A 1–3, 1C 5, 1D 7, 1Q 27, 2B 37, 2P 61, 3A 63, 3C 66, 3G 72, 4C 93–95, 4F 107
Manuscripts, xxii, 1H 13, 1I 14–15, 1N 22, 1R 32, 2E 43–44, 2J 51–52, 3B 64, 4H 110–11, 4L 118, 5D 131–32, 5L 146–47, 5M 148, 5O 151–52
Marcus, Jacob R., xv
Märendichtung, 5Q 155
Market *or* Marketplace, xvi, xvii, 1H 13, 2I 50, 3A 63–64, 3C 66, 3H 74, 3N 85, 4C 95, 4J 115–16, 5K 144–45
Marriage, xvii, 1I 14–15, 1K 18, 1L 19–20, 1Q 31, 1R 32–33, 2B 37–38, 2J 51–52, 2K 53–54, 3M 83–83, 5E 133, 5F 135, 5I 141, 5L 146
Marriage contract. See *Ketubah*
Martyrdom. See *Kiddush haShem*

Meals, 1B 4, 1P 26, 1Q 29, 31, 2E 43–44, 2F 45, 2L 55–56, 5L 146
Meat, 1F 10–11, 2E 44, 2F 45, 2L 56, 4A 88, 5I 141
Medical professionals, 5H 138–39
Medicine, 3J 78
Meir son of Barukh of Rothenburg (*Maharam*), xix, 1K 18, 1L 19–20, 1N 22, 1O 25, 2J 51–52, 2K 53, 3C 66, 3D 67–69, 3F 71, 3H 74–75
Midwife, 5H 139
Mikveh, (Ritual bath), xiv, 1D 7, 1E 9, 1F 10, 1J 16–17
MiQua, 2H 49, 5Q 155
Mishneh Torah, 2L 55
Mitzvah (pl. *mitzvot*) *or* commandment, 1Q 36, 2A 36, 2K 53–54, 2L 55–56, 2M 57, 5H 138–39
Money, 1K 18, 1Q 28–31, 2K 53, 2L 56, 2O 60, 3A 63–64, 3B 65, 3C 66, 3D 67–69, 3E 70, 3F 71, 3H 74–75, 3I 76–77, 3J 78–79, 3L 81, 4A 87, 4C 95, 4G 110, 4J 115–16, 5B 124–25, 5J 143
Moneylending, 3A 63–64, 3D 67–69, 3G 72–73, 3I 76–77, 3J 78–79, 3K 80, 3L 81, 4E 103, 5B 123–24, 5D 128
Monks, 4D 100–101, 5C 126, 5J 142, 5K 144–45
Mordekhai son of Hillel haCohen, 2K 53–54, 3F 71–72
Mosel (river), 4C 95, 99
Moses (biblical figure), 1L 20, 2G 47, 4F 108, 5D 129, 5L 146
Moses of Coucy, 2L 55
Moses son of Guthiel, 4B 89
Moses son of Menahem and Minne, 3K 79–80, 3L 81–82
Mothers, 1Q 28, 2C 39–40, 2J 52, 3K 79–80, 3L 81, 4C 98, 5J 142

Mourning, 1B 4, 1N 22–23, 1Q 31, 2E 44, 4C 94, 96, 5A 121–22
Murder, xii, xiv, 1H 12–13, 2C 39, 4C 95, 4D 100–102, 4E 103–6

Names, xi–xii, xxi–xxii, 1A 1–3, 1I 14–15, 2D 41, 2O 60, 3C 66, 3D 67, 3H 74, 3K 80, 3M 83, 5C 126, 5J 142
Narrative, 4L 118–20, 5J 142–43, 5P 153–54, 5Q 155
Neighbors, xiv, xvii–xviii, 1B 4, 1M 21, 1O 25, 1Q 31, 3I 76, 3J 78, 4C 94, 5A 121–22, 5D 128, 131, 5M 148, 5N 150, 5P 153
Neighborhood, 1C 5–6, 1D 7, 1O 25, 5C 126, 5F 135
Networks, 3C 66, 3I 76–77
New Year's day. See *Rosh haShanah*
Niddah, 1F 10–11, 1J 16
Night, 1N 22, 1O 24–25, 1Q 28, 2J 51–52, 3E 70, 4C 99, 4E 106, 5H 139, 5J 143
Nobility *or* noble, 1Q 30, 1R 33, 3J 78–79, 3L 81–82, 4E 103–104, 4K 117, 5M 148, 5P 153–54
Nordhausen, 4L 118–20
Norwich, 4D 100–102
Nuns, 5F 135–36, 5J 142–43
Nürnberg, 5C 126

Objects, xvi, xx–xxii, 1I 14, 1Q 27–31, 3E 70, 3I 76–77, 4B 90, 5L 146
Oath, 2D 42, 2P 61, 3A 63–64, 3D 68–69, 3I 77, 4B 90, 4C 93–99, 4F 107–8, 4G 109–10, 4I 112–14

Palace, xiv, 1C 5–6, 1D 7, 4B 90, 4C 93–99, 5D 128
Parents, 1Q 29, 2J 51–52, 3H 74, 5J 142–43
Paris, 4J 115–16, 5A 122, 5K 144–45, 5L 146

Passover, 1H 12–13, 2D 41, 4C 93–94, 4D 100, 4E 106, 5L 146, 5O 151
Pawns, 3D 67–69, 3J 78, 4G 109–10, 4H 110, 4I 112–13
Penance, 1F 10–11, 1N 23, 2N 59, 3M 84, 5I 140–41
Persecution, xv, xvii–xviii, 1C 5, 4C 93–99, 4D 100–101, 4E 103–6, 4I 112, 4K 117–18, 4L 118–20, 5C 126–27, 5F 135–36
Peter the Hermit, 4C 93–94
Philip (Philippe) IV (King of France), 4J 115–16, 4K 117
Piety *or* pietism, 1N 22, 1O 24–25, 1P 26, 1Q 27, 29–32, 2C 39
Piyut (pl. *piyutim*), 2E 43–44, 5L 146–47
Poetry *or* poet *or* poem, xxi, 2C 39–40, 2E 43–44, 4J 115–16, 5L 146, 5M 148, 5P 153, 5Q 155
Polemics *or* polemical, 5K 144–45
Poison, xiv, 1H 13, 4K 117–18
Pope *or* papal, 4J 115–16, 5A 121, 5D 128–32, 5E 133–34, 5J 143
Prayer, 1E 9, 1G 12, 1M 21, 1P 26, 1Q 27–31, 1R 33, 2C 39–40, 2E 43–44, 2L 119, 5L 146
Privilege, 1C 5–6, 1D 7, 4A 87–88, 4B 89–92, 4C 99
Property, 2D 41, 2K 53–54, 2O 60, 3G 73, 3H 74, 3I 76, 4A 88, 4B 90, 4C 95, 4G 109, 5D 129, 5E 134, 5G 137
Public sphere, 3E 70, 5D 129, 5I 140

Queen, 3J 78–79, 3M 83, 5P 154

Rabbis. See *specific people*
Rabbinic school. See *Yeshiva*
Rabbenu Tam. See Jacob son of Meir of Ramerupt
Rashi. See Solomon son of Isaac

176   INDEX

Regensburg, 1G 12, 2F 45, 5F 135–36
Register, 3M 83–84, 5I 140–41
Rent, 2D 41–42, 3G 72–73, 5B 124–25
Responsa (sing. responsum), xxii, 1K 18, 1L 19, 2D 41–42, 2K 53–54, 2N 59, 3B 64–65, 3C 66, 3D 67–69, 3F 71, 3G 72–73, 3H 74–75
Return to Judaism (after conversion to Christianity), 5F 135–36, 5I 140–41
Rhine (river), xi, 1D 7, 2B 37, 3C 66, 4C 95
Rhineland, 4C 95–96, 4F 107, 5N 150–51
Ring, 1L 19–20
Rintfleisch Massacre, 3J 78–79, 4I 112–14
Ritual bath. See *Mikveh*
Ritual Murder, 4D 100–102
Romanesque, 1E 8–9
Rosh HaShanah, 1C 6, 1Q 27, 5L 146
Rouen, 5I 140
Rüdiger of Speyer, 1C 5–6, 1D 7, 4A 87

Sabbath, xvii, 1O 25, 1Q 28, 31, 2E 43–44, 2L 56, 2M 57–58, 2N 59, 3E 70, 4E 106, 4L 119, 5F 136, 5L 146, 5P 153
Sachsenspiegel, 4G 109–10, 4H 110–11
Salian (dynasty), 1D 7, 4B 89
Salman the Scribe, 2O 60
Seals, 3B 65, 3K 79–80, 3L 81–82, 4B 92, 4F 107–8, 4I 112–14, 5B 124
Seder (Passover), 1H 12–13, 5O 151
Sefer Etz Haim, 2L 55–56
Sefer haRokeah, 2C 39, 2G 46–48
Sefer Hasidim, 1G 12, 2F 45, 5C 127, 5F 135–36
Sefer Mitzvot Gadol, 2L 55–56

Servants, 1H 13, 2B 37–38, 2F 45, 2H 49, 2I 50, 2J 51, 4A 88, 4C 94, 4F 108, 4G 109, 5N 150–51
Sexual relations. See Intercourse
Shavuot, 1N 22, 2G 47–48, 4C 96
Ships, 3C 66, 5N 151
Shrouds, 1K 18, 4L 119
Sicily, 5P 154
Singing, 2E 43–44, 4L 119
Slate, 2G 47, 5Q 155–56
Solomon haCohen, 1O 24–25
Solomon son of Aderet (*Adret*), 1P 26, 2I 50
Solomon son of Isaac (*Rashi*), xix, 1B 4, 1Q 30, 2L 55
Solomon son of Samson, 1C 5–6, 1D 7, 4C 93, 99
Spain, xiii, 1O 24–25, 1P 26, 1R 33, 2E 43–44, 2I 50, 3I 76, 4D 102, 5D 130
Speyer, 1C 5–6, 1D 7, 1E 8–9, 3C 66, 4A 87–88, 4B 89–92, 4C 94–95
Spices, 1H 12–13
Suicide, 1N 22–23
Sukkot, 1O 24, 2G 46
Synagogue, xiv, xvi–xvii, xxi, 1A 2, 1C 5–6, 1D 7, 1E 8–9, 1J 16, 1L 19, 1M 21, 1O 24, 1Q 31, 2C 39–40, 2E 43, 2G 46–47, 2H 48–49, 3N 85, 4B 91, 4C 97, 4D 101, 4I 112, 4L 119, 5H 139, 5L 146, 5P 153

Takkanah (pl. takkanot), 2A 35–36
Tales, 1Q 31, 5A 121–22, 5J 142, 5N 150–51, 5P 153–54, 5Q 155
Talmud *or* Talmudic, xxii, 1B 4, 1H 12–13, 1K 18, 1N 22, 2A 36, 2D 42, 2K 53–54, 2L 55–56, 2M 57–58, 3A 63–64, 3B 64, 3E 70, 3H 74–75, 5N 150
Tanzhaus, 1L 19
Tax, 3H 74–75, 3J 78–79, 3N 85, 4C 95, 5B 123–25

Thomas of Cantimpré, 5J 142–44
Thomas of Monmouth, 4D 100–102
Torah, 1C 6, 1Q 28, 30–31, 2C 39, 2E 44, 2G 46–48, 2K 54, 3B 65, 4C 96, 4L 119, 5L 146
Torah scroll, 1A 2, 1E 9, 2A 36, 4C 94, 5H 139
Tosafot or *Tosafists*, 1L 19, 1R 33, 2L 55, 3B 64–65, 5P 153
Tournaments, 1R 32–33
Travel, 1N 22, 2A 35–36, 2F 45, 2N 59, 2P 61, 3C 66, 3E 70, 3I 76, 4B 90, 5C 126, 5I 140
Trier, 4C 93–99
Tuscany, 5P 154

Vernacular, xviii, xx, xxii, 1G 12, 1H 13, 2E 43–44, 5P 153
Vienna, 2I 50, 3G 72
Violence, xiv–xv, xvii, xviii, xix, 2C 39, 4B 90, 4C 93–99, 4D 100–102, 4E 103–6, 4G 109–10, 4I 114, 4K 117–18, 4L 118–20, 5D 131

Water, 1F 10–11, 1J 16, 2F 45, 4B 91, 4C 99, 4K 117–18, 5A 122, 5N 150–51, 5O 151
Weapon, 1R 33, 5M 148
Wedding. *See* Marriage
Weissenfels, 1R 33
Westphalia, 2M 57, 4K 117
Widows, 1A 2, 1I 15, 1K 18, 1Q 31, 2D 41–42, 2K 53–54
Wiener Neustadt, 2I 50, 3G 72

Wife, 1F 10–11, 1K 18, 1O 25, 2A 35–37, 2B 37–38, 2C 39–40, 2D 41–42, 2J 51–52, 2K 53–54, 2L 55–56, 2M 57–58, 2O 60, 3A 63–64, 3F 71, 3H 74–75, 4E 105, 5E 133, 5P 154
William of Chimilli, 5B 124
William of the Church of St. Mary, 5B 124
William of Newburgh, 4E 103, 106
William of Norwich, 4D 100–102
Wills, 1O 24–25, 1Q 27–31
Wine, 1F 10, 1L 20, 2E 43–44, 2F 45, 2L 55–56, 3J 78, 3N 85, 4B 91, 5I 141
Worms, xi, 1D 7, 1F 10, 1K 18, 1M 21, 2C 39, 2G 46, 2P 61, 3C 66, 4C 94–95, 4L 118–19, 5H 138–39, 5I 141
Würzburg, 3J 78–79, 3N 85, 5C 127

Yehiel son of Asher, 1O 24–25, 3I 76–77
Yeshiva or Rabbinic school, 1N 22, 1O 25, 2I 50
Yibbum, 2K 53–54
Yiddish, 1M 21, 5P 153–54, 5Q 155–56
Yom Kippur, 1J 16, 1O 24, 2E 44, 2M 57, 5H 139, 5L 146
Youth, xii, xvi, 1L 19–20, 5P 154

Zurich, 3K 78–80, 3L 81–82
Zuzim (sing. *Zuz*, currency), 2D 42

TEAMS
DOCUMENTS OF PRACTICE

Love and Marriage in Late Medieval London selected, translated, and introduced by Shannon McSheffrey

Sources for the History of Medicine in Late Medieval England selected, introduced, and translated by Carole Rawcliffe

A Slice of Life: Selected Documents of Medieval English Peasant Experience selected, translated, and with an introduction by Edwin Brezette DeWindt

Women and Monasticism in Medieval Europe: Sisters and Patrons of the Cistercian Reform selected, translated, and with an introduction by Constance H. Berman

Regular Life: Monastic, Canonical, and Mendicant Rules second edition selected and introduced by Daniel Marvel La Corte and Douglas J. McMillan; first edition selected and introduced by Douglas J. McMillan and Kathryn Smith Fladenmuller

Medieval Notaries and Their Acts: The 1327–1328 Register of Jean Holanie introduced, edited, and translated by Kathryn L. Reyerson and Debra A. Salata

John Stone's Chronicle: Christ Church Priory, Canterbury, 1417–1472 selected, translated, and introduced by Meriel Connor

Medieval Latin Liturgy in English Translation, edited by Matthew Cheung Salisbury

Henry VII's London in the "Great Chronicle", edited by Julia Boffey

Typeset in Garamond Premier Pro

Medieval Institute Publications
College of Arts and Sciences
Western Michigan University
1903 W. Michigan Avenue
Kalamazoo, MI 49008-5432
http://wmich.edu/medievalpublications